THE TRUE HAPPINESS COMPANY

THE TRUE HAPPINESS COMPANY

A MEMOIR

VEENA DINAVAHI

RANDOM HOUSE | NEW YORK

Random House
An imprint and division of Penguin Random House LLC
1745 Broadway, New York, NY 10019
randomhousebooks.com
penguinrandomhouse.com

Library of Congress Cataloging- in- Publication Data
Names: Dinavahi, Veena, author.
Title: The true happiness company / Veena Dinavahi.
Description: New York: Random House, 2025. |
Identifiers: LCCN 2024040972 (print) | LCCN 2024040973 (ebook) |
ISBN 9780593447659 (hardcover) | ISBN 9780593594636 (ebook)
Subjects: LCSH: Dinavahi, Veena. | East Indian Americans—Biography. | LCGFT: Autobiographies.
Classification: LCC E184.E2 D56 2025 (print) | LCC E184.E2 (ebook) |
DDC 305.8914/11073 [B]— dc23/eng/20240927
LC record available at https://lccn.loc.gov/2024040972
LC ebook record available at https://lccn.loc.gov/2024040973

Printed in the United States of America on acid-free paper

1st Printing

First Edition

BOOK TEAM: Production editor: Andy Lefkowitz •
Managing editor: Rebecca Berlant • Production manager: Maggie Hart •
Copy editor: Martha Schwartz • Proofreaders: Megha Jain, Karina Jha, Lori Newhouse, and Courtney Vincento

Book design by Fritz Metsch

The authorized representative in the EU for product safety and compliance is Penguin Random House Ireland, Morrison Chambers, 32 Nassau Street, Dublin D02 YH68, Ireland.
https://eu-contact.penguin.ie

For my children, my younger self,

and anyone else seeking small answers to big questions

CONTENTS

PART I: HITTING ROCK BOTTOM 7

PART II: TRUE HAPPINESS 55

PART III: THE ROLE OF A WOMAN 149

PART IV: GRAY AREAS 217

Endnote 291

Acknowledgments 299

THE TRUE HAPPINESS COMPANY

AUTHOR'S NOTE

As a teenager, I used to think there were two kinds of people: the intelligent and the naive. I assumed intelligent people were immune to things like marketing scams, toxic friendships, and any kind of emotionally or physically abusive relationship. I certainly would have categorized anyone who winds up in a cult as naive. But then I realized I was in one.

This book is a quiet exploration of the question that plagued me afterward: How did *I* fall for *that*?

After I got out, I needed to understand my gradual transformation—to identify the turning points that felt subtle in the moment, yet obvious in retrospect. I wanted to excavate the choices that were obfuscated and presented to me as foregone conclusions. In writing this book, I've re-created these pivotal moments of my past and presented them to you with as minimal retrospection as possible, so that you can experience in real time the slow and then unexpectedly sudden process of having your reality altered by degrees.

When I was Mormon, people in my congregation used to say that the devil gets you not by telling ten lies, but by telling you nine truths and then slipping in one lie. I've never really believed in the devil, but I hope that my story allows you to recognize that one lie—namely, those instances when your decision-making is being unduly influenced by someone else's ulterior motives. I hope that it inspires you to identify and trust your own instincts. Or that it will allow you to view people in similar circumstances with a bit of grace, compassion, and depth. I wrote this book to highlight the myriad of factors that can leave a person vulnerable to manipulation—cultural scripts, gender roles, mental health struggles, and the sheer power of coercive techniques.

Reclaiming the trajectory of my life required me to shed those black-and-white ideas of "intelligence," "naivete," and "true" happiness that I held as a teenager and to embrace nuance instead. While the result can be sloppy and disorienting at times, I believe it is also deeply delightful.

Almost all of the names in this book have been changed, including Bob and the True Happiness Company. In some cases, identifying information has also been changed.

PART I

HITTING ROCK BOTTOM

1

June 2011

I didn't know what to expect from the True Happiness Company—crystal healing? bloodletting?—but I didn't expect Bob Lyon.

Amma first found Bob on one of her infamous late-night Google searches. Amma—my very sweet, very bright former cancer research scientist mother—has two master's degrees, in biochemistry and biotechnology. She also once nearly accepted a job scooping eyeballs out of dead bodies, despite the fact that she faints at the sight of blood. People think it's easy to know yourself, your boundaries and fears and limits, but decision-making is a convoluted process. Necessity has a way of overpowering all other considerations. A frequenter of Tony Robbins seminars and an inspirational speech addict, Amma has a long-standing history of finding sketchy people on the Internet and paying them too much money to do whatever they promise to do: turn our sad, dying lawn into a lush blanket of green, teach her how to get rich quick in the stock market or, in this case, save her daughter's life.

She called Bob on her way to work.

"Pull over," he instructed. "Pull over right now."

Alarmed, Amma pulled over on a side street of Baltimore.

"If you do not bring your daughter here, she WILL be dead."

It is one thing to have a worst fear nebulously haunt the back of your mind and quite another to hear it pronounced as an inevitability by a strong, commanding voice who has published more than a dozen books and hosted seminars worldwide. Emails were exchanged. An appointment was made.

I didn't know it at the time, but Amma hadn't found Bob's website on her own; she'd first found a blog written by a woman whose son had been suicidal. Amma called her, and the woman said, "Take your daughter to see Bob Lyon *now*."

If you are a parent, if you have ever been confused and desperate and aching for your children, then you know the tug of a fellow mother's heartfelt advice. Amma made all her parenting decisions based on these kinds of recommendations; I ended up playing the violin because she sat next to a woman at my first orchestra concert who insisted that once you allow a child to quit one thing, they become a quitter for the rest of their lives. I was in the third grade and spent the next ten years taking private violin lessons in the home of a woman who collected hot sauce and owned eight cats. Shelves and shelves of hot sauce filled the entryway, the living room where I had my lessons, and the kitchen, of course. This teacher fed squirrels out of her hand on her back porch during my lesson while I dreamed of playing the flute. When I asked Amma years later why I hadn't been allowed to switch, she shrugged and answered, "I sat next to this woman who said . . ."

If the confident word of a stranger could dictate what instrument I played, imagine how much more weight it carried when Amma was faced with a suicidal daughter she could not seem to save.

The first thing I said to Bob Lyon was, "I don't have to do shit," as I flounced into the soft corner creases of a once-white couch in his living room.

At least, that is his version of our first meeting: me waltzing into his home in backcountry Georgia and cursing before he can get a word in edgewise. Though I'm certain he spoke first, I've since forgotten what he said that put me on the defensive. At age nineteen, I didn't typically curse at adults—part of that Indian "respect your elders" thing—plus cursing tended to go over poorly. But Bob Lyon was unperturbed.

"No," he said. "You really don't."

I flinched. His response was disconcerting because he was the first adult I'd met who I couldn't unnerve. Had he not spoken first? Was I making it up? Was I the kind of person who dropped expletives unprovoked? This feeling of disorientation—this constant second-guessing of myself—pervaded our entire relationship. My memory buckled under the force of his confidence.

Bob Lyon looked like a giant, unamused teddy bear when I showed up in his living room that day. "Living room" was a misnomer: nothing about that room inspired the will to live. Instead of the framed diplomas you'd find on the walls of a typical psychologist's office, his walls boasted gold-framed animal prints—one of a Siamese cat and another of two intertwined peacocks. The two couches formed an L shape facing the center of the room. A plastic chandelier was fixed to a stippled ceiling overlooked by the past two decades of decorating trends. To my left sat a textured gold floor lamp that looked like it worked weekends at the Olive Garden. A tiny statue of Jesus on his fireplace was the only indication that he was Mormon—but I wouldn't learn of this fact for another four years.

In the center of the room sat Bob, this big, old white man in a rocking chair. The chair was wooden, the kind you'd expect to find on a wraparound porch with Buffalo Bill kicking up his cowboy boots, resting a rifle on his lap. Bob wore an untucked plaid shirt and blue jeans. He wore no shoes, just thick, white socks. My first impression of him was "redneck." This is also my final impression, though my feelings toward him have taken a wild detour to arrive back where they started.

"You're right. You *don't* have to do anything. But," he said lightly, "I know something you don't."

"Okay." I knew I was being set up. Still, I wanted to get to the punch line more than I wanted to fight. "What?" I conceded.

His eyes bored into me with such intensity that I felt like I'd been caught naked on the shoulder of the expressway. I wet my lips and averted my eyes.

"I know how to be happy." He spoke quietly now. "Look, kid, you're stuck here for three days. Your parents won't let you leave. You're welcome to go back downstairs and watch TV. Or go outside and walk the grounds. We've got some nice woods out here and a lake behind the house. But you are so miserable that your life couldn't possibly get any worse. You've got absolutely nothing to lose."

That was it. His big pitch. Looking back, I did have things to lose: my agency, my values, the sanctity of my body. How could I have known that a shot at his version of happiness meant trading it all in?

In the eight years that I was in his orbit, he would recount this story of how we met so many times, to so many different people, that it became canon in the True Happiness community. He'd emphasize how I "flounced" to convey my spunk and how much he liked it: She didn't just sit, she *flounced.* He'd flick his wrists to illustrate my miniskirt bouncing onto the pleather surface of his couch. Then he'd point to the corner where I sat. Here, he'd interrupt himself to observe how he remembered exactly where everyone had sat the first time they'd met him. He always phrased it that way: they *met* him. There was an air of immutability and pleasant anticipation in his telling. The meeting of two great minds.

But very different feelings pervade my memory of our first meeting. Anger, as I climbed into the back of my mom's minivan in our Maryland suburb. Resentment, as the ride progressed, and I approximated how far south we had traveled by averaging the number of Cracker Barrel signs on the roadside. Fear, as we pulled into a nondescript driveway in the middle of nowhere at midnight. Disbelief, as my mom fished a crumpled piece of paper out of her handbag and smoothed it against the dash, insisting she had instructions to "follow the lighted stairs to the basement guest quarters." Unease, as I watched my parents disembark and do as they were told.

I did not choose to be in his living room, but choices become limited when you have spent the past three and a half years sort of trying to die. There is some debate over whether my actions were suicide *attempts* or suicidal *gestures*. I am unclear on the distinction here. All I can tell you is that killing yourself is harder than it sounds. Between the ages of fifteen and nineteen, I swallowed pills over and over. I drank ant poison (doesn't work on mammals). I tried to hang myself but didn't know how to secure the rope to the ceiling.

Living is hard and dying is harder.

People assume that when you attempt suicide, in that moment, you have reached rock bottom. This is not the case. Attempting is an act of hope—that the pain will end. Those who wronged you will repent. Your eulogy will be delivered by a tearful boyfriend who realizes too late he was in the presence of greatness. Or, okay, ex-boyfriend.

It is after you've attempted and failed too many times that you hit bottom. Your cries for help are the stale potato chips abandoned at the bottom of the bag after all the good ones have been eaten. You've swallowed the pills ("I am going to start her on twenty-five milligrams of Zoloft"), swallowed the other pills ("Give her these vitamin D supplements and we'll test her blood again in a month"), agreed to the acupuncturist's tiny needles ("Are your feet always this cold? How bad do your menstrual cramps get?"), consulted the environmental therapist ("Have you checked the basement for mold?"), and been subjected to a slew of plain old regular psychologists that speak to you as though you have the IQ of a cantaloupe.

Rock bottom is a beige couch in an old man's living room in the middle of nowhere, Georgia.

*

There are always signs, moments when your intuition kicks back in. Even before we made the trip to Bob's house, something nagged at Amma. She opened her laptop on the dining room table one day, pulled up his website, and started browsing his YouTube videos.

"Are we really going to take Veena to him?" she asked Nanna. "He seems like a salesman."

Nanna rested a hand on Amma's shoulder and said, "We paid so much money for her education. What is all of that worth if our daughter is unhappy?"

Nanna often functions as the voice of reason in our house. In addition to being a literal rocket scientist, my dad is a certified yoga instructor who uses too many GRE words in regular sentences and frequently complains about the spelling of the English word "knife."

My parents embraced and details were finalized. Payment was wired. I knew nothing of this at the time.

Point is, everyone has doubts. But by the time you hit rock bottom, your options have dwindled and consolidated to a single point. It no longer matters how many bottles of hot sauce your violin teacher may own or what kind of person has a framed poster of a Siamese cat in his living room.

Skepticism is a commodity only the complacent can afford.

2

I'd never been a happy kid. Look at my family photos and you will find me scowling in all of them, aged eight months to thirteen years. Amma describes pushing me in a stroller through Macy's and being accosted by the perfume ladies.

"Ohhh, what a beautiful baby!" they'd squeal. They'd spend the next five minutes making faces, tickling my tummy, wiggling my toes, and playing peekaboo while I stared back, stone-faced. By the sixth minute they'd sigh and say, "Not today, huh?"

Not tomorrow either, Amma tells me. She'd take me and my older brother, Venkat, to a portrait studio, and all the photographer had to do was say "Boo!" and Venkat would erupt into laughter—something he still does today. I don't know if the photographer conceded faster than the perfume ladies, but his eventual defeat is immortalized by my chubby scowl in our family photo albums. Venkat is all smiles, with his windshield-wiper eyelashes, a Dinavahi trait. That, and hair covering every available square inch of our skin.

Venkat sauntered into adolescence with his easygoing ways and became so absent from our home life that the fact that I even had a brother became a running joke among my friends. While Amma and Nanna never kept tabs on his whereabouts, I could never leave the house without hearing: *Where are you going? Who are you going with?*

Will any boys be there? What are their parents' phone numbers? When will you be back? There were a million cultural wars being waged in our home on any given day. We literally spoke different languages; Amma and Nanna reprimanded me in Telugu, and I snapped back in English. The result was a state of perpetual friction—pieces of dry wood incessantly rubbing against one another, always seconds away from smoke, then fire. When Venkat grew tired of our bickering, he would pull me aside and offer practical advice.

"Just lie to them, Veena. Tell them what they want to hear and do what you want."

That system worked well for Venkat, who was always out smoking weed with his friends, scraping by with mediocre grades in school, but still beloved by our parents for being their easy baby. I, on the other hand, collected achievements like my violin teacher collected hot sauce: I played rec soccer, performed in the Children's Theater of Annapolis, and played in the Greater Baltimore Youth Orchestra. But none of my accomplishments impressed Amma and Nanna quite like Venkat's smile.

On the occasions that I didn't resent my brother, I'd reply, "Lying would be wrong. If I explain myself well enough, they'll understand."

Venkat would sigh. "They're our parents, Veena. Maybe they're not meant to understand everything."

Like all Indian parents, Amma and Nanna seemed to have built-in GPSs that led them directly to the good school districts. They chose our home based on that sole criterion—Severna Park High was blue-ribbon, one of the top one hundred public schools in the country. That's why we landed in a largely white, upper-middle-class suburb in Maryland, where the only places that stayed open past nine p.m. were a Taco Bell drive-through and a twenty-four-hour Donut Shack. I was one of three Indians in my grade and forever fielding questions about whether or not Abhi Chopra was my brother ("No, guys, stop.") or if our parents would force us to marry when we came of age ("Okay, first—gross. Second, that is not how arranged marriages work. Third, I have a boyfriend!"). The boyfriend was, like the rest of the school, white.

Despite its many academic accolades, Severna Park had one remarkable feature that stood out among the rest—its suicide rate: 136 attempts among the 1,800 students between 2008 and 2016. Twenty suicides in as many years. My high school's nickname was Suicide High. It's not in every wealthy suburb of America that the youth kill themselves with such rigor and regularity.

It's an odd place to become a person, Severna Park.

Until December 18, 2007, I'd only seen people cry at my high school because they didn't get accepted to their first-choice Ivy League college or they discovered that they'd been cheated on. But when I walked into upstairs G hall, there were so many people crying so vigorously that I knew something was off. My best friend, Eliza, approached, all fiery red hair and freckles, clutching her metal Union Jack lunch box and a Diet Dr Pepper. We usually spent our days watching *Monty Python's Flying Circus,* knitting scarves we'd never finish, and debating art history and politics, but this time she looked uncharacteristically serious.

"Have you heard?" she said. "Sarah Rose committed suicide."

My brain skipped a track. I sank into my chair and Eliza took a step back, startled by the expression on my face.

"Veena? Are you okay? Did you know her?"

I'd heard Sarah talk about how she alphabetized her books at home, how she'd freak out if her sister borrowed one and returned a *P* to the *Q*s. "Um, kind of," I said. "I know her a little bit. Knew her." What Eliza really meant was: Did I know her *well*?

Sarah was a popular senior on the lacrosse team and I was just a nerdy sophomore. We knew each other only because we were in the same multivariable calculus class.

I had math that day. There were only eight of us in the class. Well, seven now—if you counted the empty seat in front of me. During our usual exams, wisps of Sarah's blond hair would sweep across my desk, and I'd try to slide them off with my pencil without her noticing. But on that day, our unit test was canceled.

A woman I didn't recognize appeared in the doorway and introduced herself as the school psychologist. I hadn't known the high school even had a psychologist on staff. My ears felt full of water, and I barely heard what she said. As she left, we shared a beat of intense eye contact before I could look away. My heart jumped at this pointed attention, feeling like something had slipped out of me and into her.

"Why don't we pull our desks into a circle," our teacher, Mr. Clark, suggested. "What do you all know about what was going on?"

"She left a note in her car," Marcus said.

The car was found on the Chesapeake Bay Bridge. Sarah had jumped.

Marcus was her best friend in the class. His expression was blank, and his apparent stoicism bothered me. I wanted some recognition that her life had happened. I wanted to peel open the chests of everyone she had touched and find her thumbprint on their hearts.

"Yeah, she never got over what happened with her boyfriend."

From the conversation, I pieced together that her boyfriend had shot himself in the head the previous year. The summer before that, the boyfriend's best friend had killed himself. Pulling on the thread of this girl's death was like tugging a macabre endless scarf out of a magician's hat. Or like some sadistic God had lined up Severna Park students like suicidal dominoes. I didn't know who sparked this chain reaction, because I couldn't figure out how far back the pattern extended.

I tuned out, struggling to ground myself in this surreal new image of Severna Park. Mr. Clark took a Bible off his shelf and cracked it open. Listening to him read a few verses somehow both soothed and irritated me. Amma said we all found different paths to the same God. But it had been years since I'd felt connected to something larger in that way: I couldn't believe in a God who would rip high school students out of their desks and leave empty space where there used to be wisps of hair.

"Right now, I'm wondering if I'm allowed to be mad at her. Just at all," said one of my classmates, rubbing his forehead.

Mr. Clark closed the Bible and pursed his lips. "I don't think emotions are right or wrong. I think they are just things we have to deal with."

I wish I had appreciated the value of a trusted adult giving us permission to feel a full spectrum of emotions—even the difficult ones.

The whole school caught its breath that week. The whole school wept. Two weeks passed and inevitably, the whole school moved on. I could not.

I wandered around like a drunk looking for sobriety between couch cushions, as if sanity were a lost stick of gum or a misplaced nickel, disjointed thoughts slipping and slithering off my tongue as I fixed my wet eyes on whoever happened to be around, hoping someone would be able to explain the unraveling taking place inside me—to help me understand my reaction to this girl's death. I spent hours crying in the girls' bathroom and many more weeping in the school psychologist's office and even more hours talking to friends and neighbors and kind strangers, hoping someone would tell me why I was allowed to live when Sarah could not, why bad things happened to good people, but no one had these answers for me.

In a way, we all knew Sarah Rose: the college-bound eighteen-year-old, full of promise.

Back home, I sleepwalked into the kitchen and dropped into the stiff, wooden IKEA chair. Venkat, home from the University of Maryland for Christmas break, sat across from me, engrossed in his laptop.

"My classmate jumped off the Bay Bridge."

Venkat blinked and looked up. "Oh. Shit. Sorry, Veena."

I chewed on my lip. "It doesn't make sense. She was popular. She was funny and had lots of friends. Pretty, too."

Venkat craned his neck around his laptop to get a look at me. "I know what you mean. There was this kid in my grade, Eddie Reed, that shot himself in the head."

I leaned in and slapped my hands on the kitchen table. "Right! I heard about that."

"You did? It's crazy. We weren't close or anything, but he seemed happy. You think the emo kids are the ones who commit suicide. The ones who dress in black and listen to depressing music. But this kid had a sense of humor and was easygoing. He had friends."

My limbs were heavy. If Sarah had all these friends, why didn't they notice something was wrong? Did anyone care? Or did the world keep turning, indifferent to the brief life and death of one insignificant teenage girl? Or three teenage lives? Did we just brush our teeth tonight, eat our bowls of cereal tomorrow morning, and check our mail like we always did? If I died, would anyone notice? Or would I slip noiselessly into the deep, without so much as a ripple?

Venkat returned to his laptop. Did my parents even know that I was home?

The school psychologist called home at the start of winter break, concerned about me. I'd been spending more time in her office than I had been in class. Amma and Nanna assured her they would talk to me and find me an independent psychologist. But mostly Nanna insisted I take up meditation and regular exercise. Never underestimate the power of good eating and sleeping habits, he said, as if a brisk jog and a plate of steamed broccoli would settle my questions about life and death.

On the way home from my holiday orchestra concert, I waited for an opportunity to tell Amma I was still struggling.

"Shit!" she exclaimed, jerking the stick shift. She hated driving Nanna's car. She adjusted the rearview mirror, craned her neck to see out of it, glanced out the back window anyway, and turned back to the road in front of her. "That was a beautiful duet you and Melanie played." Her eyes flicked over at me. "Veena? What's going on?"

My crying was silent now. "Remember I told you that my classmate committed suicide?"

Amma nodded in a way that left doubt as to whether she actually remembered. The light turned green, and she stomped on the clutch, grunting. The car stalled.

"I went to her memorial."

It was my first time in a church. My chest shuddered and released at finding what I sought: proof that Sarah had mattered. The building, dark and dotted with candles, gave grief an ethereal quality. Sarah's friends and relatives barely fit inside the chapel. They squeezed into hallways, the main room, and the balconies. Part of me wanted to count the number of people in attendance, to quantify her importance, to solidify her into something durable. Who would show up for my memorial? How many people was I worth?

The car lurched forward. I waited for Amma to ask about the experience so I could share it with her.

"Ah. I see," she said. "I know what you're going through, Veena," Amma started, eyes fixed straight ahead. "When I was your age, I saw a classmate die in front of me."

I listened, paralyzed with fear and curiosity. My parents dispensed personal information like rations during a nuclear winter. I knew neither of their ages, just a wide range they likely fell into. I knew them only in relation to me, not as people existing in the world. For years I told everyone that my parents were from Hyderabad. Nanna had recently informed me that this was incorrect, though he failed to supply me with the correct answer. Now when people asked, I shrugged and said, "South India."

"We were on a school trip, and we stopped for lunch next to a waterfall. We weren't supposed to go near the waterfall, but kids went anyway, to wash their hands. There was this boy in my class who just . . . fell in. We all watched him drown. I watched him die, Veena, and there was nothing I could do."

It was dark and her voice cracked, but she did not cry. The story she told to help me feel understood twisted my insides instead. I didn't want to imagine Sarah's final moment, but now that the thought was implanted in my head, it was impossible to shake. What was it like for her, standing on the edge, breeze in her thin hair? What went through her mind in the moment that she inhaled and jumped?

"But, Veena," Amma continued, shifting the car's gears, "we have relatives coming over for the holidays. We all go through difficult times, but you must keep going. It is not fair to burden our family with our problems. They are coming here to have a nice time. Cheer up, okay?"

I took a deep breath and promised to do as she asked.

I hadn't felt like I had the right to experience unhappiness ever since I was eight years old and first realized my idea of "difficult times" might be nothing compared to the daily living conditions of so many people in different circumstances. In second grade, Venkat and I went on a trip to see relatives in India. We took the flight by ourselves and Bamma, our paternal grandmother, met us outside the airport gate, gray hair pulled into a severe bun, lightweight sari draped over her shoulders, and a permanent scowl etched into her face. Bamma had picked us up by car and spoke to us first in Telugu, then in a loud, slow English—as though she doubted our ability to understand either language.

A gaggle of children loitered around the car. They overlooked my brother but swarmed me as I neared, a picture of privilege, with my shiny new sneakers and blue plastic purse. The children, similar to me in age, grabbed and tugged at me in a clear plea for money. Bamma rolled up the newspaper in her hand and swatted at their heads, yelling at them to get lost. I felt sick with a sudden awareness of everything I had taken for granted. The crowd dispersed and our four enormously stupid suitcases were Tetris-ed into a car far too small to hold them. The windows were rolled up, separating Venkat and me from the other kids, searing their image into my mind, forever redefining my understanding of hardship. My comfortable home in the suburbs didn't feel quite comfortable after that summer. I still haven't figured out how to hold space for my own emotions in light of others' suffering.

There is a saying in Hindi—a language I don't speak—that goes like this: *Dhobi ka kutta na ghar ka, na ghat ka*. The *dhobi,* or washerman, goes to the house to retrieve the laundry and then to the river to wash it. His dog, or *kutta,* follows him between the two places. The idea is that the dog doesn't know if he belongs at the house or the river. But I've seen stray dogs in India, and I think the dog knows it is not wanted anywhere.

When you grow up in a place like Severna Park, happiness is incumbent upon you. If the dog lands in a nice house in the suburbs, she is expected to let go of the river and the history it carries. When your parents have left behind their villages in India, left their mothers and brothers and sisters and entered this new world for you, with its manicured lawns and blue ribbons and cul-de-sacs, you take the weight of everyone who has passed—both your grandfathers who succumbed to heart attacks far before their time, your mom's classmate who washed his hands in the wrong place, your classmate who left a note in her car—and you take the guilt of your continued existence and you forge it into gratitude.

At least you try.

3

January 5, 2008

It is hard, sometimes, to live when everyone around you keeps dying. I didn't wake up deciding that January 5 would be the day that I tried to kill myself. I just woke up wanting a little break. A rest. To stay under the covers indefinitely.

I had a fight with my parents that morning—something about my unwillingness to eat breakfast and give yoga a real chance—that ended with me getting grounded for the weekend. It is hard to look at someone who struggles to get out of bed in the morning and believe *This person is trying,* but I was, truly. I ate a banana. I went for that brisk jog. I drew the line at yoga (death seemed preferable), but everything else I was supposed to do, I did. I sat in the school psychologist's office every day while she looked strained and told me, *This too shall pass.* I talked to teachers discreetly, I tried to talk to my parents, I tried to be grateful for my home and my family and the American dream. I tried so hard that on that day, I walked over to my neighbor's house and cried while his mom made stromboli and told me stories about how her older daughters didn't have boyfriends until college.

Well, bully for those ladies, but I wasn't looking for true love, just a reason—literally any reason—to live.

I stopped at Eliza's on the way home. She eyed me curiously from inside her doorway, her red-lacquered nails wrapped around another Diet Dr Pepper.

"Your parents called," she said. "I don't think they know where you are."

I nodded casually. "I was at Jake's house. His mom taught me how to make stromboli."

"Ah." She nodded along with me, pretending it was totally normal for Jake's mom to be teaching me how to make stromboli on Saturday morning and that my eyes were not puffy. I loved her for not pressing further. We stood in silence for a minute until she said softly, "I think you should check in with your parents. They sounded worried."

She was right, of course.

As soon as I got home, Amma and Nanna started yelling at me for leaving the house while grounded. Even Venkat, who always took my side, started lecturing me about how the neighbor had called and how I'd frightened our parents. Whatever tender nostalgia I'd gathered to convince myself that things had been good once was instantly crushed by the obligation of needing to be okay for the people around me. I'd never be able to carry this weight.

I snapped at Amma and Nanna, stomped upstairs to my room, googled "Tylenol overdose," read about how it would cause liver failure in two to three days, swallowed slightly more than the overdose warning, and then I sat down and finished my French homework; I hated loose ends.

Several hours conjugating French verbs and reading about the Hapsburgs quelled the fire in me. I went downstairs and startled Amma and Nanna with prolonged silent hugs. I apologized for worrying them and promised to communicate more clearly. Not disappointing anyone for forty-eight hours felt doable.

In the evening, Eliza came over and we watched YouTube videos of college kids doing stupid pranks and I thought, *Am I really never going to college?* That panicked me because what if things did get better? What if I was switching channels right before the good part? The thing is, how do you tell someone that you've swallowed half a bottle of pills and you think it was a mistake?

I mumbled something about Tylenol.

"What?" Eliza asked. "You want some Tylenol?"

"No," I said. "I've had enough."

Eliza froze. I didn't know it at the time, but our friend Melanie had an older sister who had overdosed on Tylenol just weeks before.

"Veena," Eliza said, "did you take Tylenol? How many did you take?"

"Don't worry. Nothing will happen for two to three days."

Her jaw hinged open. Suddenly she was downstairs, sobbing to my parents that I had taken a bunch of pills. Screaming and crying ensued. Someone walked Eliza home. I lost track of Venkat. Amma and Nanna argued over where the car keys were, which hospital was closest, how cold it was outside, and which coats they should wear. I sat in the back of the minivan, singing quietly to myself, as Amma and Nanna argued over driving directions, thinking, *This was supposed to be the part where they cared about me*. Surely, we had skipped over the part where someone, anyone, hugged me and told me they loved me. I kept thinking about Sarah's memorial service and thought mine would suck. My parents would fight over driving directions on the way there. The neighbor would make stromboli, forgetting my parents are vegetarian.

A nurse in the ER checked my blood pressure. Around me were bright lights and big machines and people rushing around. My parents hovered behind the nurse, bouncing on the balls of their feet, prepared to jump to my aid at a moment's notice.

"Did you know that she is in multivariable calculus and she is only fifteen years old?"

"She makes very beautiful paintings, you know."

It shouldn't have surprised me that my parents would recite my résumé to the ER nurses. In my mind, I was still the person they described: adept and lucid.

"Calculus three?" the nurse echoed. She stuck a needle in my arm.

I hated needles.

"You must be a very smart girl," she said.

"Hmm. But I guess I lost brownie points with the whole trying-to-kill-myself thing," I mused.

She laughed. "I like the way you word that."

My blood filled up three tubes. Red, red, red. My arm felt funny, like rubber.

"How many pills did you take, sweetie?"

"Two hundred!" Amma shouted.

I almost laughed. It was my first glimpse into my mother's state of mind; there couldn't have been more than twenty-four pills in the whole bottle. "Whatever the overdose warning was, slightly more than that. About fifteen."

"Fifteen!" the nurse repeated. "That's too many! You're going to have ulcers before prom."

So, I am going to live. The thought incited no reaction. My parents left and a doctor entered the room. He asked why I was there.

"Well, my classmate killed herself." The more I repeated the words, the more bizarre and inconclusive they sounded. What was the dotted line that led from point A to point B?

"So, you thought that was the cool thing to do, huh?" he said.

"What! No. I . . . No."

The doctor stared at me over his spectacles for several seconds.

"Well, there is nothing physically wrong with you, so hopefully we can get you out of here quickly and open this bed up for someone who actually needs it."

He went on to his next patient and I was left feeling like an abscess, ready to burst.

Not much medical attention followed, and I was left to infer that I wouldn't suffer from a single side effect. My parents reappeared.

"You can never do this again," Amma blurted. "Or . . . or I'll kill myself, too!"

Her words sucked the air out of my lungs.

Nanna scowled at Amma. "What kind of nonsense are you talking?" He then turned his scowl to me, "Veena, this was so irresponsible of you."

I was used to Amma making threats; she'd threatened to leave Nanna once or twice and called him from a gas station hours later, chagrined. But she'd never mentioned suicide before.

"Promise, Veena! Promise you'll never do anything like this again!"

In the time it took for Amma to say this, all my existential musings about life, death, and purpose folded into resolve. I could not cause my parents any more pain.

"I promise."

I'd do better. I could do better. Thirty seconds into finding out I'd live and already I was tired.

Eventually, I fell into a fitful sleep on the hospital bed, not knowing where my parents were. When I woke, Venkat was hanging confusedly by my bedside, crying. I'd never seen him cry before.

"What happened to all your plans, Veena? I thought you wanted to write a book and learn Italian and travel the world."

There was so much unsaid between us. It surprised me to see him here now, in pain at my pain, intimately aware of the things I wanted for myself. I didn't know how to explain. (What's the thirty-second elevator pitch for depression?)

"Hey, Venkat, check out these socks. They have grips on both sides.

Isn't that funny? So, if I want to walk on the tops of my feet, I won't slip."

"Do you not even care, Veena?" he asked, aghast.

As if anyone thought being strapped to a stretcher in a backless hospital gown was a fun way to spend a weekend. Everyone wants to live. Some of us just don't know how.

It wasn't until Eliza and her mom visited me in the ER that I realized I'd attempted suicide on my best friend's birthday. (Depression makes a person stupidly selfish.) Eliza gave me a souvenir from the Philadelphia Museum of Art and the unhappy realization set in.

"Oh my god," I gasped. "It's your birthday. Eliza, I'm so sorry."

We'd planned the museum day trip for her sweet sixteen. For the first time since I'd arrived at the hospital, I cried, holding the cube of Gustav Klimt paintings.

She held my hand and whispered, "I'm just glad you're okay."

"Silly Eliza." I laughed through the tears. "On your birthday, *other* people are supposed to give *you* presents."

She cried and chuckled and gave my hand a gentle squeeze. "I'm just glad you're okay."

Later in the day, I was transferred to the back of the hospital to await a psych evaluation before I could be released. The room I was deposited in had four white walls, a bed nailed to the center, and no sharp edges, just rounded corners. I'd seen similar rooms in movies, with a thin, sallow person wearing a straitjacket and rocking in the corner, mumbling incoherently. That portrait of a hypothetical crazy person stood in stark contrast to how I understood myself. I was missing an orchestra concert and dance rehearsal to be in that featureless room. My thoughts still felt crisp and well-developed. I didn't belong there.

I perched on the edge of the bed, clutching my copy of *Wuthering Heights* that my parents brought me from home. I liked to match books to the occasion. Bringing a ghost story to a hospital felt fitting. In a way, Sarah felt closer to me now than when she was alive. I wondered what other kinds of people were closed behind the rest of the doors in the hallway, if they felt like they belonged there. With nothing else to occupy me, I decided to practice my ballet routine to focus on something constructive. *Tombé, pas de bourrée, pirouette*. I was productive. *Tombé*. I was sane. *Pas de bourrée.* I didn't belong there. *Pirouette.* My eyes swept over the room on my last pirouette, and it occurred to me that doing ballet in a crazy person room at the hospital might not be considered the peak of sanity. Deflated, I sank onto the bed.

I stepped into the hallway to read a poster titled Patients' Rights—it felt important to know, given the circumstances, but before I could finish a sentence, a nurse at the desk barked at me to get back in my room. I wondered whose idea it was to display patients' rights in a hallway where patients weren't allowed and decided that their sanity should be in question, not mine.

Bland hours passed. There was a knock on my door and a woman introduced herself as Dr. Linda. As I spoke, she nodded a little too aggressively and wrote furiously, more words than I could have said. I went through the already familiar steps.

"So, then you tried to hurt yourself," she said. She avoided the words "kill" and "suicide" just like the rest of the nurses and doctors.

"Sure would seem that way, wouldn't it?"

Dr. Linda looked up sharply. "Were you or were you not trying to hurt yourself?"

The dry humor that worked so well with the ER nurse did not land well with Dr. Linda. I made a mental note to tread carefully.

"No, yes—I was," I replied, in earnest.

She hugged the clipboard to her chest. "Okay, Veena. Basically, it is my job to decide if you are well enough to go home tonight. Do you want to go home?"

"Absolutely."

"Okay. Then I would need to see some indication that this was an isolated incident and won't happen again."

"Naturally."

I knew I made another misstep because she gave me that look. In my mind, I was still the overachieving nerd who helped her team win the Georgetown History Bowl. It didn't occur to me that, to the psychologist, I was a suicidal fifteen-year-old in a hospital gown. I could handle being alive or dead, but nothing in the past twenty-four hours had prepared me to suddenly take on the identity of "mentally ill."

She continued. "Yes. So what can you tell me to convince me that this won't happen again?"

"I promised my mother."

I don't know why I've always been convinced that other people's perceptions will align with mine if only I can explain myself calmly and clearly enough, but that is a trait that will continue to get me in trouble for years to come.

Dr. Linda passed her pen from hand to hand. "Ah, okay. Is there nothing else you can say to reassure me that I won't be making a mistake by sending you home?"

"I promised my mother," I insisted.

"Well, okay. I'll go talk to your parents now and have a decision for you."

Winded with every kind of exhaustion, I crawled into one of the rounded corners of my room and huddled up. Maybe they were right about me. Maybe I was crazy.

I fell asleep, and when I woke later, the brightness of the room was disorienting and there was a stain of drool on my shoulder. Amma was waiting for me, her face rigid.

"Well? How did it go?" My attempt at optimism rang flat.

She fiddled with her purse, and her eyes grazed the floor before finding my face. "Not good, Veena. They want to keep you here. They said you showed no remorse."

I didn't know what everyone wanted from me. First people wanted me to be happy when I was sad and now people wanted me to be sad when I was happy. Or, at least, people wanted me to look sad when I felt fine.

"What do you mean 'keep me here'?" I asked. "They can't do that, right? You won't let them."

"No, Veena. They told us that if we try to take you home now, we won't be allowed to visit you in the future."

The air felt thin like a paper cut. Who was "they"? I wished I knew what the sign outside my room said about patients' rights.

"What's going to happen to me?" I asked.

"They will keep you here for tonight, and in the morning they will transfer you to a children's psych ward."

My head swam and I swallowed empty mouthfuls of air. "You can't let them! You can't let them."

The course of my life shifted underneath me. If I stayed the night, it would mean something big had occurred. I wouldn't be able to go home and pretend that the past twenty-four hours never happened. I kept gasping, but no air came in. Amma looked around frantically until a nurse came in with a paper bag she placed over my mouth until my breathing calmed.

Amma rubbed my back. "Veena," she ventured, "I can stay with you tonight. Would you like that?"

I nodded. I wanted to say *Don't leave me alone,* but I don't know how you ask for tenderness after you've hurt someone that much.

"Okay." She wiped her eyes. "I'll go ask them for a bed."

I collapsed into another rounded corner. After some time, I returned to the bed and hid under the covers.

After some more time, a nurse brought in a stretcher for Amma to sleep on. A hand pushed back the covers from my face and stroked my hair. I let her. Amma was still crying.

4

January 7 to 21, 2008

To understand why Bob Lyon's charisma was so compelling, all you have to do is step inside a children's psych ward and take one look at the deadened affect of the staff. Unlike Bob, whose personality felt large enough to swallow me at any moment, the psychologists at Johns Hopkins Hospital wore desensitized expressions that gave no outward indication of caring whether I lived or died. While Bob's animated voice could persuade my mother to pull over to the side of a Baltimore highway through a single phone call, the practitioners at the psych ward spoke with dry, detached tones—when they spoke at all. They more closely resembled a board of directors than a team of mental health professionals.

Every morning started with me sitting at the head of a long oval table while eight to twelve indistinguishable psychologists coughed politely and reached for the rolling carts behind them. Then they each picked up a large binder with my name on it. Only one of them ever spoke. The rest avoided eye contact and pored over their files.

"Any thoughts of hurting yourself or anyone else? Seeing or hearing things that other people aren't seeing or hearing?"

I gave them the same stale answers.

"Okay, thank you, Veena. That will be all. You can send Jordan in now."

They put the binders with my name back on their wheeled carts and retrieved the ones with Jordan's name.

"Um, excuse me?"

Eight heads stopped what they were doing and looked up. I didn't know any of their names.

"I just wanted to ask—when can I go home?"

One of the men removed his reading glasses and set them on the table. "Well, Veena, that's why we're meeting with you every day. That's what we're trying to determine."

"Not today, then?"

What was it that they wanted to hear? What were the answers that would get me home?

"No, not today. We'll let you know when we think you are ready."

I scrunched up my mouth in poorly concealed disappointment and slid my swivel chair out from under the conference table. If that was the extent of our interaction, I didn't know how they expected to assess my mental health—or, more important, how they could help me. Though Bob Lyon was never a licensed professional, he at least had a pulse; and in contrast, that would seem like enough.

A typical day in the psych ward went: vitals, conference room, free choice, group, lunch, outside time, group lesson, free choice, meet with your caseworker, meet with a psychiatrist, free choice, dinner. After reading *Girl, Interrupted* and *The Bell Jar,* I had very particular expectations of the psych ward: the gnashing of teeth, unidentified screams, etc., etc. In reality, I stayed in a room with a baby blue ceiling with clouds painted on it and spent the days playing board games and trying to convince the nurses to change the hallway TV channel so I could watch Hillary Clinton's 2008 presidential campaign on CNN. The most excitement I experienced was during a rousing hospital-wide game of bingo. I won a Mr. Potato Head, which I sent home to Eliza as a sorry-I-tried-to-kill-myself-on-your-birthday gesture.

Though the hospital was only twenty minutes away from Severna Park, it was a different world entirely. Johns Hopkins was located in downtown Baltimore and the demographics of the inpatients reflected that. People were admitted to the psych ward for all kinds of reasons, most of them unclear. There was an eight-year-old Asian girl who seemed perfectly normal. She either did not know or would not share why she was there. Two Black teenagers, one who lost his memory and another who overdosed on ecstasy. A white girl who attempted suicide so many times that she'd been in the ICU for three months with tubes down her throat and could barely talk above a whisper. There was a girl with Tourette's who moaned back and forth loudly and screamed for her brother at odd hours. A Latina girl who had tried to jump in front of a D.C. Metro car. A boy who wore tank tops that showed off his prepubescent muscles, who was admitted for beating up his younger siblings.

Halfway into my stay, my classmate Bianca arrived. I'd seen her name written on a door but didn't believe it was really the Bianca I knew until I saw the outline of her head in a conference room. The suicide epidemic at my high school was that bad—you were more likely to run into a classmate at a psych ward than the local grocery store. There were twelve documented attempts at Severna Park High that year. Bianca and I quietly wondered what we were doing there, surrounded by people who faced dire, immediate, and inescapable problems. What do you say to a girl whose mother forces her to act handicapped so that she can receive a disability check? What do you tell a child who doesn't know when their next meal is coming? Whatever mixture of feelings I experienced—sadness, survivor's guilt, a fear of the future, a suspicion of my own unimportance—was overpowered by a new flavor of guilt. Ever since my childhood trip to India, when I first encountered poverty, I could not stop comparing my unhappiness to a greater degree of suffering that existed in the world. I had a comfortable home. Loving parents. Supportive friends and a great school system. By every calculation, I *should* have been happy and grateful. So why wasn't I . . . ?

Too many layers of softness and privilege separated Bianca and me from the rest of the inpatients. During group, Bianca and I were the only willing participants. We were dubbed "cooperative" and allowed to choose our meals. I had this idea that a psych ward would be a great equalizer—we're all equal in life and death, right?—but it was not like that at all.

The psychiatrist assigned to my case reminded me of the porcelain dolls I'd played with as a child, like she might shatter if I spoke too loudly. Pale skin, pale hair, and glazed eyes. She'd pull up a blue plastic chair and sit across from me in my assigned room. I'd smile. Her eye contact stuttered, much like her speech.

"So, Veena, tell me. How are you feeling today?"

She crossed her slight legs at her slight ankles. Took the spectacles hanging around her neck and placed them on her nose. Readied her clipboard and pen. I anticipated therapy the way some girls anticipated a good manicure; my depression would be clipped like an overgrown cuticle. A desperate mantra ran through my head: *She is trained. She can help me.*

"I feel okay," I said. "Still a bit sad and confused."

She asked further questions. I answered eagerly. She'd come back every day and we'd repeat the same conversation, me with a notch less enthusiasm, her with the same impassive expression. I scrutinized her hands, wondered what she was writing on her clipboard, scrutinized her face, wondered if I was the one who was depressed or she was. When I couldn't stand it any longer, I interrupted myself.

"I—I'm sorry. But do you have any kids?" I needed to know if this doctor had ever experienced human emotion.

She looked up, the slight shake of her blond bob the only indication of surprise. She attempted a smile that slid off her face like lukewarm water. "I have a dog."

There's no way she can help me.

When I think back on that moment, I realize that woman must have been highly trained and educated. But she was timid, and, at age fifteen, it was easy to conflate confidence and competence.

"Ah. Sorry." I gestured to her notes. "Please, continue."

The two relevant words on her clipboard: "situational depression." The term sounded like such an oxymoron (Was the problem with my brain? Or with the situation?) that I didn't bother to look it up for years and no one bothered to explain it to me either.

After two weeks in the psych ward, I was released abruptly back into the world, like a fish too small to eat.

Eliza came over the day I was discharged. She gave me a Doodle Bear that all my friends had signed; even Payton Miller, my first kiss, had signed it—though he didn't know why I was in the hospital and wrote "GET WELL SOON" on the forehead.

"Veena," Eliza said, "I would do anything to take this pain from you. I'd—I'd cut off my arm if it would help you."

"Jesus. Thank God I don't need your arm."

She wrapped herself around me and we lay on the floor of my room like that for a while, watching the paper cranes hanging from my ceiling refract light from the window.

My stay at the psych ward spliced my life into a clear Before and After. Amma and Nanna avoided any direct mention of the words "depression," "psych ward," and "suicide" like we were playing some elaborate, prolonged game of Catch Phrase. When forced to reference that time, they referred to it as "the Incident" and quickly changed the subject. When addressing me, it was "your Incident," as if to remind me that I alone bore the responsibility for everything that happened. But they were gentler than ever; Amma planned museum dates for the two of us and Nanna left CDs of Broadway show soundtracks on my pillowcase.

In the months that followed, I was presented to a string of psychologists who were the same but different; all perfectly nice women who wanted to know: *How did that make you feel?* I remained cooperative until roughly the fifteenth one.

"But you're young, beautiful, and have your whole life ahead of you. How can you be depressed?" All those things had been true of Sarah Rose, and not one of them made her any less dead.

I dragged my sneakers across their carpeted offices. "Aren't my parents paying you to answer that question?"

Mr. Carl came after the acupuncturist, the homeopath, and the environmental therapist. The six-foot-tall old white man leaned back in his swivel chair and told me that he partied and drank so much in college that he almost lost his football scholarship. The only major left that he could complete in time was psychology, back when psychology was still "for sissies."

"Since I'm going to ask you about yourself, I figured it was only fair I told you about myself."

Now this was a guy I could work with. Mr. Carl tested me extensively for personality and mood disorders. I filled in all the bubbles on the questionnaires. I read Kay Redfield Jamison's *An Unquiet Mind* and didn't relate to her experience of bipolar disorder. I chewed my fingernails as he flipped through my results.

"Well. Seems like you're pretty normal, kid." He tossed the paperwork on his desk. "I think they were spot-on when they told you that you have situational depression."

I should have felt relieved, but part of me wanted a more dramatic diagnosis to explain the abrupt left turn my life had taken—if for no other reason than to have a clear answer for the next person who asked:

But how could you *be depressed?* Maybe it was subconscious, but I was hoping for an answer that didn't seem quite so simple.

Since no pills, needles, or supplements could cure me, I was left caring for my mental health in the ordinary, boring ways: Mr. Carl drew me the cognitive behavioral triangle and explained how our thoughts generate feelings, which spur actions that can create positive or negative feedback loops. During the week I journaled, and at our appointments, I passed along the pages to Mr. Carl. He helped me identify potentially harmful thought patterns.

"You said you'd never resented anyone so much. But it seems like your previous psychologist was only trying to help you. We can't change her, but you can change your thoughts about her, and then you'll feel different."

Slowly, *I feel sad, I have always felt sad, and will always feel this way* turned into *I feel sad, but I haven't always felt this way because I can remember many specific times when I was happy, and I don't know how I will feel tomorrow because it is a new day*. Mr. Carl helped me place one foot in front of the other without feeling like I needed to tear off my skin with my teeth. But therapy has its limits; it couldn't answer questions like "What is the meaning of life?" or "Why do good things happen to bad people?" or my personal favorite, "How do I have the right to live when Sarah Rose is dead?"

I like to think that if I'd stuck with Mr. Carl for longer, I never would have needed Bob Lyon, but I don't know if that's true. Psychologists couldn't promise me a happy ending; Bob did.

5

2008 to 2011

I wish I could show you the beauty I found in life even while I questioned the meaning of it. My mom could brew us a pot of her chai, we could sit at my kitchen table and I could tell you about the surprise murder mystery party she threw for my sixteenth birthday, and we could laugh about that one time she accidentally burned a pair of socks to a crisp by warming them on a space heater. I wish I could take you backstage during tech week at my high school musicals, show you the part of the auditorium floor where I had my first kiss, and introduce you to my good friends and favorite teachers. I led the mock trial team to the state championship, maintained a GPA of 4.36, and was nominated most likely to succeed. My mental health had stabilized so much that I'd stopped seeing Mr. Carl—and he'd even invited me to intern for him the following summer. Even when things were bad, they weren't all bad. But for you to understand why the True Happiness Company could draw me in, you need to understand my state of mind—a state overpowered by my worst moments. Things were going well until I found out my childhood best friend, Kate, committed suicide.

Kate had been sending me messages for months throughout our junior year of high school, saying she missed our friendship. I missed it, too. It was Kate who introduced me to Britney Spears and hair straighteners. When we both got our periods, it was Kate, not Amma, who gave me my first pad and told me what to do. But I hadn't spoken to her since sixth grade, when she started hanging out with a different crowd, cutting class to smoke cigarettes in the alley behind the school. Our lives, which for those formative years felt like a single entity, were cleaved apart in the way you halve a crisp apple. She'd moved to a different neighborhood, and attended a different high school, but rumors about her dating her drug dealer made it across town. Things were going well for me, and I couldn't jeopardize that.

After Kate's fifth Facebook message that fall, I finally caved and invited her over, only to discover that we had nothing left in common. Her large eyes were rimmed with eyeliner as thick as a finger. Her strawberry blonde hair had been dyed black, but her demeanor carried the same inexhaustible energy. She told me her favorite band was KISS and talked about the latest WWE matches she'd watched on TV. I feigned interest. It had always been difficult to keep up with Kate's personalities. When it was my turn to speak, I talked about my new boyfriend too enthusiastically while Kate grew politely bored. As she was leaving, Kate left me with a standing invitation to her house. She was only twenty minutes away. I knew then that I should tell her I'd come by, but I was tired. I said goodbye and wished her well.

Three months later her brother found her hanging from her bedroom ceiling. I felt sick for him and obsessed with imagining Kate's final moments, as I had been with Sarah. I pictured Kate in my room, so nearby and so recent, but gone entirely.

Amma and Nanna forbade me to attend the wake; they didn't want me to see the body. I ran into Kate's mom in town months later and she asked me why I wasn't at the service. All the pictures were of the two of us: Halloween, summer camp, in our backyards. I felt like Kate deserved better than an excuse, so I just didn't answer. Her mom said she had a box of Kate's things for me, but I never went by to pick it up. I think I was scared to face her mom again. Even in Kate's death I wasn't there for her.

I didn't know how her classmates responded, but only a few kids at Severna Park cried for Kate. Other people described it as "unsurprising" because she had been "unstable." I heard rumors that before she died, she wrote "DON'T YOU MISS THESE TITS" across her chest in Sharpie and lay topless across her ex-boyfriend's windshield while his girlfriend was in the passenger seat. I didn't know if the rumors were true and I didn't care. I wanted to stomp on the faces of anyone who spoke about her breasts or her "drug problem." People can act superior all they want (Had I once thought I was better than her?), but in the end, we all die. I couldn't shake the feeling that if I had said something—if I had shared my experience with depression—maybe Kate would still be alive, organizing her days-of-the-week underwear and talking too much about KISS.

After Kate's death, I spent the senior year of high school occasionally cutting myself with razor blades in places no one could see and swallowing pills—either because I knew nothing would happen or because I was hoping something finally would. I thought that once I graduated high school, I could lay the tragedies of the past to rest. I had a vision for college that involved students in bright hoodies emblazoned with school crests, drinking at the fountain of knowledge. It was a metaphorical fountain, but my vision included a literal fountain as well—likely a result of the informational brochures I'd consumed before matriculating at William & Mary as a physics and philosophy double major. College was meant to be the happy marriage of my two cultures: the quintessential American coming-of-age experience and the only thing my parents loved more than their firstborn—education. Even Venkat had grown into himself when he'd left the house; the pothead I once knew was pursuing a master's at Stanford.

But my freshman year didn't go as planned; I was plagued by a recurring dream where Kate would come back to life and we would pick up where she left off. I was so happy she had returned that I could not call these dreams nightmares. But I was so angry at her for leaving in the first place, so riddled with fear that her body would fall apart, like Frankenstein's monster's, unable to stave off death, that I spent these dreams eyeing her pallid skin for signs of decay, while Kate, as she did in life, grew exasperated with my fussing and told me to loosen up. I started staying awake until the sun came out, and then inadvertently slept through my morning classes.

When the nightmares got to be too much, I finally broke down and opened up to a college friend, Ben Hewitt, about my past at Suicide High. Instead of the cathartic release I was hoping for, all I got was the false rumor that I was sleeping with him. Everyone thought we were cheating on our high school sweethearts. Even after we corrected the rumors ("Ah, actually I come from this town with a weirdly high suicide rate? And I was crying? That's why the door was closed. No, we weren't having sex.") everyone still looked at me like I was a pariah. By the end of the day, the people who I'd thought of as my friends—in this new college life where everything was supposed to be good, clean, and unmarred—were calling me a slut. I stopped speaking to Ben and everyone in my dorm. Shame is corrosive.

Things weren't going well with my boyfriend, either. He was three years older than me, we'd been dating long distance on and off, and we'd spent most of our two years together fighting.

Drag a relationship past its peak and all you can do is watch giddiness corrode into resentment. It feels passive and inevitable while it happens but, in truth, you actively compound the problem. His silences grow longer. His replies, when they do come, are gruffer and terser. You want to be gruff and terse in response, but instead your sentences expand to fill his silences and you're worried the effect is whiny.

Maybe falling out of love was normal for other people, but I knew that everything could end in an instant. Life was capricious and death gave no warning. He could get into a car accident. I could have a seizure and never wake up. Each conversation could be our last, so how could I risk letting him go because what if no one ever picked me up and told me I was worthwhile again? I was still hung up on that question by the time he broke up with me.

All I wanted was someone to know my depths, but everyone drowned before they reached the bottom.

Unsurprisingly, by the end of my first year in college, I did not find myself. I was solidly back to square one, scrolling through my phone and wondering *Who can you really call when you need help?* Eliza and I had had a falling out and I hadn't kept in touch with the rest of my high school friends. I had some texts from Venkat I'd forgotten to answer, but we'd never had the kind of relationship where we could open up to each other.

I texted my ex-boyfriend: I feel like hurting myself and don't know what to do.

He replied: Good. I hope you actually kill yourself this time.

Our relationship—bad in all the normal ways—was made yet more unbearable by my depression and his sporadic cruelty and kindness. I laughed and cried as I read the text, knowing, somehow, that I deserved it. I had taken a nice boy and I had worn him out, like thin sneaker soles.

I had one final exam left the next day and then my freshman year of college would be over. It was a beautiful balmy day, and I sauntered across campus, laughing at how good the sun felt on my skin and how unhappy I was in spite of it.

Back in my room, I collapsed on my desk chair, found bottles of Tylenol and Advil, upended both containers on the desk, and swallowed all the pills as fast as I could. I flopped over on my bed and thought about Kate—what she would have been like if she were the one lying on the bottom bunk in a college dorm instead of me. If she could've been happy here.

I tried to hold back the mounting nausea, but the taste of the medicinal candy coating was too overpowering. My eyes flew open, and I rushed to the communal bathroom. I ran into the first stall and vomited before I could shut the door. My hall mate Lacy looked up from the mirror where she was carefully applying mascara.

"Aw, Veena. Rough night?"

"Um. Yeah."

The little pills came falling out in a disgusting pink waterfall. The taste sharpened. I flushed and watched it swirl away. The word "blossom" hung in my mind. *You'll just blossom in college, Veena.* That was what my high school psychologist said before I left Severna Park. I approached the sink next to Lacy, leaning both elbows across the counter and cupping my hands for water.

"You all right?" She rubbed my back gently.

I swilled the water around in my mouth, nodded deeply, and spit. "Yeah. Thanks for asking."

Back in my room, my heart jumped around in my chest as I considered what to do about my one remaining final. I couldn't focus enough to sit through a classical mechanics exam and I'd heard the student health center could give you a note to postpone a final. Apparently I hadn't learned from my first psych evaluation, because when the psychologist at the health center asked about my mental health history, I was again overly honest. I answered every one of her questions, starting four years ago, with Sarah Rose. The mousy psychologist reached for tissues during my story and dabbed her eyes. I stared, certain that the tissues were meant to be for me.

"Are you having any current thoughts of self-harm?"

I paused slightly too long before saying no. She deposited me in the waiting room and disappeared without explanation. I watched the clock on the wall plod from 1 p.m. to 5 p.m. and lost hope that this woman would return. I picked up my bag, hoping to meet some friends at the dining hall but the secretary stopped me.

"No, no, honey. I think she wants you to stay."

At 8 p.m., my parents burst through the doors, agitated and confused.

"What are you doing here?" I asked, standing up in alarm. They lived three hours away and must have had to take off work to be here.

"Veena?" Amma squeezed me. "Is everything all right? The dean wouldn't explain anything to us. She just said we had to come get you."

Nanna hovered behind her as he had in the emergency room, bewildered and panicked.

"They didn't tell me they called you. I'm sorry you came all this way for nothing. I just wanted a couple more days to take my final."

Both of their faces were taut, and I knew they didn't believe me. A dean of students I'd never met before sat us in a conference room and told us that, given my mental health history, I was too much of a liability to have on campus. I would be leaving with my parents and allowed to return once I had "demonstrated considerable effort toward resolving my issues."

I laughed out loud. She said it as if I just hadn't *tried* hard enough to live for the past three years. My parents exchanged worried glances and spent the next eight minutes apologizing profusely to the dean.

The ride home was tense and awkward. I complained about missing my final to avoid noticing that my parents were terrified of me.

"I think the dean is just worried about you," Nanna said. "We are worried about you."

I had a different interpretation of the dean's priorities but I didn't argue. I wondered if her life had played out as she expected it, if it was everything she had dreamed it would be as a child. Because I did all the things I was supposed to do and I still couldn't find the happiness that was supposed to be the prize at the bottom of this cereal box.

I didn't know that in just a couple of days, we'd be packed into the minivan again, heading south instead of north, past William & Mary, past the life I thought I would have, on our way to meet the man who promised answers to all our questions.

6

May to June 2011

It is unclear what Amma typed into Google that night we got back from William & Mary, after we quietly unloaded my things. What do you google when your daughter who planned on getting a PhD in theoretical physics can't even finish her first year of college—for reasons you suspect but no one will confirm? How do you put that fear into words and then feed those words into Google? "My daughter won't stop trying to kill herself" and "What is the meaning of life?" are equally likely contestants. Google dredged up some woman who told Amma to talk to some man, and Amma brought her findings to our emergency meeting with my psychologist from home, Mr. Carl.

"There's this guy in Georgia," she said as we all gathered in his office, "and he helps families like us. We would go see him for a weekend."

Nanna sat beside her, blinking rapidly.

"I . . . don't think we loved you as well as we should have, Veena," Amma continued. "He can teach us how to do better."

"That's ridiculous," I snapped. "You are great parents. Nanna? You agree with this?"

Nanna tried to speak but couldn't. Finally, he nodded and put his arm around Amma's shoulder. "Yes," he said. "I think we failed you, Veena."

I didn't know what to say. I'd tried to kill myself to stop being a burden on them while they'd spent this entire time thinking my unhappiness was their fault. All three of us sat there thinking we'd failed each other.

There was no way I could have known then that they'd already spoken to Bob—that he'd already blown their preexisting insecurities out of proportion. Even in hindsight, it's hard to tell where Amma's and Nanna's natural fears as parents ended and Bob's manipulation began.

I tried to catch Mr. Carl's eye.

"I wouldn't go that far," he said. "But even though your parents are great, there are some things they're not qualified to handle."

"Wait," I said. "You don't actually think this is a good idea?"

"Why not?" he asked me levelly.

"For one, the guy lives in Georgia."

"I looked at his website. He's written a lot of books. Some of the stuff he's saying makes sense."

I won't bother to look at the website for years, but in retrospect, I'll wonder how Mr. Carl could have gotten past the grating stock photos of generically happy adults frolicking through fields.

"Do you have a different suggestion?" he asked.

I did not.

As soon as we got home, I made a cup of Earl Grey tea and sweetened it with Raid I found under my bathroom sink. Amma and Nanna were downstairs, arguing over something. I drank the whole sickly-sweet concoction before discovering it doesn't work on mammals. By that point you'd think I would have learned to read the bottle first.

Amma was sitting at the table when I rolled into the kitchen the next day, eyes flitting about and fingernails tapping the surface. It must have been a weekend. Time melted around me and I didn't register the passage of days. She sprang to her feet when I entered.

"Hey, Veena. Here's that thing that we talked about. You just have to sign this."

She pushed a piece of paper and a pen in my direction. If she were capable of looking me in the eye, her eyes would have pleaded with me. Instead, they raked over kitchen tile. Everyone spoke to me as if I were a fire hazard.

I glanced down at the paper. No one uses the name the True Happiness Company for anything other than a cult. You sort of know this already and I sort of knew it, too, when I first looked at the paper and laughed. I offered my mother some colorful suggestions about what she and her waiver could go do together. I wish that could have been the end of it. I wish that I could have chosen some kinder words for Amma and listed out each red flag: the hyperbolic company name, the man's lack of a medical license, and the fact that his services—whatever they were—required a legal waiver. Maybe she could have listened and we would have had a funny story to tell at family gatherings about the time we almost drove down to Georgia on a quest to fix me. But that's not what happened.

"*THIS* is the guy you want me to see?" I exclaimed. "I'm sorry. You didn't tell me he calls himself the True Happiness Company. This is bullshit."

"Veena, please don't use that kind of language." Amma wrung her hand. "You agreed to try it."

I had reluctantly agreed, but during that first discussion with Mr. Carl, she had left out several key details, such as the company name and what the treatment actually entailed.

"How much is he charging you? Where did you find this guy?"

"I—I was googling something and found his website," she said, faltering.

"How much are you paying him?" I repeated.

"Please, Veena. Money doesn't matter to us. We would pay anything if there is a chance it could make you happy."

I didn't know they paid almost half of my annual college tuition for two days with Bob Lyon, but from Amma's refusal to answer, I could guess the number was high. To burn money in this way couldn't be the culmination of my parents' hard work—of the miles that my father walked barefoot because he didn't own a pair of shoes until his college professor bought him one. His efforts had to count for something greater than the ability to write a large check to some stranger in the hopes of fixing a daughter who quite literally had it all but still couldn't manage to get it together.

My stomach turned and I went to the sink for a glass of water, making a mental note to never take advice from boys in psych wards. The twelve-year-old kid had suggested ant poison when he'd heard I'd tried Tylenol. Or was it rat poison? The image of a rat wasting away crawled into my brain and languished there. I gagged into my hands.

"What is going on here?" Nanna asked in a voice at once quiet and loud. Every argument in my family was settled by that tone of voice from my dad. He had entered so silently that I hadn't noticed until he spoke.

"Veena is saying that she doesn't want to go to Georgia anymore," Amma said, relieved that the backup had arrived.

"That's not a question, is it? We decided we would go. We are going," Nanna pronounced.

I considered protesting further, but I knew the scene too well to bother. I looked at my parents' tired faces, picked up the pen, and signed away my "considerable future legal rights."

Signing that waiver marked a turning point, but in that moment, it didn't feel like my life was turning at all. It felt devoid of movement. Maybe if I hadn't gotten in the car I would have wound up at another inpatient facility. Or maybe Bob was right when he told Amma I'd die young if she didn't take me to Georgia immediately. I don't know. As far as I was concerned, I had two options: I could die (successfully, this time), or I could forcefully choose to live. Continuing to limp along in this wan, diluted manner was unacceptable.

The next day we piled into Amma's minivan for the twelve-hour drive. The last time Nanna drove the minivan was on a family road trip. Typically, Venkat would sit in the back with me, but at that moment, he was in California getting his master's. No one remembers what they told Venkat or when. He had such a go-with-the-flow attitude that it was easy to forget to keep him in the loop. I didn't think of him often, but sometimes I remembered the way he wept over me in the ER and wondered what he thought of his unstable sister. When I'd comment on Venkat's absence, Amma would say, "He said he texted you, but you didn't text back." I'd scroll through my messages later in private and, sure enough, would find his unanswered text. Somehow his messages escaped my notice.

I sat in the back of Amma's enormous Toyota Sienna, with a full row of empty seats separating me from my parents that forced us to yell to hear each other over the length of the car. Nanna hated driving Amma's minivan. His own car was a ten-year-old stick shift BMW in immaculate condition. The leather seats were heated and spotless; he had a strict no-food-in-the-car policy. In Amma's minivan, on the other hand, the cupholders were caked with half an inch of not quite dry chai. Nanna cursed each time he reached for his water bottle and came away with sticky residue on his hands. Amma clucked her tongue when he complained, her way of letting him know it's not a big deal and could he relax, *please,* for once. You could always smell but never quite locate an overripe banana somewhere in the van.

"Keep a lookout for the next Subway sign you see," Nanna said.

I groaned. "Not Subway again." We had already stopped at Subway for lunch, and every Subway on the Eastern Seaboard seemed to be owned by an Indian family who would smile at us and ask, "From India?

Which part?" And my parents would be drawn into a lengthy conversation about the motherland while I waited for my Italian B.M.T.

Nanna glared at me in the rearview mirror. "If you have a different suggestion, fine. Otherwise, no complaining."

I leaned forward in my seat. "What about Sonic? My friends say it's a drive-in restaurant where the waiters bring you your food on roller skates."

Amma clapped her hands and cooed into Nanna's ear. "Wow, roller skates?? Let's go to Sonic!"

Nanna took the next exit, fuming but accepting defeat. We pulled in and scanned the menu.

"Hot dogs . . . hamburgers . . . cheeseburgers." Amma's face fell. "Only meat."

We ate dinner at the nearest Subway.

It was midnight when we arrived in Georgia. We turned onto a quiet suburban street, and I pressed up against the window, trying to make out the shapes of individual houses. I asked when we were getting to the hotel, assuming we must have made a wrong turn. But Nanna pulled into a nondescript driveway and announced, "We are here." With the engine off, I could make out the sound of unusually loud frogs in the distance. As the air-conditioning dissipated, the muggy heat of Georgia began to seep into my skin. That's when Amma pulled the wrinkled paper out of her purse and read aloud the instructions to "follow the lighted stairs to the basement guest quarters."

I laughed into resounding silence. "Wait, are you serious right now?"

Amma and Nanna unloaded their bags. I stayed in the car, alone. If you get a sinking feeling in your stomach right about now, that is a good thing. I had that feeling, too. Apparently, that was my gut feeling. Now, people tell me to trust my gut, but when I was nineteen, people told me, "You're overreacting."

I sat with this unease for another minute before ripping my backpack out of the van and stomping down a set of brick steps strung with a single strand of Christmas lights in the heat of June. The steps led under a porch, to a glass basement door with a keypad. Amma stood under the outdoor lights, punched a number into the keypad, and opened the door.

To the right was a standard, well-stocked kitchenette, the counters replete with coffee, teas, and a bowl of perfectly round, perfectly green Granny Smith apples. To the left was a living area with a TV and plush couch, chosen by someone who obviously valued comfort over style. The hallway past the kitchen led to three separate bedrooms. The basement was, at least, a separate apartment, though it did not make up for the fact that we were sleeping in the basement of some random man's house. My parents and I were the only ones there. Amma and Nanna settled into the room with the king-size bed. I picked the far bedroom with two twin beds, huffed down on one, and sent Venkat an angry text about our parents' lack of judgment.

Wow, came his reply. They must be really desperate.

I smirked and shot back: You have no idea.

PART II

TRUE HAPPINESS

7

June 4, 2011

I wake up uncomfortable and disoriented. I have to remind myself, *Right. I'm stuck in the basement of a stranger's home in backcountry Georgia, waiting to see a man who calls himself the True Happiness Company.*

The basement is empty. I shower using a body wash I find in a bowl of single-use soaps on the bathroom counter. I dress in a floral silk blouse, a black miniskirt, and suede flats. I'm going for the polished look that says *I'm sane; we're done here*. My parents climb down the basement stairs and inform me that they just met with Bob and now it's my turn—though it remains unclear what it is my turn to do: sound healing, holding hands and singing to Pete Seeger, or doing a deep dive on my star chart. Amma and Nanna point me to a set of stairs that connects to the main home at ground level. I ask several times if I'm really supposed to just climb the stairs into this man's home. Finally, I do.

I find myself in the kitchen with a towering woman whose appearance and demeanor make me think both "gentle giant" and "friendly troll." She smiles broadly at me—as if she regularly has suicidal teenagers traipsing through her kitchen. While brewing a cup of tea, she introduces herself as Bob's wife, Barbara.

"He's in there waiting for you."

The gentle giant has a Canadian accent. Barbara gestures to a thin set of folding doors that open to the living room. I walk in and she shuts the doors behind me. In the center sits an old man in a rocking chair. Behind him, an unused fireplace. A Black woman sits at a desk before a window with the curtains closed. Her presence calms me; it's a relief that I'm not alone with this strange man—and that there are at least some people of color in his circle.

"You slept in."

No matter how he will tell this story later, those are the first words we exchange. His voice is clear and commanding and belies my initial impression of him as a redneck. Bob rocks back and forth impassively and clears his throat. "I like that. You get up when you're ready instead of worrying about being on time."

He has a talent for delivering what, at surface level, appears to be a compliment but leaves you with the feeling that you've done something wrong. Am I late? I've been awake for hours, but no one told me when I was expected. I pause behind the couch. My flats sink into the thick carpet, and I debate whether to apologize, but ultimately decide that if he wanted me there at a certain time, he should have made it known. Bob Lyon nods toward the couch in front of him, indicating for me to sit. I perch on the edge and fold my skirt neatly over and under my thighs.

"So, while you're here, you have to keep an open mind."

I arch my eyebrows and reply calmly, "I don't *have* to do shit."

"No." The syllable hangs in the air with quiet ferocity, derailing my thoughts. "No," he repeats with one firm shake of the head. "You really don't."

Bob's eyes do not leave mine.

"But," he says lightly, "I know something you don't."

"Okay." I want to get to the punch line more than I want to fight. "What?" I concede.

"I know how to be happy." He speaks quietly now. "If you want—and only if you really *want*"—he emphasizes these last words, cranes his neck down to get a good look at my reaction, and waits while I half nod—"I can teach you how."

He straightens in his chair, waiting for my reaction to a line he's probably delivered a thousand times.

I roll over the phrase "only if you really want" in my mind, like a jawbreaker along the tongue, the idea too big and too dense to bite into at once. I've seen a parade of mental health professionals and not one has asked me what I want. You don't ask a totaled car if it wants to be repaired. You take it to the shop and fix it. Spit on the seats and rub out the scuffs. Replace the shattered windshield. Change the tires. Or scrap it for parts.

I have no witty retort, too winded by the thought that what I want could matter. Bob's large, weathered hands grip the wooden armrests as he watches me.

"All right. What do you want?" I grumble.

"Me? Nothing. I don't need you to do spit." He practically spits when he says the word. He leans forward in the chair, hands spread out in front of him to illustrate the situation. "Look, kid, you're stuck here for three days. Your parents won't let you leave. You're welcome to go back downstairs and watch TV. Or go outside and walk the grounds. We've got some nice woods out here and a lake behind the house. But you are so miserable that your life couldn't possibly get worse. You've got absolutely nothing to lose. So, you might as well listen to what I have to say." Bob reclines in his chair, knowing he's scored for the home team.

Well, I have been half-heartedly trying to kill myself for the past three and a half years. Maybe the man has a point.

• • •

THERE IS A texture to people. There are things you feel before you know, things you know before you know why you know them: she has an open heart and would donate money to charity; he'd make a loyal friend; they're searching for something they'll never find. You find these clues in an upturned face, a pair of used sneakers, a moment of eye contact. These hints are so fleeting that they melt out of your periphery before they have a chance to crystallize. The signs disperse but the feelings they inspire solidify into convictions. Bob Lyon not only has a texture but a weight to him.

"Tell me a little about yourself. Why are you here?" he asks. He hangs his thumbnail between his teeth and settles in for my answer.

"I'm here because I have no choice," I snap. "My classmate killed herself and things went downhill from there."

"That must have been very scary for you." His response seems so natural, so obvious, but it's one I've never heard before. Every therapist has forced me to explain and re-explain how traumatizing the incident was.

"Yes. It was scary."

He stares at me, chewing the inside of his cheek. "But it's not why you're here."

I fold my arms across my chest and smirk. Thirty seconds in and he's already trying to explain my own life to me.

"All this pain you've felt," Bob says, waving his arms about, "is the result of a lifetime of not feeling loved. Most of the wounds you're experiencing now began in childhood."

I unstick my thighs from the couch. "Uh, I do feel loved. And you're implying that my parents didn't love me."

"I'm not implying anything. I'm saying it outright: your parents did not love you." He leans back. "They didn't know how."

"That's absurd," I say, already bored with this game. This old man knows nothing about my parents or where they come from. Behind him on the fireplace mantel are pictures of smiling, clean-cut white American kids and grandkids. He has no concept of the sacrifices my parents have made in order to carve out a life for my brother and me in this country, no idea about the family they've left behind or their commitment to care for me no matter how far I push them beyond their comfort zones and value systems. Amma and Nanna may express their love differently from whatever ideal Bob has in mind, but I have nothing to learn from anyone who would dismiss everything they've given me with a single sentence.

The kind-looking woman in the corner smiles to herself as she writes something on her notepad and Mr. Lyon follows my gaze.

"Did I forget to introduce Enid? Sorry. She'll be taking notes for you. I can never remember what I say, so Enid will jot down things you're learning. When I met Enid, she was a wreck. Her three grown children hated her. She was on the verge of divorce. She had nothing. Angry all the time."

Enid nods emphatically. Something in her expression pulls tears to my eyes.

"*THERE*," Mr. Lyon says, pointing at my face. "You felt something."

I blink away the wetness before it escapes onto my face. "I—I don't believe in pitying people," I stammer. I've never had someone notice my own emotions before I do and the effect is deeply disconcerting.

"Not pity. Empathy. A minute ago, when I was just speaking, you felt compassion for Enid. And I can help you, like I helped her."

"Okay," I say. "What are you suggesting?"

"Loving someone and caring about them are two very different things. Your parents care about you very much, but they were never taught to love you unconditionally."

This strikes me as semantics. "According to you, what is the difference between loving and caring?"

Mr. Lyon reaches for one of three plastic water bottles on the floor beside him, arranged in a pyramid like bowling pins. He cracks open the seal and takes a long swig, all with one hand. "Unconditional love is when we care about the happiness of another human being without expecting anything in return. We all care. We all want to love each other. But simply wanting to understand calculus doesn't make you capable of doing complex math. You have to be taught. When we're not taught how to love unconditionally, we end up rewarding our kids when they are 'good' and withdrawing our love when they are 'bad.'"

Something about the way he frames this concept gives me pause. Of course my parents care about me . . . but haven't they made their share of mistakes? Haven't they trained me to be "good"?

"Like patting a dog on the head when it rolls over," I say slowly. I start reevaluating my parents' worst moments, like reading a horoscope for any conceivable truth: the time Amma told me I was adopted because she was mad at me, the time Nanna pinned me against the wall because I wouldn't eat breakfast. "But even if this were true—and I'm not convinced it is—what does all this have to do with my depression?"

Mr. Lyon takes another drink from the water bottle. "When we don't get the love we need, it creates a gaping hole in our lives and we grab at anything that might temporarily ease the pain: money, sex, praise, power. The danger of these things is not that they don't work but that we think, 'If only I can get enough, I'll be happy.' It's never enough. Sooner or later, something disrupts that process. Your classmate dies." He gestures at me. "You don't get the promotion you were promised. Someone breathes on you in the wrong way. It takes very little to bring it all down. We mistakenly assume those events lead to depression. The pain was there all along. We just couldn't see it because we were medicating it."

The weight of my accomplishments lies heavily on my chest: the AP credits, the mock-trial championships, the soccer trophies, the violin awards. He's right; I *have* been taught that if I succeed enough, earn enough, look good enough, act nice enough—then I'll finally be happy. But I'm not. And if no amount of achievement can bring me happiness, what can?

"I used to be the youngest eye surgeon in the country with my own private practice, had enough money to do anything, buy anything, had five beautiful children, and I had to get addicted to narcotics for twelve years before I ended up in the woods back there," Mr. Lyon says, pointing toward the drawn window, "with a gun to my head thinking, 'This can't be it,' before I finally learned something."

I sensed our shared history instinctively—pain recognizes pain—but hearing it confirmed is an analgesic for a constantly inflamed wound.

"I don't know if I actually wanted to die." The words roll out of my mouth before I can reel them in.

Mr. Lyon shimmies his rocking chair so close to me that his thick blue jeans brush my knees. "You didn't."

The finality of his pronouncement takes me aback. He rests his elbows on his knees and his face in his hands. I catch my breath, so I won't exhale on him.

"All you really wanted was for someone to listen to you. You wanted someone to care. You wanted to matter."

The truth of his words reverberates through me, jangling my insides like a cowbell.

"You just didn't know that it was possible. You didn't dare believe. So being dead was the next best thing. But we can do better than dead," he says. "We can do happy."

The hope I start to feel is so delicate and so novel that I don't make any sudden movements. If there's a chance that what he's saying is true, I'll do whatever it takes to fix me.

8

June 5, 2011

I sleep easy. The basement guesthouse, which seemed like the set of a crappy murder mystery last night, now feels quaint and homey. My skin feels soft and exposed as if I've been rubbed down with sandpaper. The tension between my parents and me has dissipated. Mr. Lyon told me to sleep in, but I wake early, energized, and spend the morning exploring his backyard. Deer scamper off into the woods. I take a seat on a swing hung between two trees, enjoying the early sun on my arms and the feel of cool chain links in my hands. Around eight, I enter his kitchen from the outside stairs to his deck. Enid is making herself a cup of coffee.

"Doesn't this whole thing feel weird to you?" I cannot help but ask her. "Staying in some old man's house in Georgia?"

When Mr. Lyon first introduced Enid, he mentioned that she lives in Baltimore, twenty minutes away from me. She laughs and pours cream into her coffee. "Honey, it is *so* weird. I have known this man for twenty years. I was one of his very first guinea pigs before he really figured out what he was doing. I have thrown his books across the room more times than I can remember and yelled, 'I am never talking to that crazy white man again!'" She shakes and opens two packets of Splenda.

"But you heard him. Before I met him, not one of my children would speak to me. My husband and I were on the verge of divorce. He got me my family back."

I nod. It's hard to argue with an endorsement like that. Mr. Carl may have taught me some useful skills, but I can't say that he's drastically altered my life. Enid seems to have an unmistakable ease of existing in the world that functions as its own kind of endorsement. She finishes her coffee, and we assume our regular positions in the living room. When Mr. Lyon joins us, there is no preamble this time.

He squints at me. "Were you ever diagnosed?"

I've filled out more mental health questionnaires than standardized tests. My parents dragged me from office to office, and the diagnosis was unanimous: "Uh, they just told me I have situational depression."

Mr. Lyon nods. "If you had ever been properly diagnosed, they would have told you that you have borderline personality disorder."

Before I even know what the diagnosis means, my body floods with relief. All the times people asked, "Did you know her well?" and "But how can you feel this way because you have great parents and a great house?" I never had an answer that satisfied them. Now, in the span of seconds, Bob Lyon can finally explain why I've been feeling this way with a reason so compact and travel friendly that it fits into just three words. My hall pass to experience emotions deeply.

In this moment, I'm not focusing on the fact that Bob is a former eye surgeon without any training in psychology. In this moment, I'm not thinking about his credentials at all.

"Now, I'm not huge on labeling people," he continues, "but I am telling you this because it will explain your entire life to you. In order to qualify for the disorder, you have to meet five of nine criteria." He counts them out on his fingers. "Feeling dissociated from reality, distorted and unstable self-image, turbulent relationships, extreme mood swings—and I'm not talking about having a bad day. We're talking one minute you're on the top of the world and the next minute you're at the center of hell. You've never known happiness, will never know happiness again for the rest of your life, and then the next minute you're bored. Look it up when you get a chance. Borderline personality disorder. You'll sit there thinking, 'This just described my entire life.'"

Even though I've just met him, it feels like he's known me forever. Within hours, this man, who labels himself the True Happiness Company, has figured out what all the licensed psychiatrists could not. For some truths, you don't need fancy psychology doctorates or tedious questionnaires. For some things, you can just look at a person and *know*. At least in the mind of a suicidal nineteen-year-old.

I will look up the diagnosis later but only to confirm his vision. I won't question Bob's interpretation of borderline personality disorder for years; the diagnosis will leave me too busy questioning my own judgments.

"Honey, you're not aware that you do this, but you are such an expert at manipulating people that no one in your life has ever had the courage to tell you what you need to hear."

The word "manipulate" burrows into my stomach. My ears get hot, and my face feels unclean as I struggle with the gap between who I thought I was and who he is telling me I am. No one has articulated this about me before. Not the high school teachers I'm still in touch with, not my psychologists, not my friends. Amma always says I'm honest to a fault, and I get my integrity from Nanna. She calls it my "honesty problem," but what does she know? With all the pain I've caused, there has to be something wrong with me, some deeper rot inside.

I fidget with my skirt. "Why should I trust you when you're describing things about me that no one else sees?"

"Would you trust one hundred blind people? Or the one person who can actually see?"

And that's it; the self-image that I've pieced together over the years rattles away like a handful of dry leaves carried by a single, powerful gust of wind. I feel sick as I realize I'm an unstable, manipulative girl, but it also feels good—finally having an answer. It means I can do better.

I really want to do better.

"If you walk away from this"—he gestures between us—"no one will tell you this again for the rest of your life. I have seen your story too many times to have any doubt. You will either eventually succeed in killing yourself, or you will end up permanently institutionalized by the time you're twenty-one. And, honey," Mr. Lyon says, "that would just break my heart."

A chill shoots up my spine. If the way the dean of students treated me is any indication, Mr. Lyon's right.

"Honey, I can teach you how to change all this. I can teach you how to live differently."

"Wait, what? You're going to tell me what to do?" Part of me wants to vomit at the thought, and yet another wants to weep with relief.

"Yes," he says, emphatic now. "You didn't think that I was just going to sit here, make you tell your story until you went blue in the face, and then send you home to the same exact situation you left?"

Stunned silence softens me for a moment. "That's what everyone else has done."

"I know!" he shouts, smacking the armrest. "I believe you! That's what everyone is *trained* to do. But we are not going to do that here. We will make sure you have everything you need and an actual *plan* before you leave."

"Okay, so what do we do?" I ask, holding back tears. "I don't want to be like this."

"We'll get to that. First"—Mr. Lyon comes so close to me that our noses almost touch; his breath smells like buttermilk—"I love you."

I recoil. "You don't even know me."

"True," he replies, undeterred. "I've known you for less than a day. Incidentally, I know you better than anyone in your life ever has. What would I need to know in order to love you? Your résumé? Your high school GPA?" He works his jaw in the silence. His lips are thin, his nose narrow. Everything about him is focused. "What would you need to know about someone who is drowning before you decide to reach in and help them out of the water? Their middle name? Their favorite hobby?"

My mouth hangs helplessly open. How have I gone through life never asking myself these questions? What deems a person worthy of love? Worth saving? I don't know.

"I love you because you need it. It's as simple as that. You are so used to earning affection that you have no idea what unconditional love even *looks* like. I love you exactly like I love my own grandchildren. When they were born, when they were itty-bitty babies, I didn't ask them to perform circus tricks before deciding to love them. No, I just *did*. Right now, you are a baby. No exaggeration." He rests his hands on my knees. "So, no, I don't know you. *And* I love you all the same."

"Why does this matter? I have plenty of people in my life who love me. Or 'care' about me," I say, adjusting myself out of his reach.

"Until you've completely opened up to one person, you'll always be holding back. There will always be a part of you that thinks, 'You wouldn't love me if you knew . . . fill in the blank.'"

I go quiet, reliving the biggest regret of my life. Months after I got out of the hospital, during a depressive episode, I texted Eliza to ask if she could come over, but she was hanging out with a boy she had a crush on instead. She texted back: We can't always hang out in your dark room. We have lives too.

Hurt and angry, I cut up the Doodle Bear she had given me when I first got out of the hospital. Then I rang her doorbell and put it in her arms without a word. My heart hurt as soon as I saw the look of concern on her face, but I couldn't speak. Eliza followed me home, worried out of her mind. I wanted to scoop up every kind thing she'd said and place it back in her mouth for safekeeping, for someone more deserving. Her mom forbade her to see me after that, but Eliza ignored her and stayed up all night, sewing the bear back together, hoping it would make me whole. She kept reaching out, trying to absolve me of that moment—something she'll continue to do for a decade—but I stopped speaking to her after that. If no one else would punish me for my bad behavior, it was my job to insulate them from whatever I had become.

After I finish telling the story, Mr. Lyon is silent for a long moment. I'm crying so hard that my face is slick. He continues rocking impassively back and forth in his chair, and I regret speaking. No matter how many times I had talked over this mistake with Amma and Mr. Carl, I can't scrub myself clean. They might write it off as the mistake of a depressed fifteen-year-old, but I still think no one would love me if they knew how I treated Eliza. No one *should*.

"Your problems," Mr. Lyon says, "would have been completely crushing to your high school friends."

I hadn't thought it was possible for me to feel worse, but here we are.

"Heck, your problems were crushing to *you*. They were overwhelming for your parents and your psychologists—all of them. But you had no way of knowing that. You had no better way to handle yourself. It never occurred to you that your friends didn't have the necessary tools to help. How could it?" His face is relaxed and easy. "But I can help you, sweetie. I'm an old man. I've been around. Nothing you can tell me is going to shock or disgust or overwhelm me. You don't ever have to go through something like that alone again."

Finally, someone I can't hurt. The feeling of discomfort persists, though I no longer regret sharing the story. "Yeah, I just . . . don't like to think about how I acted. . . ."

"You really hate yourself."

More fat tears roll down my cheeks. "I hate myself, Mr. Lyon," I wail, digging my nails into my thighs.

"Listen closely, honey. All the things that you have come to think of as yourself? They're not *you*." He jabs a finger at my chest. "They're not even close. You're not a depressed *person*. You're not an angry *person*. You've been depressed and angry for such a long time that you think those are your character traits. They're not."

"I—I don't understand."

"If I videotape you from the chest up, and then stab you in the leg with a fork"—he mimes the videotape and the fork in my thigh—"what would you look like to an outside observer? Let's say I play that video to someone and ask them to describe what Veena is like. What would they say?"

"That I'm a crazy person."

"Yes. They really would. Because all they would see is you flailing around and screaming. *They wouldn't be able to see the fork.* Get it? All this time, you've been in more pain than you ever realized. More pain than you realize right now, even. And all those things—angry, depressed—they were a reaction to the pain. *They're not you.* Not even close."

A helium balloon rises in my chest. "But without all that . . . who am I?"

"Exactly. You have no idea who you really are. Cool! As you begin to feel loved, we'll find out together. It's like you're covered in shit and you're looking at yourself in a mirror going, 'Gosh, I look terrible.' Not you, sweetie. Just the shit. We get rid of all the shit, all these defense mechanisms, and then we'll see what you're actually like underneath. And you'll *really* like what's underneath."

"How do you know? What if it's just more unpleasant things?"

Mr. Lyon shakes his head. "Not possible. Happy people have this incredible positive energy about them. When you know someone loves you, you become fearless. Invincible."

His description of the transformation affects one in me as he speaks.

I clap my hands together. "Then I'm excited to find out!"

Mr. Lyon laughs, his whole body quaking from the gut up. "Me too, kid. Me too."

He stands from his rocking chair, the top half of his body pitched forward at the waist to maintain his balance. He lowers himself next to me on the couch, like a gradually lowering forklift. Instinctively, I pull away. Still facing forward, he reaches out a hand and tugs my arm upward. I pull further away and look at him in confusion.

"Stand up," he says finally.

He has to repeat his instructions before I rise awkwardly to my feet and stand facing him. He rotates me to face the fireplace and pulls me down onto his lap. My knees resist before buckling. One of Mr. Lyon's thick, hairy arms turns me sideways and wraps around my back so that he is cradling me like a baby. His other arm snakes under my thighs. He takes great care to ensure my clothing does not ride up or expose me in any way, but I'm still relieved I chose pants today instead of yesterday's miniskirt. My arms hover awkwardly in front of my chest, preparing to spar. Mr. Lyon extricates them and places them around his neck. My muscles are rigid, coiled with tension. What is happening right now? I glance over my shoulder at Enid for her reaction. Mr. Lyon's gaze follows my thoughts.

"Oh, you can bet I've held Enid like this," he says.

She smiles in confirmation. I don't even know how that would be possible logistically since she is bigger than Mr. Lyon. But her smile is so placid that this must be normal for them. Normal enough that she is not intervening on my behalf. My mind starts racing for a way to get out of the situation without causing a scene.

"This is what we all need, honey. This touch. Connection"—he scratches my back with his fingers—"but we're all too worried about being polite. So, we stay alone."

I'm too nonplussed to speak, but I wonder if there is truth to what he says. As wildly uncomfortable as this is, the idea of being held has some abstract appeal, especially if it were my parents or friends doing the holding. I used to cuddle with my friend Melanie when we felt sad, just for companionship, and the physical touch helped ground me in my body. It sounds socially abnormal to say it out loud, but it felt healing to be near someone I cared about. Right now, though, all I want to do is run out of the room.

Mr. Lyon looks deep into my eyes and places his nose near mine. He tells me I'm done being alone; I've got him now. My body stays tense and I try to look away.

"You notice how I didn't ask for your permission to hold you?"

My eyes widen and I give a tiny, quick nod. I had indeed noticed.

"It's not an accident," he says. "People are so scared and confused that they don't know what they need. I use the rocking chair on purpose, too. That way I can scoot closer and closer to people without them noticing. Pretty sneaky, huh?" The skin near his eyes crinkles. He chews his lip and winks at me. I laugh, increasingly focused on a pain in my back, wondering how to unstitch myself from his arms.

"Your mom, bless her heart, told me, 'Veena doesn't like being touched.' Well, I've been doing this for years and if your mom knew what you needed, you wouldn't be in this situation to begin with." He laughs, Enid chuckles, and I mentally thank Amma for trying to establish my boundaries. "You hate being *used*. Turns out, you love being touched—when there are no ulterior motives. When someone is not trying to *get* something from you."

I smile politely. Finally, it occurs to me that I can use the uncomfortable position as an excuse to get up.

"Sorry, my back is hurting," I say. "Can I sit up again?"

"Oh! Sure. Sure." Mr. Lyon suggests we take a ten-minute break. Enid flips to a new page on the legal pad. It's only halfway through my second day, but I feel like an oversaturated sponge, in need of a good wringing out before I can take in any more.

"Did he touch you?" Amma asks when I go downstairs. "I asked him not to."

"Yeah . . ." I say, rubbing my arm. "It was weird, but it was only for a second."

Amma relaxes. I can tell she wants to ask more questions, but I am physically and emotionally exhausted from reconfiguring my entire sense of self in the span of twenty-four hours. I lie down in the room with the twin beds and text Venkat: Weird old man in Georgia: not as bad as I was expecting.

He replies: That's a relief. Glad he didn't turn out to be a serial killer.

After another one-on-one session with Mr. Lyon, we all meet as a family. I was nervous about meeting all together, but Mr. Lyon assured me that I've never had him on my side before and that I'm going to like it. He drums his fingers on the armrest. "She's much happier," he says abruptly. "And we've only talked for one day. Can you see that?"

My parents smile with an uncomplicated brightness I haven't seen in years. "Yeah," Amma says, reaching over to touch me. "She is much calmer."

"Yes! She's *softer*. She's *tender*. I'm thrilled that you both can see the change in her already."

"Guys, I'm right here."

"Sorry, dear," Mr. Lyon says, grabbing my knees and knocking them around. "*You* are softer. More gentle. Less afraid. Hopeful, even. Do *you* see that?"

I inhale and exhale. "Yeah. Yeah, I do."

"So, what are the things you usually fight about? Anyone can speak up. This is how we learn: through everyday, real-life examples."

Amma opens her mouth and looks around to confirm her needs are most urgent. "Bob, I feel like I have a good relationship with my son, but when Veena is at college, she never calls me. How do I get her to call me more often?"

Out of all the concerning aspects of my life, of course this would be the most pressing one for her. If I were dying in a ditch somewhere, Amma—along with every other Indian mother—would worry about how good the cell service was at the bottom of my ditch so she could call to make sure I'd been eating three meals a day and sleeping at "normal hours."

Mr. Lyon pets both her knees, preparing to let her down gently. "Sweetie, listen close. When your daughter calls you?"

Amma nods eagerly.

"Throw a fucking party."

I lean back and look between them. Who is this guy and where has he been all my life? If I spoke to my parents like that, you would find me hanging from a meat hook in a dark freezer somewhere. No one is allowed to speak to my parents in that manner, but Amma just flashes a painfully confused smile.

"I mean it. Buy balloons. Whatever you need to do. It's not our kids' job to love us. They need us too much."

From the look on her face, Amma believes Mr. Lyon as little as I do. I've seen many a Bollywood movie where the heroine marries the hero based on a parent's dying wish. The movies always end with those couples living happily ever after, having honored their parents' legacy. And this white man is telling me it's not my job to make my parents happy?

"When kids are in as much pain as Veena, most of them refuse to interact with their parents at all. Now, did you notice that as soon as you started speaking, Veena tensed up?"

This observation resonates enough to reengage Amma. "No, I didn't notice."

"That tells me this isn't the first time you've had this conversation."

"*THANK YOU!*" I burst. "I would talk to you more if you didn't spend the entire time complaining about how I don't talk to you."

Mr. Lyon does not break eye contact with Amma. "Do you see what Veena just did? She *gave you the answer*. Most kids don't. If you stop nagging her, she WILL talk to you more."

Watching Amma's reaction is like watching daybreak across a dark sky. "Oh. Okay. I didn't realize that. I can do that!"

"Anything else on your minds?"

Nanna shakes his head. "No. We are just very happy to be here."

"Wonderful."

"I've got something," I say. "My dad is pretending to be humble—"

"Hmmm, abstemious," Nanna mumbles. This is a thing he does, interrupting conversations to function as an out-of-context thesaurus—a holdover from those GRE days.

"Yeah, whatever. But that's not actually how he feels. My parents complain about me all the time, but now that we're here, he's pretending to be all supportive and Zen."

The rocking chair inches toward me, and my rambling peters off.

"Let's assume that your dad is making this up about twenty percent. Or forty percent. There would still be sixty percent of him that genuinely means this. Your dad is so used to withdrawing emotionally that when he does open up and express some tender emotions, it sounds foreign to you. You don't believe it." Mr. Lyon pauses. "Give your dad the benefit of the doubt. He's trying to do something he's never done before. I bet they don't encourage men to express their emotions in India, do they?" he says to Nanna.

Nanna stares at his feet. "No." He chuckles. "My mother didn't have the time or the energy to teach us all that."

He still has scars across his knuckles to show for Bamma's form of educating her sons. When Nanna was eight, his father took a nap during a family picnic and never woke up. It's not difficult to imagine that Bamma—as a single mother with three boys who were always stealing the neighbor's goat, setting the mattress on fire, or burning the concrete floor with hydrochloric acid—had limited opportunities for emotional sensitivity training.

"You are adorable, little man," Mr. Lyon says, squeezing Nanna's knees.

"Adorable" and "little." Two words I've never heard used in conjunction with my dad. Mr. Lyon reads my mind and turns back to me to say, "I've heard this guy has been pretty scary to you, all that yelling and stuff. Turns out he's a marshmallow. Earlier he started crying simply because I pronounced his name correctly. Apparently, no one has taken the time to do that."

The last time I saw Nanna cry, I was nine. He's crying now. Mr. Lyon has that effect.

The rest of the session continues in this way, with each of us taking turns airing our grievances, and Mr. Lyon helping us find solutions that feel obvious in retrospect but felt impossible to find on our own. Enid occasionally chimes in with stories about her own children. It's 5:00 p.m. when we stop—we sat there for seven hours in total. I have instructions to call him every day when I return home. Enid gives us her phone number and says she'll connect us with a local True Happiness group in Baltimore. I text Venkat.

Me: Heading home! Confirmed Georgia man is not a serial killer, just weird.

Venkat: lol

There is a story in Hindu mythology about Ganesh and his older brother, Kartikeya. As with many Hindu stories, no two people can agree on the details, but the way my parents told it, Lord Brahma gave Shiva and Parvati a magic fruit—a mango. Whoever ate the fruit would gain wisdom and knowledge. Shiva and Parvati had two sons, and they could not choose who should receive this blessing. They decided that the son who circled the world three times first would win the mango. It wasn't much of a race; Ganesh, the plump elephant-headed god, had only a mouse as a pet and vehicle, while the athletic Kartikeya immediately jumped onto his peacock and set off. In the meantime, Ganesh called his parents to sit together on Mount Kailash, mounted his mouse, and circled his parents three times.

"Now give me the mango," Ganesh said.

His parents looked at him in confusion. "But you haven't fulfilled the terms of the competition."

Ganesh replied, "As my parents, you are the world to me. When I went around you three times, it was equal to going around the world."

There's no consensus on how Kartikeya reacted when he returned, whether he flew into a rage or accepted defeat graciously, but the tale ends with Ganesh winning and eating the fruit. Amma and Nanna have always told me that the moral of this story is to honor your parents, but growing up in a white suburb, I had a difficult time appreciating the parable. Sure, respect your elders and all that, but I wanted a world that was not limited to my parents. Why didn't Shiva and Parvati simply cut the mango in half? Why did they give one brother a mouse and the other a peacock? Why had they been made to compete for resources? If Mr. Lyon told the story, it would probably involve Shiva and Parvati circling their children three times. That version would make sense to me. This weekend has not altered any physical circumstances of my life—and yet the entire axis of my belief system has shifted.

We pack up our bags and pile into the minivan for the twelve-hour drive home.

9

July to August 2011

It was Amma and Nanna's idea for me to spend the summer with Venkat while he's in graduate school. But I'm certain that stealing kegs from frat parties and getting drunk at trivia nights with Venkat's friends was not what they had in mind when they referred to "sibling bonding."

One of Venkat's friends tries to open a beer bottle without an opener but succeeds only in taking a chunk out of the kitchen counter.

Suffice it to say I have not spent the summer months calling Mr. Lyon every day like I was supposed to. We talked once, that first week after we went to see him. But the conversation was awkward, stilted, and short. I had nothing to discuss with a sixty-year-old man over the phone, no matter how glorious it felt to be finally understood. I had, however, read all the books Mr. Lyon gave me: *True Happiness, True Happiness in Dating, True Happiness in Marriage,* even *True Happiness in Parenting,* because, as Mr. Lyon says, doing something halfway is like jumping halfway across a canyon. His writing is terrible, and the covers are tacky. He even signed some of them. (I can't imagine what prompted him to do this when his handwriting looks like a five-year-old's and no one has asked for his autograph.) I figure I can learn the principles like I learned Newton's laws and apply them just as easily.

Venkat's friend walks out to the porch to smoke a joint, and Venkat stands up, some strange plastic device in hand.

"What's that?" I ask.

"This? You use it to roll joints. Veena," he says, waving it in front of me. "One day hundreds of years from now, archaeologists are going to uncover this—this plastic joint roller—and they are going to pore over it and wonder, 'What purpose did this serve? Was this the pinnacle of society?'" He laughs maniacally. "And people just used it to get high."

The years of distance and misunderstanding between Venkat and me, exacerbated by my hospitalization, are sloughed away like dead skin, without needing to be directly addressed at length. We share one key to his apartment and lock each other out by mistake—so often that I learn how to juggle and slack line because once, when I was locked out for hours, the Stanford juggling team was practicing on the lawn. I don't know if it's possible for the past to be wiped so clean, but my brother's apartment doesn't feel haunted in the way Severna Park does or isolating in the way William & Mary feels.

Nothing difficult or sad happens this summer. No one calls me a slut. No one dies. I talk my way into a graduate level particle physics conference being held at the particle accelerator. I nurse hangovers by alternating between water and coffee. Ultimately, it is the most ordinary event that motivates me to pick up a phone and call Mr. Lyon: a boy who won't text back. Even though Venkat and I are getting along, he asks me for advice more than I rely on him. I want to talk to an adult who can challenge my way of thinking and teach me something I don't already know—not a friend who will agree with everything I say.

"Mr. Lyon, I met this really cool guy here and I want to be friends with him. But he's been pretty clear that he's not interested. He stopped responding to my texts and—"

"You're right," Mr. Lyon interrupts. "He *HAS* been pretty clear that he's not interested."

I've never met anyone so unconcerned with protecting my ego. His manner feels as clarifying as it does unsettling. "But I can't let it go."

"Honey, I love you, and you've got to. This lesson is too important. There are going to be people in your life who don't like you. Any time we try to control people, we're *using* them—in the same way we'd use a candy bar or pint of ice cream to feel temporarily better about ourselves. Are you seeing how ugly this is yet?"

He has a way of saying the word "ugly" that makes me want to take a Mr. Clean Magic Eraser to my life. I sigh. "Okay. I'll work on this."

When I'm about to hang up, I hear, "And, Veena?"

"Hmm?"

"If you want to be happy, you've got to stop sleeping around. It's not a moral judgment—just a practical one."

Normally, I'd never let a comment like this slide, but he sounds so chill about it that I take him at his word. I won't reevaluate his position until years from now, when I wind up in a church and watch a youth leader teach a lesson on virginity by chewing up a stick of gum, holding out the resulting wad to a group of teenage girls, and asking: *Would any of you want this now?*

He's probably right; sex would be too distracting for me right now.

"I didn't actually sleep with this one. . . ." I trail off. Not that this guy hadn't tried. I wait for the lecture that is sure to follow but Mr. Lyon remains silent.

"You're right." I sigh. "I need to focus on my mental health."

We hang up with a renewed plan for me to call him regularly.

Of course, I don't. For the rest of the month, "focusing on my mental health" looks a lot like fountain hopping with Venkat on drunk summer nights, talking Stanford professors into letting me conduct research in their physics labs the following summer, and assiduously ignoring Mr.

Lyon's direction to stop "sleeping around" with a couple other boys who catch my attention. When I reluctantly return home, I meet Enid for a weekly coffee date at a Barnes & Noble café in downtown Baltimore.

"My coworker said, 'Enid, what is wrong with so and so?' and I told her, 'Honey, I'm still trying to figure out what's wrong with *me*!'" Enid laughs. "You want something to drink, sweetie?"

I order a drink that's more chocolate than coffee.

Enid has come by the house a couple of times now and introduced us to a group of women in the area who practice True Happiness. Enid is more grounded than the rest of the group. Maria, a Latina single mom, talks about how to raise her teenage son with patience. She's cool, but if you open your mouth, she will try to solve your problem even though she doesn't understand much. Gladys, a nanny who is scared of pretty much everything, complains about her boss and explains each of her fears at length. Her friend Emma, a quiet, reserved woman, puzzles over how to date in an honest way. Betty, a four-foot-tall artist, is mostly unintelligible. She talks in a shrill, energetic voice and the way her dyed blond hair sticks up and bobs as she's talking reminds me of my dog. Even though I don't understand what Betty says when she speaks, she is my favorite. She has good energy.

None of these women have met Mr. Lyon but they get together weekly to discuss his books and how to implement the principles in their lives. Apparently, Mr. Lyon has written over a dozen books, he just got back from a seminar in China, and he operates a network of coaches around the world. As I get to know them better, I learn that the women from group don't want to meet Mr. Lyon in person. His interventions cost thousands of dollars; they've heard that he holds people in his lap and find it weird; they agree with some of his principles, but not all. All valid concerns, but, then again, there are a lot of things you can't learn from a book. Part of me thinks they just don't have the guts to change. When people say they're scared of Mr. Lyon, I think it's really their own behavior reflected back that scares them.

Amma goes to group on occasion, mostly to talk about me. I've gone with her a couple times. It's a rewardingly bizarre window into her world, understanding with a new intimacy the way I have hurt her. Overall, though, I prefer my solo coffee dates with Enid to listening to eccentric middle-aged women talk about middle-aged things and occasionally comment on how heartwarming it is to see a mother and daughter communicate so well. Gladys is exhausting after the first thirty seconds. Emma is fine. She's boring but nice. Betty remains fabulously incoherent.

They may have their quirks, but in some ways, I have more in common with these women than I do with anyone else in my life: we share the single-minded goal of becoming good people. Plus, the mother who has spent years telling me that blood is thicker than water, who has looked for support from her family and not found it there, who has only found judgment in her Indian community—she has finally found people who accept her. After spending years trying to silence me, convinced it was for my own benefit, Amma has begun to open up. Finally, she can talk about what it has been like trying to keep me alive. These women offer her empathy without condescension. It is nice to see my mother smile.

Enid tells Amma about some conference calls led by True Happiness coaches around the world. They're free and scheduled almost every day of the week: Monday's is led by a coach in the Bay Area; Tuesday's is led by Bob's wife, Barbara; Wednesday's by a couple who are both coaches in the UK; Thursday's by a woman in Phoenix. You dial a number to call in with the other eightyish participants and listen as they tell stories about their familial problems. The structure of the calls varies by coach, but mostly they just use True Happiness principles to suggest loving courses of action. Tell your sister you will not speak to her if she yells at you during conversations. Impose natural consequences for your children without anger. That kind of thing. Amma never talks when she calls in. She'll listen, muted, while she's cooking dinner, but the circumstances people share vary enough that Amma always manages to learn something without exposing herself.

Before the semester begins, I have a call with the William & Mary dean of students to convince her that I have exerted "considerable effort toward resolving my issues." My parents and I are standing in the same kitchen where we fought over the True Happiness waiver just three months earlier. They hand me the phone and offer a collective four thumbs-up for good luck.

"So, Veena. Your mother tells me you learned a lot about yourself this summer." Her voice is as curt and unemotive as I remember. If this woman told me her name, I can't recall it.

"Yes. The biggest thing that I learned"—I glance back at my parents, who encourage me onward—"is that I wasn't as loved as I thought. People tried their best, but that wasn't enough."

"How do you deal with that now?"

"My parents took me to see this guy who explained all this to me. He's capable of supporting me in the way that I need, and I've been calling him since I left." This is true; I finally started calling Mr. Lyon every day to prepare for this conversation. My college education hangs in the balance. I can't afford to mess this up.

"And how is that going to work when you return to campus? Or when he no longer has the free time to talk to you?"

"That's not the permanent solution. He's not just making me feel better when I talk to him. He's teaching me how to sustain happiness in my own life by not blaming other people and making them responsible for my happiness. By noticing when other people are trying to care about me and being grateful for it. By learning how to care about other people, and as a result of that, developing healthy relationships instead of unconsciously using everyone I come into contact with."

I'm taking breaths before instigating fights now. Explaining how I feel instead of reacting. Making specific requests for what I want from my parents: Could you listen to me instead of giving advice? I could use a hug. Could we continue this conversation in thirty minutes? No single change feels earth-shattering in itself, but in aggregate it feels like a real path forward. I think about how my relationship with Eliza would have been different if instead of cutting up the Doodle Bear, I had asked her—or another friend—for a hug. If, instead of yelling at my parents before I swallowed Tylenol, I had asked for some time to gather my thoughts. Certainly it had felt like I'd tried everything, but in the moments when it counted most . . . had I?

At this, the dean falls silent.

"Once I get more experience, I won't need to talk to Bob." This is Mr. Lyon's constant refrain. Psychologists might want long-term clients, but Mr. Lyon's goal is for me to outgrow him.

"If we decide to let you back on campus, what is your plan if things don't go well?"

"I'm learning how to identify when I need help before it becomes too late. And how to ask for help from the people who have it to give, like my parents and Bob, rather than my friends, who are already swamped with their own problems. I could also get a psychologist in Williamsburg."

"Oh, we'd require that you see a psychologist weekly if we did allow you to come back."

Months ago, her smugness felt unbearable, but now that I'm focusing on the support I do have instead of the support I don't, all she does is amuse me. I don't need this woman to care about me; my parents do. Mr. Lyon does.

"Right. So, I'd see a psychologist."

"All right, Veena. We will be in touch."

Amma and Nanna pull me into a family hug and Amma jumps up and down like an energetic puppy.

"I'm so proud of you, Veena! I'm so happy that we found Bob and that you are happy now!"

"No matter what the dean says, we are so proud of you."

Two days later the dean calls back and I am readmitted to the College of William & Mary.

After I return to college, I continue calling Mr. Lyon a couple of times a week. I quietly exit the back stairs of my campus apartment and pace by the dumpsters as he gives me advice on how to divide the dishwashing chores with my roommates. Each time I ask: *What are we going for here? How long am I meant to keep calling you? I think I'm good now. Nothing to share this week.* And each time he says he will let me know when it's too much, but right now he says I need more. Sometimes he reminds me that he charges people who can afford it for these follow-up conversations but, for me, they are free. These reminders only make me uncomfortable and more reluctant to call. I reach out to Enid and ask again, "Isn't it weird talking on the phone to a random man in Georgia?" Again, she says, "Yes, sweetie. It is weird. And it saved my family."

So, I call him like I'm supposed to. Initially, I schedule calls with Mr. Lyon via email. Once I call two minutes past our appointed time and he says I don't value his time or my mental health and that I should reschedule via email when my priorities are clear. Now that we text more often, I sometimes ask if he can speak and he will text: Call now or Can you talk in 20 minutes? And if I miss the window, it's gone, so I've learned to check my phone more often. Punctuality is one of those lessons that will stay with me.

I call between classes, in the morning, sometimes late in the evening if I have to. It feels safe to open up to this disembodied voice in my ear, and it's easy to forget there is an actual person on the other end of the line. I get a job at a candy shop in Colonial Williamsburg and tell Mr. Lyon how we haze new employees by making them try the double salt licorice, and I think, *There is no way this can be interesting to him.* He says that I'm so mature that it's a wonder I'm able to put up with these people, and the next time my manager tells the latest hire that the double salt is delicious, I feel slightly detached and annoyed at the whole scene, but I can't pinpoint what's changed. Conversations that I would've had with my debate teammates and lab partners are now re-routed to Mr. Lyon. And the results are a vast improvement to being ghosted, called a slut, or told I should die. I do not miss the volatility of opening up to my peers. I'm so lucky to have Mr. Lyon.

10

November 24, 2011

It's Thanksgiving Day and I'm sitting in the back of a car on the way from New York City to the suburbs of Connecticut. Next to me is Charlie, a skinny awkward kid from the Johns Hopkins debate team who I accidentally started dating four weeks ago. His mom is driving. I'm clutching a homemade pumpkin pie that probably didn't come out right, watching the houses that roll past grow exponentially in size. When Charlie invited me to Thanksgiving dinner with his mom, I accepted; his sister was spending the holiday with their dad, and I assumed I could handle the mom. What he neglected to mention was that his mom spends Thanksgiving with her childhood best friend's entire extended family.

Charlie and I met on the debate league. I've been spending all my weekends at debate tournaments. Even though it's been nearly a year since the people in my freshman dorm called me a slut, I still spend as little time on campus as possible. And I'm applying to transfer so I can get out of the south. Suffice it to say that even with Mr. Lyon's support, college sucks. No one on my thirty-person debate team wanted to partner with me so they instead paired me with some random guy from another college who wasn't even on the debate team and just published an article in their school newspaper about how date rape is actually a good thing because it means ugly girls can finally get laid. My teammates told me this story, laughing, with the warning: "Just don't accept any drinks from him and you'll be fine." Ultimately, as a debate partner, all he did was mumble incoherently for seven long minutes.

In comparison, Charlie seemed harmless—if not my first choice. He's known on the debate league for wearing incredibly tight skinny jeans, V-neck T-shirts, and headphones around his neck at all times; for constantly telling people he's from New York (the city, not the state); and for using the kind of biting sarcasm that leaves people in tears. Last year he completely ignored me, so I filed him under both "not interested" and "probably gay." But this year, he—and his short, even more socially awkward debate partner—had been following me around for months. When I found out the guy I was actually interested in wasn't single, I brought Charlie home instead, but I billed it as a "sleepover" so questions about his sexuality remained. I asked if he wanted to kiss, and he said he didn't know. I asked if he wanted to leave, and he didn't. We spent an uncomfortable night together. I fully expected the morning to be even more awkward, but Charlie was uncharacteristically at ease. Not wanting him to get too comfortable, I finally asked pointblank what he was going for. "I just got out of a long relationship and I'm really not looking for another," I said. "It kind of feels like you are?"

Charlie fidgeted and looked pointedly at the corner of wall to my left, all the bluster and confidence of debate rounds washed clear from his voice. "Oh . . . I, um . . . well, if you would like to, then . . . I think . . . that . . . would be nice."

"What?"

He took a breath. "I would . . . like to date you."

I stared, unsure what to make of the boy in front of me. I was wary of dating; my high school boyfriend started as a summer fling, dragged on for three years, and ended disastrously. This was the first time I'd been single since I was fifteen and it felt important to develop some kind of independence before jumping into something else. I was just beginning to understand that my first relationship may not have been healthy. Then again, that relationship was so ruled by passion, in the way we both loved and fought, that maybe the lack of passion between Charlie and me could be a good thing. Maybe healthy relationships begin in this calm, considered way.

"Give me a week to think about it?" I asked.

My roommates weighed in on the matter. "I've always suspected that Charlie might be super sweet on the inside once you get past that prickly exterior. Of course, I don't know since he's never let me close enough to find out . . . but he might let you!"

So I said yes, based on this idea of who he might be if only you got to know him well enough.

A week later, Charlie and I became another debate couple. My roommates and I threw a Halloween party. Charlie dressed up as the mouse living under our oven and I dressed as the exterminator. When we were drunk together Charlie referred to himself, alternately, as "one hundred and ten pounds of fury" and "Charlie Jones, man, myth, legend."

As soon as I called Mr. Lyon and told him, "There is this boy," he said I wasn't ready to date. And, okay, maybe that was technically true—I mean it had only been like five months since I was drinking ant poison in my tea and, yeah, the prudent option would be to wait until I had sustained emotional stability. But since when did it become a good idea to take dating advice from a sixty-year-old man? Nanna always said a woman shouldn't date until she has her own steady income, but, please. I told Mr. Lyon I was going to date the boy anyway. I waited for the reprimand but instead a tense silence followed. I knew he would likely cut off communication now that I'd gone against his advice; Mr. Lyon refused to take calls from anyone who started dating while first learning True Happiness. He said dating was so distracting that it was the equivalent of being on drugs.

But what does he honestly expect? I am nineteen. We are young, we have time, and we look adorable together. I can always end things if it feels too serious.

But five weeks after telling myself I would take it slow, I'm in Charlie's mom's car on the way to Thanksgiving dinner for—technically?—our first actual date.

"That's the house?" I exclaim as we pull into a winding driveway. It looks like it shamelessly swallowed three of the houses I grew up in.

"No," Charlie says. "That's the guesthouse. The main house is up there." He points past the tennis court and swimming pool.

I ask how many people are coming and swallow as he says, "Like eighty." I step out of the car in my beige lace dress, clutching my pie, while his mother introduces me with a hint of pride as "Charlie's girlfriend." I can tell I'm his first. The host, a close family friend, pronounces, "You're beautiful!" with a tone best described as shock. I wait for Charlie to display this same pride, but he hangs back, biting the fingernails of his left hand, with his right hand shoved into his back pocket. His mother's friend gasps at my pie. "You brought a pie! You're so sweet. Let's go put it on the pie table." I'm led into an enormous, bustling kitchen where my well-intentioned pie is placed among a small fleet of gourmet pies from boutique New York City bakeries. Several turkeys are being basted on the white marble kitchen counters, each in its own specific turkey-roasting appliance. The murmur of polite conversation mingles with the clink of glasses. Charlie stays slouched in a corner, and I glance back at him, unsure who to talk to or how. I'm rescued from a conversation with somebody's drunk grandmother by a kind stranger, and that's when I finally corner Charlie, who is still hunched in the entryway, scrolling Reddit on his phone.

"That's it?" I ask.

"What?"

"You're not going to introduce me to anyone?"

He shrugs. "I don't know most of these people." A teenage girl in cutoff denim says, "Hi, Charlie," as she passes through the hallway. I raise my eyebrows, but he does not comment further. "Do you wanna leave?" he asks, chewing a fingernail. He does this when he is nervous, but for some reason he also does it when he is calm.

"What? Of course not." We've just arrived, and his single mother already has to spend Thanksgiving without her daughter. I replay the conversation in which Charlie initially asked me if I wanted to spend the holiday with "just me and my mom." I had agreed because it sounded so casual—but, wow, could he have picked a better first date? Now that we're here, the least he could do is be present.

His eyes drift back to Reddit. I stalk outside, heels sinking into the soft earth, composing a breakup speech in my mind, and text Mr. Lyon about how weird Charlie is acting.

He responds immediately: Call now.

I pause. It's afternoon on Thanksgiving Day.

Me: Are you sure? I can wait until the holidays are over. I don't want to bother you.

Mr. Lyon: Call now

I spend thirty seconds trying to apologize and thank him for making time for me when I'm sure he'd rather be with his family. He interrupts that I am not to thank him, that we *are* family now. I'm just glad he still decided to take my call even though I didn't listen to his advice.

"Well, sweetie," he says after hearing about Charlie's behavior. "I hate to say it, but I told you that you were not ready to date. Have you asked to leave?"

"Well, he offered but—"

"That's great! Hey, have you told him about me?"

"Uh, yeah, I told him you help me when I'm feeling down." I haven't told most people about Mr. Lyon; the explanation is so long and convoluted. My debate friends don't know about my past, so it's just easier not to mention it. When Charlie and I started dating, I had to explain who I was calling. I mean, there's no reason for me to hide the fact that I call an adult who helps me manage my mental health. This is what progress looks like: being proactive instead of riding the mercurial wave of my emotions.

"And he's okay with that? He's not weirded out or anything?"

"No."

In fact, he was oddly accepting when I mentioned it. Obviously, I'm happy to have a supportive boyfriend. But somehow, I expected more questions. Then again, Charlie had had his own therapist whom he had called at odd hours of the day.

"Hey, these are great signs, honey!"

"Really? He's not talking to anyone. Isn't it concerning that he'd make his mom leave for me?" The idea of making this woman drive all the way back to New York City for a girlfriend his son barely knows is insane. Doesn't he have any principles? A sense of loyalty toward his mother?

"No, sweetie, it means he values you more than being there."

This, too, concerns me—that he doesn't value being here, among family and friends. But what do I know? I'm borderline; I am the kind of person who cuts up teddy bears and ruins nice things. Maybe I should listen to the happily married sixty-year-old man who quite literally wrote the book on dating. The idea of "trusting yourself" has become so popular, as if one grand truth or feeling clearly rises above the rest and all you have to do is cling to it, like a life raft. But what if your gut feelings have led you astray in the past? What if, on your own, you gravitate toward toxic partners? My parents' arranged marriage is a testament to the fact that you can start a successful relationship based on logic instead of romance. Amma and Nanna have always said that relationships come first and feelings come later.

Maybe Charlie is just an awkward boy who cares about my happiness. Awkward doesn't have to be a deal-breaker. Maybe what's next for us is a heartwarming montage where I teach him how to be an attentive boyfriend.

"Tell you what," Mr. Lyon says. "Don't break up with him yet. See how the evening goes and check in with me later."

I pocket my phone and put off my decision to break up with Charlie.

Right now, there's no way I can guess at Bob's motivations, in part because I'll never discover one single clear answer. Even in retrospect, it will be difficult to separate his own personal dogma from the bits and pieces of Mormon-inspired doctrine that he cherry-picks to suit his needs.

I rejoin Charlie at one of the large circular tables in the dining room, smile at him, and try to make the best of the situation. I glance at the table settings and ask myself how many forks one person could possibly need. But there are many questions I do not ask myself in this moment—and will later wish I had. This is an uncomprehensive list:

Is there anyone left in my life who Bob does not approve of?

Why is Bob so invested in my dating life?

Why did he change his stance on Charlie so quickly?

Do I even want to date Charlie?

And perhaps the most important question anyone can ask themselves in any relationship: What happens if I say no?

11

December 14, 2011

Amma does this thing where she semiannually goes through the house and donates 90 percent of everything inside of it. Our home is like a *Highlights* magazine picture puzzle: *Can you spot the 2,124 objects missing in the picture on the right?* Venkat and I frequently find our most prized possessions missing and learn later that they've fallen victim to the Salvation Army. Our favorite stuffed rabbit disappeared one summer, only to show up two years later on a shelf in our cousin's house in India, missing his bag of carrots, his right eye, and the majority of his fur.

This time, I'm home for winter break and my favorite shirt is the item in jeopardy. You'd think the natural place to find my favorite top would be in my closet, hanging where I left it, but, no, I find it hours later in a corner of the basement in a black trash bag labeled for Goodwill. I yell that I wouldn't be surprised if Amma tries to donate me next; she yells at me not to speak to her like that; I storm upstairs and slam my door.

This fight, however, is not like the rest, because within minutes, she is on the phone with Mr. Lyon.

"Veena," she calls out, "Bob wants to talk to you. I'm leaving the phone in the hallway outside your room. Please come and get it. You agreed to talk to him regularly."

Now that I know how busy he is, I don't understand why he's so determined to get me to call every day. He juggles interventions, back-to-back calls, and seminars. Plus, he's a sixty-year-old man offering to talk on the phone daily to a teenage girl. At first, I figured "call me every day" was just a thing he said to suicidal people—like saying "God bless you" after someone sneezes.

"We will be telling Mr. Carl and the dean of students if you are not upholding your agreement to take care of your mental health," Amma says.

This guy certainly knows how to teach them leverage, I think as I wait until there is silence in the hall. Then I crack open the door and put the phone to my ear.

"Hey, kid," he says. "I hear you've been having a difficult time with your parents. Sounds pretty tough to handle on your own." There's a note of mirth in his voice.

"Yeah, yeah, okay," I say. "After seeing you and learning about unconditional love, all I can see are the mistakes my parents make. Why is that? They have their loving moments, right?"

Growing up I was also so certain that my parents loved me. They had sacrificed so much for me and Venkat. But ever since I read the True Happiness books, that clarity has become muddled. Logically, I know that even if Amma can't recognize my favorite shirt, she cares about me in a myriad of other ways. But on some deeper level, I just want her to notice what is important to me as evidence that I am important to her.

"Imagine that you're meeting me for the first time," Mr. Lyon says. "For the first nine minutes you're with me, we have a fantastic conversation. You feel warm and understood and safe. Then for the tenth minute, I chase you around with a butcher knife. What would be your overall impression?"

"I'm gonna go with"—I scrunch up my face in consideration—"not good."

"Right. Unfortunately for parents, pain hurts more than happiness feels good. You might not want to go out of your way to spend time with them right now."

"That's okay? That seems unloving." His suggestion contradicts everything I know about the importance of family and my role as a daughter. I think of the story of Ganesh circling his parents. No Hindu parable ends with Ganesh dismounting his little mouse, abandoning his parents on that mountain, and setting off to find himself and explore the world on his own.

"It is unloving, but it's only temporary until it no longer stresses you out. Consider this your doctor's note."

When he says it like that, it makes sense. It feels radical—permission to distance myself from my parents, avoid them even, until I can hold a conversation with them without yelling.

"Hey," he says, "how are you doing otherwise?"

"Honestly, I've been feeling kind of depressed again. . . . I've been thinking about transferring schools."

Sadness has crept back into my life like lead into drinking water. I know Mr. Lyon says people can be happy anywhere, but then he's never been a brown girl at a college south of the Mason-Dixon line. I haven't been able to find my group at William & Mary. Every girl I meet wears Lilly Pulitzer and tries to convince me to rush a sorority. I'd give anything—my firstborn, a limb, any internal organ of choice—to recapture that feeling of belonging I felt with my brother this past summer. But he is all the way in California. When I try to talk to my parents, they just tell me that story about how my grandmother sold all her gold jewelry to pay for Nanna's entrance exam and God, I get it (sort of), but I'm just trying to make a friend or two and not fail my classes. I've filled out applications to places like Georgetown, Yale, and Amherst, and all I have to do is hit send.

"Come see me again," Mr. Lyon says.

"You mean all the way to Georgia?" My stomach turns even though I'm not sure why. "I'd rather not. . . ."

"Sweetie, I care about you enough to tell you that if you don't address the problem internally, no external solution will work," he says. "If you end up in the hospital a second time, you're going to wind up permanently institutionalized. Come down here again. Bring your parents and bring Charlie. I won't make you pay anything. I *NEVER* do that. Ask my wife, Barbara. I care about you—you in particular—that much. In fact, come down *THIS* Sunday. You shouldn't have to live another day like this, kid. Let's do something about it."

And yet, I really don't want to go back. Feeling understood by Mr. Lyon the first time felt amazing, but overall, learning how to be happy doesn't feel as good as I thought it would.

After I hang up, I go to my parents' room to apologize for raising my voice over the missing shirt. They're both sitting on their bed and anxiously awaiting the results of my call. I climb onto the bed and take hold of their hands.

"I'm sorry. I shouldn't have overreacted like that. You guys do so much for me. All the stuff that I own is what you bought me anyway. I appreciate that. Not just that you buy me stuff, but that you raised me, and you put up with me when I'm difficult and still try your best to love me. For nineteen years, too."

Nanna wipes away tears of disbelief.

"Amma, I just don't like it when you touch my stuff. If you could—"

"I got that! Loud and clear. From now on, I am *NEVER* going to touch anyone's stuff again."

It's the kind of blanket assertion I've heard many times in the past, but I let it go. She's trying. With Mr. Lyon's help, I can see that now. Nanna squeezes my hand and tells me that they spoke to Mr. Lyon and think it's best for all of us to go see him again. Remember how I didn't want to go the first time and how well it turned out? They just want to see me happy. I'm not aware of this at the time, but my parents do pay him for this—and every single visit. Between Amma, Nanna, and I, none of us knows what he's told the others. We only know what he tells us.

Mr. Lyon instructs me to bring Charlie: he doesn't conduct interventions with individuals alone; there's no way to address their target behaviors without a counterpoint perspective. I understand his reasoning—people might swear up and down that everything is perfect, have a wonderful three days, and return to the same miserable conditions they left. Even though my parents are coming, we now barely speak. And to be perfectly honest, things aren't much better with Charlie. Ever since we started dating in October, our relationship has felt more like a project than a partnership. I try to teach him how to read body language, how to communicate, how to ask me out on dates. Every other week, I try to break up with him, and he buys a pound of gummy sharks with his dining dollars, stress eats the entire thing, and promises to learn how to be a boyfriend. Then I feel guilty for stressing him out and, after talking to Mr. Lyon, I think maybe I should stay with the boy willing to put in work to better himself for me. But I can't help but wonder what my life would be like had I agreed to go on that date with the enormous football player who stopped me on the way to the dining hall to tell me that he likes Indian food.

So the next time Charlie visits, I go for the kill, half expecting, half hoping he'll break up with me in response.

"Remember that therapist I told you about? The one in Georgia?" I ask. There is no way in hell the words "True Happiness Company" will ever come out of my mouth. "Therapist" feels like the most concise description.

"Yeah."

"Would you have any interest in driving down to see him with me and my parents?" I say the words quickly so I won't have to consider what I'm asking.

"Sure."

I wonder if I've heard him correctly, like when you take one more step than there are stairs and expect your foot to be met with resistance but instead feel it fall through free air. *Huh. That was easy.*

Amma, of course, found it odd, bringing my new boyfriend to our therapist, but it takes a certain kind of broad-mindedness to usher a suicidal daughter into each subsequent year of life. The process involves eradicating your preconceived notions and placing your faith in a foreign health care system. It involves talking to your coworkers at the nation's third best hospital and leaving the conversation with long lists of names and phone numbers. You and your husband shuttle your daughter to office after office, encouraging her to believe in the condescending assholes, when you yourself do not believe in them, because they are the experts and that is supposed to count for something. You feed her little green pills with a Dixie cup of water and still your daughter withers. All these professionals failed her. The accumulating cost is greater than any of the home renovations you take upon yourself and you are exactingly careful to never mention money in front of your daughter, though you and your husband both know she knows. You field prying questions from the Indian families who sublimate your deepest pain into gossip, pumping you for information the same way they tried to pump you for your son's SAT scores years prior. All these people failed you in your moment of need. Anyone who has the luxury to judge has never experienced the threat of suicide like a vise around the neck.

What else can you do? Who else can you trust? When you struggle, you discover how small the world really is. There must be people who have faced this problem and overcome it. This thought leads you to Google and you systematically make your way through a list of alternate paths. You are a research scientist working in vaccine clinical trials, and your husband is an engineer working in fluid dynamics, and this systematic approach appeals to your logical outlook on life.

And then it works. You meet the only person who has ever been able to reanimate your daughter. Sometimes you attend group with three or four women in the area. Here, you do begin to open up. Your own pain, which you have kept bottled up in the face of your daughter's pain, finally bubbles over and releases. These women do not ask how many AP credits your daughter has nor do they comment on the weight that she has gained and then lost. They comfort you.

So, yes, this man occasionally suggests weird things: repeating after him, listening to his conference calls, and not contacting your daughter more than necessary. But, as he is quick to remind you, there is no alternative. You've seen your daughter struggle to get out of bed before; you know where that road ends. What you do not know is where this strange man's instructions will lead you, but you are willing to find out. He is the only one who has offered you light at the end of the tunnel. So maybe it's odd, bringing your daughter's new boyfriend all the way to Georgia, but you go along with it. Your husband has always believed in the inherent goodness of people (an extension of his own strict moral code), and you trust his savvy. He tells you, *We have trusted this man and he helped us.*

Charlie and I sit in the back of my parents' minivan for the long ride. Not your typical second date, but when your first date is Thanksgiving dinner, how much worse can it get? He reads Steinbeck's *East of Eden* to me out loud and provides an extra set of eyes to count Cracker Barrel signs as we drive by. By Sunday, we are in Georgia. We walk into the local Mexican restaurant, where two tween girls are wailing into microphones. There is a sign on the wall that reads: Second Best Karaoke in Georgia!

"Really?" Charlie wonders aloud. "Only second best?"

12

December 18, 2011

He is more impressive in person than I remember—all that bulk and quiet ferocity. In fact, he feels very different now that he is no longer a disembodied voice on my phone or a faceless text. It takes a period of adjustment to connect the person in front of me to the person I've divulged so many intimate details to over the phone, to remind myself that this is a person I trust. This time there is no one taking notes; Mr. Lyon and I are alone in his ugly living room. My parents are staying downstairs with Charlie in the basement guest quarters.

"You're forgettin', sweetie."

I hang my head. He means I am forgetting that he loves me, and I know it's true. This conversation may seem uncanny, but anyone who has read the True Happiness books, blog posts, or been on the conference calls would be able to follow what Bob Lyon is saying.

Mr. Lyon tells me there's absolutely no criticism. He cares about me and wants me to be happy. If I believed that he loved me—if I felt it down to my very core—I would be ecstatic. All my life, I've been looking for unconditional love, and here I've found it. It still sounds dumb—the idea that all I need to be happy is unconditional love. But it also doesn't. At this point, I've listened to countless debates about nature versus nurture, been pushed antidepressants funded by pharmaceutical companies, and weighed the benefits of cognitive behavioral therapy compared to dialectical, but the most understood I've ever felt was the first time I met Mr. Lyon and he told me, "You wanted to matter."

"Didn't we go over this the first time I was here?" I ask.

"To a degree. I'd estimate you were truly peaceful for about"—Mr. Lyon tilts his head and looks up at the ceiling—"three weeks after you left here."

My stomach clenches at the way he rewrites my memory of an entire half year in just a few words. Except for the past month, I felt *good*. Does he know my own feelings better than I do? With my diagnosis, can I even trust my own feelings of happiness?

"But, honey," he continues, "trusting someone halfway is like jumping halfway across a canyon. You do it completely or you don't do it at all."

"What does that even look like?" I'm tired of the cryptic metaphors. I want concrete steps to climb out of this pit permanently.

"Easy. You'd do everything I suggest."

I grimace. "That doesn't sound easy."

It would have meant no sex and no dating, to start. As much as I hate rules, these particular rules don't raise any alarms because they're the same values Amma and Nanna tried to raise me with: chastity, commitment, monogamy. Even in three years, when I find out that the statue on the fireplace behind Bob is actually Jesus and that Bob is Mormon, these moral standards will not feel drastically *new*.

"No kidding. The answer is easy. Doing it? Phew. This is the part where people quit. Everyone likes getting loved. But when it comes to actually *doing* something? Shoot. Then you'd really be vulnerable."

All I can see is the expression on Eliza's face when I cut up the Doodle Bear. Someone at college described me as "acerbic" and I don't want to be this person anymore. I want to be someone bright and soft, not someone who nicks other people with her sharp edges.

"You know what?" I say. "Every time I've followed one of your suggestions, it's improved my life. Every time I've tried to do it my way, it's made me miserable. I'm done doing it my way. My way sucks."

"That's it, kid. *THAT*"—he smacks his armrest, grinning—"is trusting."

Half an hour later Charlie is shaking hands with Mr. Lyon.

"It's wonderful that you were willing to come all the way to Georgia for Veena," Mr. Lyon says. "You must like her a lot."

Charlie grins. "I do."

I look back and forth between them, trying to understand what is happening. I brought this boy I barely know on a twelve-hour drive in the back of my parents' minivan; we slept in the basement guest rooms, and now he's here, grinning at this stranger without a single comment on the entire experience. Is Charlie the weird one? Or am I? Because it took me at *least* fifteen minutes to be sold on Mr. Lyon the first time we met.

"While you're here," Mr. Lyon says, "Veena, I'm going to give you some tools to be happy and, Charlie, I'm going to give you some tools to handle her when she's crazy."

The way Mr. Lyon says "crazy," it sounds like a term of endearment or an inside joke. Once you've accepted that label, there are so many ways you'll allow a person to treat you that you never would have tolerated otherwise. With my history, I assume my craziness is as indisputable, immutable, and as readily apparent as the fact that I'm five foot three. Everyone must know and agree that the shoe fits. So, I don't wonder what Charlie considers normal or what qualifies as craziness to him. We both agree.

"Be watching each other constantly. Charlie, if you see the slightest wrinkle in her forehead, say something. Don't let it go unaddressed. It is *way* easier to deal with a problem before she jumps down the rabbit hole. When my wife, Barbara, and I are together, I watch her constantly. Periodically, I'll ask, 'How are we doing?' Most of the time she says, 'Great.' Occasionally she has to think and says, 'Um . . .'" Mr. Lyon laughs. "'Um' means 'bad.' I know I've screwed up somehow."

Charlie and I play footsie while listening to him talk. "What about after Veena's already crazy?" Charlie asks. "I'll try to do something sooner, but sometimes I don't notice."

"Veena, you need to work on noticing when you start to feel stressed out and asking for what you need—whether it's calling me or asking Charlie to hold you or whatever."

"That's true." This feels like the most crucial tool in this battle against my mental health: noticing sooner. Identifying what I want and asking for it instead of hoping someone will magically notice and provide.

"Be aware of it. You'll get better over time. Now, to answer Charlie's question, just touch her. Hold her. Usually that's enough to calm people down. Tell her to call me."

Mr. Lyon stands up and lowers himself next to me on the couch, displacing Charlie. He cushions his back with a wealth of pillows. He pulls me onto his lap and turns me sideways as he did the first time, with movements so swift and precise they must be practiced. My legs are draped over his arm and my left side squishes against his large, padded chest. Charlie watches, unflinching. Mr. Lyon turns my face toward his own to make direct, intense eye contact so that our foreheads and noses are almost touching. My muscles stiffen and I try to look away. Mr. Lyon's right hand supports my back and with his left he grabs Charlie's hand and places it on my thigh.

"Sweetie," Mr. Lyon says, tucking a piece of hair behind my ear, "you're thinking. You know how I know? Your forehead gets these *liiiittle* wrinkles in it. Don't think. Just feel. If you've been dying of thirst in the desert, and you see a well of water, do we need to stop and have an intellectual conversation about it? No. Just drink."

Everything slows.

"I'm going to give you some words to say. If you want, repeat after me. I do this only because up until now you've had a"—he looks up and chuckles—"limited emotional range at best, so these things are almost impossible for you to identify on your own. I've noticed over the years that when you say things out loud, you feel the truth in them. You want to give it a shot?"

The real answer is "hell no," but so many of Mr. Lyon's questions are not actually questions. If I am willing to kill myself, I might as well be willing to try whatever bizarre thing he suggests first. "Okay."

"Cool. Repeat after me, and don't change the pronouns. 'You love me.'"

I stay silent.

Mr. Lyon laughs. "This is a killer for people to say. Saying 'I love you' is *WAY* easier because you're in control. When you say 'You love me,' that's scary. That takes real vulnerability. So take your time. 'You love me.'"

I let the silence ride out. Then, finally: "'Youloveme?'"

"Nice. Now try and say it less like a terrified question. 'You love me.'"

"'You love me,'" I say, a little louder.

Mr. Lyon considers the wall, then turns back to me. "True or not?"

Like he promised the first time, nothing shocks or disgusts or angers him. "It's true. You love me."

"Cool. So, 'You love me like a daughter.'"

"'You love me like a daughter.'"

"I like it."

I grin. "'I *like* it,'" I repeat with feeling.

"And if I love you like a daughter, what does that make me?" he asks.

I stay silent, uncomprehending.

"That would make me your . . . daddy."

I almost gag as he says the word and glance frantically over at Charlie, who, to my shock, does not react. He is unnervingly calm. If I took any random person from my debate league and dropped them into this situation, would they immediately accept it—like Charlie does right now? Would they instantly recognize the unconditional love they've been searching for their whole life? And I don't, because I'm borderline and have severe trust issues? Mr. Lyon says that when I'm crazy, I can't tell up from down.

"Umm . . . hmmm, I don't want to say that."

"Your call, honey, but I can tell you you'll feel closer to me when you start thinking of me as your daddy. I love you just the same as my own children, no kidding."

No matter how good it feels to be understood, your brain does a hard stop when someone refers to himself as your daddy. But Mr. Lyon is an eccentric old man, and once you've put someone in the box of "quirky" there are many idiosyncrasies you excuse. Whenever he uses the word, I just replace it with "father figure" in my head.

He calls these the five truths: (1) My daddy loves me, (2) My parents and my boyfriend are doing their best to love me, (3) I like it, (4) I have everything I need, and (5) I have nothing to fear. He tells me to write them down on an index card later and repeat them to myself whenever I feel low. I never do the index card thing. His methods may be bizarre, but I get the point: to stop spiraling thoughts and replace them with grounded ones.

Mr. Lyon takes my face in his hands. His eyes are locked on mine. "How do you feel, kid?"

I feel soft. Malleable. I feel as though the past nineteen years have beaten me with a meat tenderizer, kneading me to the optimal consistency, preparing me for this moment.

"Good," I say.

"Good is a start. I would have KILLED to have someone tell me these things when I was your age."

Gratitude unfurls in my chest. Whatever he had to endure for fifty-some years, I don't. Because I have him on my side.

Mr. Lyon grabs one of Charlie's knees. "How you doin', kid? You've been sitting here very quietly."

Charlie unleashes one of his rare, wide smiles. "I'm good."

"What do you think of what I'm doing here?"

Charlie turns his bashful smile to me. "It's nice seeing Veena so peaceful."

"Oh, my Lord, isn't it? Isn't she delightful when she's happy? Because you've seen her when she's not." He howls with laughter, and Charlie and I join in.

By the end of the day Charlie is sitting in Mr. Lyon's lap, enveloped in a great big hug. My head explodes at the sight. I can't decide if it's weirder sitting in Mr. Lyon's lap or weirder watching him hold my boyfriend, but Charlie still doesn't protest. He looks so content that I don't dare let my cynicism intrude on his newfound peace, even though I want nothing more than to ask how and why he is okay with this. I try to imagine what he's feeling. Maybe allowing a trusted adult to love you like a parent really is the most natural thing in the world, but because modern society trains us to associate any physical intimacy with sex, we're left isolated and alone. Maybe I can't get past the "weird" factor because my parents never held me. But if I want to break out of my unhappiness, I need to think radically. I need to completely let go of all my preconceived notions—about life, intimacy, about what's weird and what's normal. My ideas have kept me depressed and suicidal. At some point you have to step back and realize: *this doesn't serve me*. You have to open yourself to something new.

"Oh, kid, you are just the sweetest," he says to Charlie. Then he turns to me. "Now, remember all those times you argued with me, saying that you would never find someone capable of loving you?" He pats Charlie's knee. "I'm just going to take this moment to say I told you so."

Charlie and I grin at each other.

"Having you guys here has been a delight. Most couples come here and bicker for hours. You guys have nothing to worry about. You are so young and are already in the top one percent of relationships in the world. So, Veena, keep this one," he says, motioning to Charlie. "I know it's, like, unheard of, Charlie," he teases, "but sometimes she's wondered if she should break up with you. Crazy, I know." He turns back to me. "No, keep this one. Marry him."

I half smile. He is joking, right?

13

December 31, 2011

Since Thanksgiving was such a resounding success, I find myself spending New Year's Eve with Charlie and his high school friends in one of their parents' penthouse apartments in New York City one month later. I wash my hands meticulously, eyeing the immaculate white marble of the bathroom floor and walls. When I rejoin the group, Charlie's friends are cracking open another round of beers. I politely decline; I stopped drinking as abruptly as I started—just in time to spend New Year's being the one sober brown girl with four drunk, socially awkward video gamers.

"You don't know anything about Charlie when he was in high school, do you?" his best friend asks me.

The boys laugh and I sit up with renewed interest. "No. Am I missing something?"

"Yeah, you are. Charlie, remember that time Ricardo took your drink on the bus?"

They describe Charlie forcing an entire root beer soda down a kid's throat on a field trip. Apparently, one of Charlie's signature moves was sticking his hand underneath someone's drink so they couldn't put it down and had to keep swallowing. His friends laugh as they describe how the kid gagged, sprayed root beer all over the bus, and had to remain drenched in soda for the entire field trip. I've known Charlie to have a sarcastic edge that can tip over to mean, but this image of him forcing a drink into someone's mouth suggests a level of callousness I hadn't associated with him. His friends tell story after story like this—the time Charlie "accidentally" pushed someone's toy off a penthouse roof, some girl he made fun of until she cried, teachers and classmates who couldn't stand him. I stare out at the city lights, telling myself that everyone makes mistakes, but Charlie only laughs in response to these stories.

Mr. Lyon says all that matters is a willingness to learn. And Charlie is willing to learn. But sometimes I feel like I am dating him for his potential instead of who he is today. Like I'm telling myself that I'm bound to get to this magical cream filling of empathy and kindness if only I take one more bite. But what if I never find anything drastically different inside? People show you who they are all the time. But like every other complex human, Charlie is not all good or all bad. Who he is on a given day becomes a function of what I choose to focus on: Is he the high school bully who forced drinks down people's throats? Or is he the brilliant person who has grown beyond that, who debates with me on the shifting economic conditions of other countries and discusses the finer points of Nietzsche?

Two weeks ago, I would have been the one to text Mr. Lyon to talk. But since we've come home, Charlie has been the one to reach out, slinking off to call Mr. Lyon to talk about me. I don't know when or how they exchanged numbers. I am constantly left inferring what they've discussed about me—reading into Charlie's facial expressions when he returns or Mr. Lyon's tone of voice during our next call. What initially seemed like an extraordinary gesture of support now feels like a violation. I feel like a dog who is constantly found pissing where she is not meant to.

Right before midnight, we walk up the lighted stairs to the roof deck, and when 2012 comes rolling in, the cacophony of the city is somewhat muted beneath us. Fireworks break out over Times Square. I can't get the picture of Charlie forcing an entire can of root beer down that poor kid's throat out of my mind. He leans in for a kiss and I duck. His friends pretend not to notice.

"Is everything okay? Veena? Can we talk?"

"Not here," I whisper.

But as we climb downstairs, I'm overcome by the growing feeling that I just might not like my boyfriend as a person. I don't want him to kiss me, and I don't want to be with him on New Year's. We walk back to his mother's apartment along Lexington Avenue. Limousines stir up cold glitter on the street as they drive by. Gaggles of teenagers pull down their sequin miniskirts and pass around joints, taking long drags. Tourists stumble past in plastic 2012 sunglasses and paper hats. People blow kazoos. Charlie asks me what's wrong.

I stop and turn to him on the sidewalk. "Were you ever going to tell me any of that about yourself, Charlie?"

"I don't know. Probably. Why?"

"Why? Because you were a real jerk. Maybe I would have liked to know that about you."

I can't reconcile the Charlie that Mr. Lyon sees with Charlie I know.

"I know I was mean when I was in high school. But you know me. I'm the same person. You figured it out, remember? You said it was my defense mechanism, making fun of people and all that."

I snort. "I hadn't realized you were quite *that* defensive."

Hadn't I?

Charlie holds out his hands in earnest. "I don't know what to do, Veena."

I also don't know what I want from him. I keep hearing Mr. Lyon's voice in my head: *Keep this one*. This one? I glance back at Charlie. Is Mr. Lyon seeing something I'm not?

It'll take me years to understand what Mr. Lyon sees: someone malleable.

*

We'd made plans to go to the Museum of Modern Art the next day, but when morning comes, I still have no idea what I am doing with this guy, why I'm starting the New Year in his mom's apartment, or how our relationship escalated so quickly. His mom and sister are out. Charlie showers and gets dressed while I stay in bed, reevaluating our whole, three-month-long relationship.

He looks at me expectantly while I pull the covers back over my head and groan, "I don't wanna go." Charlie stalks out of the room, annoyed. I fall back asleep briefly but wake up several minutes later to the sound of Mr. Lyon's voice in the other room saying, "No, no, no. She doesn't get to do this moping-around-in-bed nonsense."

Had I woken up feeling well-rested and empathetic, maybe I could have realized Charlie must have been concerned. When you have a history of suicidal ideation, the people who care about you become too jumpy to differentiate between normal behaviors and symptoms of depression.

"Hey!" I call out. "Can we have this conversation just the two of us?"

Charlie doesn't reply. Even though it's only been two weeks since they met, everything Charlie communicates to me is now relayed through Mr. Lyon. It's like Charlie and I speak different languages, and Mr. Lyon is our Google Translate.

"Charlie! That's *my* therapist. You can't call *my* therapist!"

Because then who do I have left to confide in?

Charlie's physical form returns to the room but based on the words that come out of his mouth, it is not Charlie—the Charlie I've come to know—who returns to the conversation.

"This behavior is unacceptable," Charlie says. "We made a plan to go to the museum and we are going to follow through with that plan. You cannot spend the rest of your life in bed." I can tell he is struggling to remember the words Mr. Lyon planted in his mouth.

I'm watching a transformation occur here. I feel like I'm witnessing that moment when a person leans back and allows someone else to take the wheel. You can't identify what it is at the time, but the most jarring thing is the loss of their speech pattern. They say things you know they would never say, but it's not just that: Their enunciation is altered. They can't see it while it is happening. The more you try to call attention to the change, the more they insist everything is the same.

I sit up. "Charlie, you're my *boyfriend*. You don't get to tell me what to do. Look, all I'm saying is that I don't want to go to the museum. Can we please talk about this?"

Charlie leaves the room, calls Mr. Lyon, and returns. "You push everyone in your life away from you when they are trying to help. You refuse to take the necessary steps to become happier and then blame me when I am trying to help you. This has been a long-standing pattern of yours for years."

He isn't responding to what I've just said. The conversation feels flavorless and unpleasantly effortful, like chewing drywall or arguing with a headstrong toddler. I almost want to laugh but I don't think he's in on the joke.

"Charlie, we've been dating for three *months*. You haven't known me for years. Can you not see that you sound like him?"

Mr. Lyon, too, hasn't known me for that long—it's only been six months.

Charlie leaves the room, calls Mr. Lyon, and walks back in. "Mr. Lyon tells you something at volume one, you don't hear it. He tells you something at a two, you don't hear it. By the time he gets to a seven, you say he's being mean and then withdraw from the relationship, and then I'm left to clean up after you because you refuse to take the simple, necessary steps, like calling him regularly."

By now, the humor has leaked out of the situation, and I need air. I try to walk out of the room, but Charlie physically blocks the doorway. I glance at the iPhone in his hand and notice that Mr. Lyon is still on the line. Charlie starts trying to force the phone against my ear, telling me that I need to talk to Mr. Lyon, that I've been avoiding him. I want to shake Charlie back and forth until this bizarre self-help automaton who is spewing phrases he doesn't understand, like some irritating version of Tickle Me Elmo, transforms back into the awkward skinny kid who debated house elves with me and loaned me his soft gray sweatshirt when I was cold. Instead, I slap the phone away from my ear. Charlie pushes it back against my face. Mr. Lyon's voice snakes into my ear against my will (I really need air) and now I am yelling, trying to grab the phone away from Charlie, yelling that I will flush his stupid iPhone down the toilet if he doesn't leave me alone. I can hear Mr. Lyon's distinct words now, telling Charlie that I don't get to threaten to break property. Alarms go off in my head (Mr. Lyon is *right*—What am I doing, trying to break my boyfriend's phone in his mother's house?), but they slip away faster than I can correct my own behavior and now Charlie is pushing me back into his sister's room and I am trying to break loose from his grip and he is skinny (only a hundred and ten pounds of fury), so I am able to break free and suddenly I am rifling through kitchen drawers looking for a kitchen knife to cut myself with but all I can find are butter knives and Charlie is wresting the butter knife out of my hand and back into the drawer and pushing me out of the kitchen and my head is spinning and he is back on the phone with Mr. Lyon. It feels sudden to me, but somewhere in the back of my throbbing mind I think there must have been many points between not wanting to go to the museum and trying to cut myself with a butter knife when I could have (should have) stopped and deescalated the situation but I cannot see any of them now (Honestly why am I still dating this guy and why the fuck is he calling my therapist?) but I hear Mr. Lyon tell Charlie, "Call the cops," and I know I have irreversibly screwed up.

My spine runs cold. A memory tugs at me. Once, a couple months ago, I was unresponsive to my parents for an hour and I heard Amma hesitantly relaying Mr. Lyon's instructions to Nanna ("He said to take her to the hospital"), and then I heard Nanna drop a few expletives ("That horrible place? Do you remember how they treated her last time? Absolutely not."), except Charlie is not like Nanna. He listens to instructions. And now I've given him good reason to. I return to his sister's room, sit on her bed, and retreat into myself.

I hear Charlie pause. "Are you sure?" There is genuine concern in his voice.

I'll only find out what Bob says when Charlie tells me weeks later. "Yes. Do it now. I know how scary this is for you, but you need to do this for HER safety."

I don't hear him make the actual call, but some minutes later, three burly New York City police officers in bright blue uniforms and black vests burst into the room. Guns are holstered to their legs. They all jump when they see me sitting on Charlie's sister's dainty bed, under the crystal chandelier.

"We got a call that you were trying to hurt yourself," one says gruffly.

I shake my head almost imperceptibly, perched on the pastel quilt. One of the officers shifts his weight to the other foot and the third glances around the room, bored. Stuffed animals sit on a doll's couch on the floor next to me. A guitar is propped up in the corner. On the wall is a Hirschfeld cartoon of the *Wizard of Oz*—personalized because Charlie's grandparents were good friends with Hirschfeld.

"Can we see your ID?"

I fish my driver's license out of my blue and white striped backpack and hand it to them, trying not to cry.

"Well . . . you seem okay. I'm really sorry, but we are legally required to take you in because, who is that—your boyfriend? Because your boyfriend called us."

I silently, numbly follow the men down in the ornate wooden elevator and pass the doormen who always flirted politely with me on my previous visits. I wonder what is wrong with me, and what they think of my escort as we exit the lobby and I climb into the ambulance that's double-parked on Lexington Avenue. Charlie's mom will return home soon, confused and concerned, but she doesn't know me, and Charlie is following my therapist's instructions. Now, I just want to expunge the past twenty-four hours, to take back how judgmental and unloving I was last night, to redo the morning and communicate better with Charlie and just go to the museum like he asked. The museum would have been nice. But none of my poor choices can be retracted, so I instead want it all to end. I pull out my phone in the back of the ambulance and scroll through the contacts list. There is only one person I cannot disappoint because he already knows everything.

I text Mr. Lyon:

I want to be dead.

Do you want to be dead or do you want to learn?

Be dead.

Sorry. Can't help you.

I shove the phone back into my pocket. The police officers apologize to me all the way to the hospital. On the outside, I must look like a normal girl. Mr. Lyon has told me so many times that a second hospitalization will leave me permanently institutionalized. I'm beginning to feel like he has a crystal ball; he knows everything that will happen to me before it happens. And in the moment, it feels good to know that Mr. Lyon will stop me when I misbehave—even if no one else will. His boundaries are like a hug, squeezing me tighter and tighter.

I still can't figure out how the day escalated so quickly by the time a psychologist at the hospital asks me for the story. I'm about to tell this woman that I did (sort of) try to cut myself with a butter knife, but I stop. I learned from both of my previous psych evaluations not to be overly honest or I'll get held against my will. How did it get to this point? The last time Mr. Lyon suggested police intervention, my parents just held me until I was ready to talk. The night ended with snuggles and a good conversation instead of another hospitalization. My instinct tells me that all I needed was warmth and understanding. The psychologist indicates that I'll be out as soon as possible—she spoke with Charlie, and it was just a big misunderstanding. I start to feel woozy with relief as I imagine getting out of New York and waking up in my own bed tomorrow. I am not going to be institutionalized. (Do people who are normal know and appreciate how normal they are, or do they not even realize it without a point of contrast?)

The psychologist stops as she reaches the door. "Oh, also your boyfriend gave me your therapist's phone number. Do I have your permission to speak with him?"

My body goes cold, but I don't know why. I want to say no, but the only real answer is yes—I can't tell a health care professional that she doesn't have permission to contact my therapist without raising a lot of alarms. "He's not really a therapist," I start to say, but I stop. In the few seconds before she walks out the door, there's no way I can explain to her that he's not a licensed therapist but actually a former eye surgeon with no background in therapy. *Mr. Lyon cares about me.* I only feel scared when I am fighting the truth.

When the psychologist returns, she bursts through the door.

"It seems you haven't been completely honest with me," she snaps, clutching the clipboard at her side, face down. She stays standing. Her face is taut with disdain.

The air is light as I wonder what I have done wrong this time.

"For instance, you didn't tell me that you have borderline personality disorder or that you were trying to hurt yourself."

She doesn't give me time to respond before announcing that I will be staying the night. Even if I had the chance to reply, she would no longer believe me. Why should she? She has seen the truth of the ugliness inside me. I bawl into my hands, sucking in air through the gaps between my fingers. She bursts out of the room as quickly as she entered. The door slams behind her.

Her words are liquid, melting their way out of my ear even after she is gone. Mr. Lyon was right—I will be institutionalized. For a second, I wonder: *What did he tell her?* But that is replaced by the question: *What have I done?*

I lie face down on the bed of my cell-like room and cry quietly, still trying to sort through the events of the day. At what point was I supposed to stop and communicate how I was feeling to Charlie? I think about my parents, who have never really shown me what quiet, calm communication could look like, and cry harder, wondering how news of my hospital stay will affect them. Who will tell them? When will I be allowed to see them again? I feel for my phone and text Mr. Lyon: I need help.

He calls. "Hi, my little sweetie. I understand you're having a tough day."

"So tough, Mr. Lyon." I cry quietly into the phone.

"Honey," he coos, "none of this would have happened if you'd just been talking to me every day. It's too late when your hair is on fire. We need to catch it before it starts, okay?"

"Okay."

In this hospital room, which is actually a cell with a plexiglass wall, my future tightens around me. The myriad dreams available to me as a high schooler—becoming a lawyer, a physics professor, a writer—dwindle and dance past my grasp. This deep into the mental health care system, even my dreams have learned modesty. My goals are now more realistic: Going back to college. Making a good friend. Keeping my grades up. Not throwing my parents into a state of panic. Yet even these dreams of mediocrity are jeopardized by my behavior. "I promise I'll call every day, Mr. Lyon."

"Hey, it's not for me, kid. It's for you. And I'm not Mr. Lyon, remember? I'm your . . ."

I wince.

"Uh, that's still weird to me."

"I know, honey—that's why I'm bringing it up. You will only feel close to me when you realize I'm your daddy."

Father figure. He means father figure.

"We wouldn't be in this situation if you'd just trusted me," he continues.

I will do whatever it takes to avoid being in a place like this again, but I still can't bring myself to say the word. "Ehhhh, okay. Okay!"

His tone changes as he lets me in on a joke. "Hey, you really had that psychologist going, didn't you? Ha! The head psychologist at a major New York City hospital and you had her eating out of your hand." He laughs. I laugh along with him, unsure what we are laughing about. I'd felt like a small furry animal in that moment—so earnest and splayed open. And then I remember that I'd withheld the truth from the doctor. I join in his laughter more genuinely, feeling grateful that I have Mr. Lyon to expose my manipulative tendencies and forge me into a more honest and dependable person.

"I had to beg her to keep you there at least a night." He chuckles.

"You—you asked her to keep me here?"

"Sure. You gotta learn the lesson somehow. There are some lines you don't cross."

"But . . . I don't know when I'll be allowed out."

"Ah. I hate telling you how to game the system, but if you want to get out tomorrow, agree with everything they say. Don't argue. And call me once you get out."

And it works. Mr. Lyon always knows what to say.

The next day I take the Greyhound bus home without saying goodbye to Charlie. How do you say goodbye to the boyfriend who called the cops on you? Even if you now believe you had it coming. Even though you've become convinced that you deserved it. You're tired and don't have the energy to communicate with a nineteen-year-old boy, even one who says he loves you. Instead, you talk to an old man in Georgia, because he says nothing you say will shock or offend him. It feels less risky—easier, less effortful, to speak to him. He gives you permission to avoid your boyfriend for a little while, just like he gave you permission to avoid your parents (even though you didn't really ask for it). He gives your boyfriend instructions not to contact you for a while. Your boyfriend listens because the man is your "therapist."

You start telling this man every thought that your mind crafts. You wonder if it's getting excessive, but every time he tells you more, you need more. More reliance, more dependence, more trust. It starts to feel unhealthy, but then he refers to himself as a father figure and you think of your own stern, withdrawn Indian father and how you wish you could reveal your inner world to him, so it begins to make sense that this man could fulfill that role instead. These daily conversations feel odd enough that you don't advertise this relationship to your friends—what's left of them, anyway. Most people in your life have no idea about the texts, the Skype calls, the emails. On the surface you seem, if not well-adjusted, then at least ordinary.

Your speech patterns have changed now, too, but you don't see it. If anyone questions this change—not necessarily in words, but with so much as a glance—they will never understand and accept you as you are. This is how communication with the outside world fades out. Relationships fall away from you like strands of loose hair. It is so much less effort to have only skin left on your head that you don't question it. When you reconnect with these friends years from now, they will say, "I don't know why, but I got the feeling that you didn't want to be in contact." Neighbors will describe being intrigued by you but getting the impression that you were closed off. You don't know this at the time. At the time you wonder why the world is full of judgmental people and why no one wants to be your friend.

Fuck what other people think. None of it matters. Because for the first and only time in your life, someone sees all of you, not just the straight As or the awards or the trophies or the screaming or crying or cutting, but the whole fucked-up mosaic of talents and fears and thoughts and what he has now convinced you is a pathological condition. You quote specific *Star Trek* episodes to him, and he understands the references. He sees all of you, not just one glimpse or one snapshot or one feature, but all of you, and he finds all of you to be magnificent. He is brilliant and understands your thoughts before you complete them. He has no breaking point, and no boredom when it comes to you. It is all you have ever wanted. You get back together with your boyfriend, but it will feel different. Other things matter less and less. People describe this experience as drinking through a fire hose, but you are unzipping your skin and allowing someone else to crawl in and rearrange your insides.

Questions/ Comments
Veena Dinavahi to Bob Lyon

Sun, Dec. 23, 2012, 1:32 p.m.

Re: our conversation a couple days ago, I feel like sometimes you forget that I am 20. Sometimes (like this month) I am just particularly frazzled. I don't always get what you're saying the first time around. And honestly, it doesn't matter to me whether your advice is technically consistent; it was confusing to me regardless, so I felt overwhelmed.

I was upset that you've never once admitted you've made a mistake with me. But I KNOW for a fact that in all the time we've talked you've at least made one mistake with me—at least one. Being prematurely stern or something. I still don't really get what you were trying to say, though . . . not really sure what message I was missing.

Bob Lyon to Veena Dinavahi

Sat, Dec. 24, 2012, 9:11 a.m.

So you're requiring that I made a mistake with you before you can trust me. That's what you're saying.

So you're needing proof that I can be trusted, despite the countless times I've loved you.

Despite all those times, you need a specific kind of proof that I can be trusted. That I made a mistake, when you can't even specify which mistake (exactly, not generally) I made.

That requirement would make a relationship pretty difficult. Up to you. If you want to specify a mistake I made, I'll be happy to admit it.

The problem?

1. How would you know for sure that what I said was a mistake? When you're feeling fearful and needing me to admit something, how would you see clearly enough to judge what I'm doing? How would you know whether it wasn't exactly what you needed? You would naturally judge what you don't LIKE as a mistake, which everyone does. Then you'd require me to admit a mistake that wasn't.
2. Even if I DID admit a mistake to you, you'd just keep requiring that I do it again.
3. You either trust me or you don't.
4. You have more evidence than almost anyone outside my blood family that I love you, and yet you are choosing to doubt it. That's your choice. Nothing I do now will change that. You already have the evidence, plenty of it, and yet you're requiring something more. It won't work. So you have a decision to make: trust me or not. If you don't, you'll just keep distancing yourself, all the while justifying it by pointing at something that I'm doing or not doing.

It's up to you.

14

2012

He never tells me "drop out of college." He rarely gives instructions that direct. Instead, he talks about how overrated and overpriced college is these days.

"My son Brian," he says, "dropped out of college. Worked for several years and then went back to get his degree and valued it that much more the second time around."

I don't return to campus after my second hospitalization. I tell Amma and Nanna I need a break to focus on my mental health. Nanna asks if I am sure and does not press when I tell him this is a temporary measure. For once he does not repeat his stories about how his mother sold her gold jewelry to pay for his college entrance exams or how his professor bought him his first pair of shoes. I don't know who told them about my hospital stay or what they were told, but Amma and Nanna now handle me with the same delicacy that I've seen Amma use with her pipettes in the lab. Temporarily, I move back into my childhood bedroom and strip the walls of my old posters of kittens and puppies to fight back the mounting sensation that I am regressing to age twelve.

Everyone wants to know what my parents were thinking. To be clear:

they always prioritized my independence. Growing up, Nanna insisted on teaching me how to change my own tires. I'd find him on the garage floor, and he'd call to me from underneath his BMW to tell me stories about how he taught Amma to drive when she first came to this country in 1986. Nanna would roll out from underneath his car to describe how she stepped off the plane and into the Michigan snow in a sari and sandals. Then he'd laugh, grab a wrench, and roll back under. She hated the cold, but she learned to drive a stick shift on the hills of Ann Arbor through Nanna's instruction. He insisted on her self-sufficiency. Here, Nanna would again pause to tell me he wanted to finish teaching me to drive a stick because those are two skills every girl should know: how to change a tire and how to drive a stick. I always managed to avoid the lessons.

I still can't do either.

And yet, it's not difficult to understand how my parents let the distance between us grow. Take a man and a woman and give them a daughter as inscrutable as a houseplant, who wilts when she is watered, shrivels when she is dry, browns in both the sunlight and shade. Give them a white savior who brings about verdant new growth. Anytime they have doubts (they will have many), walk them back through the logical steps: She needed unconditional love and you did not give it to her.

The old man says parents hate to take responsibility, but it wasn't the mailman who made your daughter this way, who made her feel like the only way she can breathe is to die. You relive the times when your child, your darling daughter, asked for the slightest bit of understanding or empathy and you let her innocent pleas for help go unanswered or, worse, met them with judgment and criticism. Though the old man doesn't say it directly, the thought that you may have actively contributed to your daughter's depression is so incapacitating that you begin to treat her like a Jenga tower, perpetually one step away from collapse.

You remove yourself, because you worry the slightest breath or comment will bring her toppling down.

And so, the two parents sit back and allow the bricks to be stacked between them and their daughter, sometimes with confusion, sometimes with guilt or sadness. There will be fights that take place on their side of the wall, but she will never know. The mother will ultimately yield to the father, as she has been taught to do. *We trusted him and he helped her. Let us not interfere now.*

• • •

I TAKE A job at the local garden center, and from my station behind the cash register I run into all the people in town I want to avoid. Parents of friends, who've told me for years that they wish their children were more like me, now stop in their tracks when they see me.

"Veena! I almost didn't recognize you. I thought you were at William and Mary?"

"I am. I'm just taking a semester off."

"Right." They touch my shoulder sympathetically. "It's good to take a break sometimes. You were always the smartest in the class! I'll tell Max you say hi."

A stay-at-home mom comes at me with three flats of African violets.

"Three flats, with twelve in each . . . so that's twenty—"

"Thirty-six," she enunciates, narrowing her eyes at me. "Twelve times three is thirty-six."

I cannot stop the tears in my eyes from welling over, but she pretends not to notice. It's only been four or five months since I took a break from college but already my math skills have deteriorated beyond recognition. I text Mr. Lyon under the counter:

I took multivariable calculus when I was 15, you know.

He replies: They can't see you like I can.

His response draws me closer like a winch.

*

Around the same time I take a break from college, Venkat drops out of his master's program to build a software startup with his friend. When our grandmother finds out, she is livid. She yells at Nanna over the long-distance phone call, asking if he is out of his mind letting both of his children drop out of school. Venkat at least has his bachelor's, but Veena—didn't she want a physics PhD? Nanna mellows her out as best as he can, and when he hands the phone to me, I pretend that I can't hear her well and give the phone back quickly, rolling my eyes and saying her hearing aid is acting up again.

Charlie visits sometimes. We've started dating again, but the whole thing feels hot like glass. He still says he wants me. I tell him he doesn't know any better because he's never had a girlfriend before me, but then he counters that he's never wanted one before me. He says he's never met anyone who cares about other people as much as I do, that I've transformed his life for the better. He's fighting with his mother less and even repairing his relationship with the father he hadn't spoken to in years.

"Being around you . . . I feel things in a way I never have, Veena," he says.

Hearing him speak like this makes me think this scrawny boy might actually love me and maybe it's incumbent on me to love him back. Maybe I just want to ruin this good thing because I am borderline.

"I know you have your struggles," he says, "but I want to help you through them."

Mr. Lyon says almost no boyfriend would have the guts to do what Charlie did for me, but it is hard to conceive that his calling the cops on me was a favor. Charlie doesn't see it that way either; he treats me the same way my parents do, like I am both the memory of his mistake and his opportunity to do better, even though he is too scared to do much of anything. Mr. Lyon reminds me that the most important factor in the success of a relationship is someone's willingness to learn and Charlie says he is willing to do anything; so I agree to give the relationship another shot.

Periodically, I tell Mr. Lyon I'm thinking of going back to school. He waits a beat and then asks, "For what, sweetie?"

I don't have an answer to this question, but I'll lose my mind if I stay at the garden center. With my AP credits, I only have one year left of school to get my degree.

He pauses again. His silences communicate so much. He tells me that I'd be making my parents spend a lot of money on my tuition without even knowing what I want. I thought I wanted to be a physics professor, but when I estimate how much money my parents have already spent on me—between therapy, paying Mr. Lyon for my intervention, and my first year of college—I cannot bring myself to ask for more. Mr. Lyon tells me I could do what he does, one day. I have a real talent for this, he says.

What "this" entails is unclear because the structure of his business remains hazy. As far as I can tell, True Happiness coaches operate independently. Some have their own websites and fee structures. Some conduct their own interventions, but others simply coach over the phone and charge hourly. All the coaches must first be certified by Mr. Lyon and Barbara. I'm not sure I want to be a True Happiness coach. But Mr. Lyon keeps talking about how I could use my talents to help people. So when Mr. Lyon says he has a girl who could use some additional support, the idea of saying no feels selfish. Of course he can pass along my contact. He doesn't charge for follow-up, so I know not to ask to be paid. I do it because life is hard and what do we have if not each other.

Fall comes. I miss the deadline for reenrollment and take a second job at Bath & Body Works. My parents move to a different part of Maryland, and I move in with Charlie in downtown Baltimore because who wants to live with their parents at age twenty?

Sometimes I look around the mice-infested apartment we now live in and wonder what I am doing with Charlie, whose life is diverging further from the pounding stability of adulthood I find myself in. He still goes to debate tournaments and tells me about the stupid arguments Rutgers kids made this time, but I'm out working until one or two in the morning, rearranging displays of Sensual Amber body lotion for minimum wage and it's getting harder to feign interest in Charlie's college experiences.

When I wonder anything big, Mr. Lyon gives me more tasks to complete: I write blog posts for him. I transcribe hours of his video chats from his website. He mentions celebrities coming for interventions—never by name, of course—but he says I'd know exactly who they are. He gives me my own conference call to host and there is no time or heart left to wonder. Next semester, I tell myself, I will reenroll in college.

But I don't have energy for much. I used to read the *Washington Post* every day, but after hearing Mr. Lyon talk about how the media is so fatalistic and fearmongering, I stop. I can't remember why I found the news cycle important and compelling before.

I fly to Georgia once or twice a year to intern for Mr. Lyon. In the past, whenever I'd walk through airports, strangers would ask me for directions. Now, they stop me to ask if I am lost. After the third time this happens, I call Mr. Lyon, annoyed.

"Do I have some kind of sign over my head that says I don't know what I'm doing?"

"Yes, sweetie, you really do. And I love you anyway. We can work on it if it bothers you."

I tell myself it's just temporary. I can go back to college if I want.

*

I don't go back. I quit my job at the garden center and take another job at Express at the local mall. I don't make friends at my new job. I haven't seen my brother in months. Mr. Lyon and I are the only people left in the world.

From Daddy

Bob Lyon to Veena Dinavahi, Charlie Jones

Sun, Jan. 6, 2013, 3:36 p.m.

1. No abortion.
2. Wait until you see where you and Charlie are going.
3. If you and Charlie stable at 8 months, stay together and raise baby.
4. If not, give baby up for adoption.

15

January 2013

I reach into the soft tissue of myself to remove the NuvaRing but feel only my own flesh. Details of the last month solidify into focus: the excessive fatigue, elevated body temperature, vomiting spells in the bathroom at work. My body knows what the test will confirm hours later: I'm pregnant.

NO, I think, pulling my head between my knees. There is a type of girl this sort of thing happens to and I am not her. I am only twenty and I'm going to get a PhD and become a professor. Sure, I've been out of college for a year. Yes, I've been working two jobs at the local mall, selling Christmas cookie–scented candles and helping people try on overpriced blazers. And, yeah, I moved back in with my parents. (Charlie and I are not doing great.) But these changes are temporary. (Did we even have sex this month?) I cannot let the permanence of a child solidify this state.

I take my time washing my hands with soap, deciding what to tell Charlie, who is making conversation with Nanna out in the hallway. I thought I'd freak out in a situation like this, but I'm just annoyed at myself for being so irresponsible. You don't know how stable you've become until crisis strikes and you stare down your reflection in the bathroom mirror and wonder dryly what all the classmates who nominated you most likely to succeed would think of you now.

I'll go to CVS for Plan B. Probably too late for Plan B. First, Charlie.

We had a fight last week and Mr. Lyon suggested I break up with him. I don't remember what it was this time—the fact that he spends forty hours a week playing Magic: The Gathering or still doesn't take me out on dates? I'm not sure what Mr. Lyon wants from me, though. Sometimes, he'll tell me to break up with Charlie, say that Charlie's just a child who doesn't deserve me. Then I'll describe something sweet Charlie's said or a change he's promised to make and Mr. Lyon will suggest I keep dating him. He tells me no one is perfect: *Charlie will never be able to understand you like I can, sweetie.* That's why you've got me. Then I wonder if this is the best relationship I can hope for. I can make it work if I know I'm supposed to, the same way Amma and Nanna worked through their arranged marriage. But listening to Mr. Lyon's contradictory advice day in and day out leaves me feeling isolated even when Charlie and I are together. Last week Mr. Lyon said, "I never told you to marry the guy."

"That is exactly what you told me!" I exclaimed. "You said that word for word: 'Keep this one. Marry him'!"

Mr. Lyon yelled that that was absurd, that he never tells people what to do with their lives, and I stopped arguing. Eccentric old men and their terrible memories. When I broke up with Charlie for real this New Year's, he actually heard what I was telling him about wanting to go on more than one date a year and said he'd call Mr. Lyon regularly to work on his emotional availability. Mr. Lyon suggested we start dating again, as if for the first time, taking it slow. Last week we went on a normal first date that Charlie planned—pizza at HomeSlyce and a trip to the Baltimore Museum of Art—and now I probably have half his chromosomes implanted inside me. So much for taking things slow.

I walk into the hallway, pull him into my room, shut the door, and sit him on the bed. "I have something to tell you."

Charlie scoots toward the door in alarm. "Okay . . ."

"I went to take out my birth control," I say. "And it's not there."

Charlie blinks. "What do you mean 'it's not there'? Like, it fell out?"

There is a fundamental misunderstanding about the nature of vaginas or NuvaRings, but I do not point this out. "I think I forgot to put it in this month." I'm only on the NuvaRing because Amma insisted all other forms of birth control utilize too many hormones. Why did I even tell her I'm on birth control?

Charlie paces the length of my bedside. "Okay. Okay. What does that mean? I'm not ready to be a father. You might not be pregnant though, right?"

I shrug helplessly under the weight of my mistake. How could I have forgotten something so simple?

"But if you are pregnant, we're both not ready to be parents, right? You'd . . . take care of that? Agreed?"

"Obviously."

The only time Charlie and I ever discussed abortion, it was in the abstract, philosophical sense. When I was still in college, we partnered together at the University of Maryland debate tournament and did so well together that we made it to semifinals. We lost to the case "Congress should provide a facilitative right to abortion." We both agreed so strongly that the government should subsidize abortions that we couldn't think of a single counterargument. I almost dropped out of my freshman philosophy seminar because I had to listen to the guy across from me talk about how women don't have the right to choose what happens to their own bodies. I even followed Hillary Clinton's presidential campaign from the psych ward.

These political beliefs feel like I've prepared for a hurricane with an umbrella.

"I'm gonna call Mr. Lyon. I need to call Mr. Lyon," Charlie says.

"Wait, can we talk about this first?"

He holds up his hand to stop me and puts his phone to his ear with the other. "I need to talk to someone right now and I don't know who else to call. You don't have to talk to him, but I'm going to."

I shrug again as he puts Mr. Lyon on speakerphone and explains that my birth control "fell out."

"What do you mean 'it *fell out*'?"

"I didn't put it in!" I yell across the room. "I forgot."

"That makes more sense. First, we need to find out if Veena is pregnant. No sense having a conversation about something that might not happen. She needs to go to the drugstore and buy pregnancy tests."

"I *know,*" I snap. "I'm going to get Plan B and pregnancy tests."

"Plan B is a shot in the dark if you haven't had birth control for a month."

I resist the urge to repeat "I know" or roll my eyes. This is my mess.

We pick up the supplies without saying anything to my parents and take them back to Charlie's apartment. I rip open the box of Plan B in the car and swallow the pills, knowing it is too late.

The apartment smells of rodent droppings mingled with the musk of Charlie's kind but hygiene-deprived roommate. The toilet bowl is smeared with the residue of whoever used it last. I gag as I pee onto the stick. Before even ten seconds has passed, the plus sign appears, ripe and red like the apple of original sin. I hike up my pants and call out, "Yup! Most definitely pregnant!"

I lower my voice, realizing his roommate might be around. Charlie demands to see the test himself and spends several minutes in the bathroom, staring at it, willing it to change. I flop onto the IKEA bed in his room and stare at the ceiling. Charlie brings Mr. Lyon back on speakerphone.

"I am pregnant," I announce.

"Now we have some decisions to make."

Charlie and I lock eyes over the phone. "I always figured I would get an abortion if this happened." Charlie nods vigorously. "I'm not prepared to be a mother."

Mr. Lyon clears his throat. "Just because you have the right to do something, doesn't make it the right thing to do."

When he puts it so bluntly, my beliefs—personal, political, philosophical—start to feel obviously wrong. It's as though he has uncovered some immutable truth about life that I have been too dumb or self-absorbed to see all this time. His suggestions are more like commandments than I realize.

Charlie paces again, slapping his hands against his thighs, saying to himself, "I'm not ready to be a dad! I'm not ready to be a dad!"

All these things I told myself—that I could break up with Charlie before it got serious, that I could go back to school, that all these decisions are undoable—evaporate like steam off a mirror. This *is* my life, this boy in skinny jeans pacing the floor and this very untheoretical bundle of cells inside of me.

"But what else can I do? I'm not ready for a child."

"You have options, honey. You could give the baby up for adoption. There are so many families waiting to receive a child. You could raise the child yourself. It would be difficult, but you could do it."

"I can't give away my own child. . . ."

The situation feels surreal, like someone has carelessly picked me up and dropped me into a scene from *Juno*. How does anyone make a decision of this magnitude? One choice whose consequences will transform the entire course of my life—or not. How do I imagine the futures, place them side by side, and pick one? How do I distill the implications of this moment personally, practically, ethically?

I want to bang on Crtl + Z and pick up where I left off. People got abortions in Severna Park; it's the instinctual response to unplanned pregnancies. I assumed it would be mine.

"Well, if you wouldn't give the child up for adoption, that narrows your options," Mr. Lyon says. "I can tell you that getting an abortion is the number one regret of all the women I talk to. It is the very last thing they tell me, the source of the most shame."

Already I am thick and congested with shame.

I hang up and spend five minutes on the Planned Parenthood website. Reading about the different options, how one of the pills effectively precipitates premature labor, the heavy bleeding that will ensue, how they might have to go back in to remove any remaining parts, and it feels much less like a philosophical issue and much more like I'm considering dismantling a child. *My* child. With Mr. Lyon's words in my head, I stop reading and don't fully explore the options. Based on the last time we had sex, I must be five weeks pregnant. According to Google, my baby is the size of an orange seed and may already have a heartbeat.

There are things that I want for myself, and as I cry on my boyfriend's bed in his college apartment, with his covers pulled over my head, slowly, I let each of them go. The physics PhD. Learning Italian and traveling the world. Writing a book one day. The hope of ever being a normal college kid with normal college experiences. And I start imagining things I want for the child who didn't ask to be inside me right now, her heart beating alongside mine. Her first words. Her school field trips that I'll chaperone. Her first kiss and driving her first car. In this world I am waiting tables without a college degree because I know Charlie does not want both of us. But the child and I can still be happy in that world. Together.

I am so small in this moment, only twenty years old and scared, but there is someone even smaller growing within me and it cannot be right to eject her from my body just because her existence interferes with the Way Things Are Supposed to Be. The only thing to do is to rise to the occasion. I rub my inconspicuous stomach and know she is mine—permanent in the most dizzying way.

I want to tell my parents immediately—I cannot get through this without them—but Mr. Lyon says that miscarriages are most common in the first twelve weeks and there is no point in telling anyone before.

Charlie hasn't told his parents. I've tried to cut him loose of any responsibility toward us. I tell him he can leave. I don't want anything from him, and I certainly don't want him to stay out of obligation. I'll land on my feet. Charlie hangs around, awkward and indecisive as always. He wants me but not the baby and he's still trying to talk me out of it. I don't blame him; it's fully my fault.

At the twelve-week mark, Mr. Lyon says it's time for us to tell my parents. Charlie doesn't want to be there, but Mr. Lyon insists that as long as Charlie is my boyfriend, we tell them together. I don't have an opinion. We are kids and life is suddenly complicated without notice. Mr. Lyon is the emergency lighting as the plane goes down and I am relieved to follow him to safety. We meet my parents at the kitchen table one night and anxiety pools in my palms. Nanna will yell. But I feel an immutability from the budding life inside me. No one will take her away. There is a strange formality in the way we arrange ourselves, with Amma and Nanna sitting directly across from Charlie and me.

"I am pregnant." I say it just like that.

Amma grins. "You're joking, right?"

Nanna locks eyes with me and shakes his head. "No. She's being serious. I knew something was wrong."

Amma's smile sears off her face, as if with acid. The kitchen stands still and silent.

"That's all? No reaction?" I've prepared a response for every objection and criticism, but I hadn't prepared for the possibility of silence.

Nanna pets the table gently and closes his eyes. "Just give us a minute, *bangaaru talli*. We are processing."

Golden daughter. My lips close. Though I've never seen this scene played out—Promising Indian Daughter Tells Immigrant Parents about Unplanned Pregnancy—this is not how I envisioned it unfolding, with quiet consideration from the father who I have known as cold and demanding. It forces me to consider how much of their characters I have misjudged, and this is not a question I'm prepared to take on. Amma gapes. Charlie stares at the tile floor.

Nanna finally speaks. A whisper. "Have you . . . decided what you are going to do?"

"I'm going to keep the baby."

Nanna nods and closes his eyes again. "Okay. We are here for you. We will figure it out." He nudges Amma in the ribs and she adds hastily, "Yes, of course, we will support you, but have you considered—" Nanna gestures for her to stop and she lapses into silence again, scarcely able to contain herself.

That is about the extent of the conversation.

I'm not sure who rang Mr. Lyon, but there he is on Skype. When he says, "Hey there, Grandma and Grandpa," my parents laugh and allow their fear to melt into excitement. Amma will spend the coming months at yard sales with me and Charlie, cooing over baby hats and insisting on buying us the Fisher-Price rainforest-themed baby swing, telling us stories about how I used to fall asleep in it.

"Let's do this thing for real," Mr. Lyon says. "Come down here next weekend. We'll do a one-day intervention and, if it goes well, you guys get married. We'll do it right here in the living room. If not, at least you tried. Everybody good with the plan?"

Everyone says yes. No one can think. It is comforting to have someone take charge.

By the time I find out that Charlie and I aren't the only ones whose marriage is orchestrated by Bob, I'll be so entrenched in his belief system that I won't question it. God hasn't come into the picture yet, but when he does, marriage begins to make even more sense: *Of course, marriage is the end goal of a life full of unconditional love—it is ordained by God.* I'll tell myself that Mr. Lyon knows better than the rest of us. We'll follow His plan. "True Happiness" sounds like such a universal good.

Re: Georgia Marriage License
Veena Dinavahi to Bob Lyon

Sun, Feb. 10, 2013, 10:52 a.m.

To Bob Lyon

Re Georgia Marriage License

So we're working on getting Charlie's birth certificate from his mom. We told my parents and we both agreed we'd like to have them there. Do you think that would be too much of a distraction?

Bob Lyon to Veena Dinavahi

Sun, Feb 10, 2013, 10:52 a.m.

To Veena Dinavahi

Nope, as long as you let me control their drama. So if they say ANYTHING that could be distracting, you send them to me. What day would they come? As it is now, we plan on this:

Saturday, you arrive.

Sunday, we work.

Monday, probably married that day, and several of OUR children will attend probably: YOU, Charlie, Noel, grandkids. Party. Your parents would arrive Saturday night? But we don't have a place for them to stay.

You leave in p.m.

16

February 18, 2013

I shiver in the driver's seat of Mr. Lyon's car. He let us borrow it for the ten-minute drive from his house to the courthouse. Charlie stares ahead with the unmistakable expression of roadkill in its last moments of life.

"I'm not sure about this," he stammers.

"Are you kidding?" As of yesterday, I wasn't sure either, but marriage feels like one of those things you do all the way or don't do at all. "Then what am I doing here, in this dress?"

It's coral and semi-sheer. Even though we are in Georgia, it's still a cold February day. I've never imagined myself in a white dress. I don't even know why my mind defaults to white when my own Telugu wedding customs call for a red sari.

The only wedding I've ever been to was my cousin's, and she wore a different silk sari for each ceremony and a full bib of uncut diamonds. It was a week-long celebration in India that fused customs from the north and south: a mehndi function where all the women applied henna while the men fed us. A slew of religious ceremonies ranging from just the two families to an entire event hall of guests. For the actual union, my cousin was carried into the hall on a palanquin. She and her fiancé walked around an open fire seven times. She put a garland around him, he put a garland around her, and we all took turns onstage throwing rice at them as congratulations. After each time the band onstage reached a crescendo, I asked Amma, *Are they married now? Is it official now?* Amma looked at me and shrugged. I'm not sure there is one moment like in American weddings. My cousin's wedding was filled with family, friends, and good food.

My own wedding takes place in less than two hours in Mr. Lyon's living room. The only people who attend are Mr. Lyon and his wife, their daughter Noel, and my parents. I'm not wearing any diamond necklace or silk sari; I picked my dress based on the criteria of (1) what was available via rush shipping, (2) what I could rewear, and (3) what was under three hundred dollars. Not a perfect decision-making framework, but none are.

"Five minutes," Charlie says. I start to protest but he repeats, "Just give me five minutes," holding up his hand to display the number.

He steps out of the car and calls Mr. Lyon, pacing back and forth on the sidewalk while I rub my hands together and wonder what the old man could possibly say to convince this boy to marry me. I fuss with my bangs, trying to make them lie flat over my cowlick. Bangs are not a good look on me. I told my hairdresser I might be getting married this weekend and she asked, "What do you mean you *might* be? Did he propose or not?" The conversation lapsed into an uncomfortable silence as I realized Charlie had never actually asked me to marry him. If anything, Mr. Lyon had proposed to us both.

Five long minutes later, Charlie opens the car door and offers me his hand, eyes shining. My eyes ask the question for me.

"I'm ready," he says. "Let's do this."

"Charlie," I start, "five minutes ago you weren't sure. I don't think we should do this if you're not sure you want me without Mr. Lyon in your ear."

He pulls me out of the car and holds me by the shoulders. "I love you. I get scared. That's all. I'm working on it. But I am so lucky to start a life with you. Please join me?"

I consider saying no for a long thirty seconds. I considered it all of yesterday, imagining a world in which I move back in with my parents. Nanna just accepted a job in California, so I'd start fresh. I could take a job waiting tables, come home to a crying baby, and argue with Amma about best child-rearing practices. Rinse and repeat until my aspirations and personality are ground out of me. Either that, or take a shot with this young man who, yes, is scared but is here with his outstretched hand. I've never had any set notions of what my ideal partner should be like. During those middle school sleepovers when my friends would stay up, imagining their perfect husbands—tall, dark, funny—I'd roll my eyes and lecture them about divorce rates in America. My friends would groan and ask, *Wait, you really don't have any preference on what your ideal partner would be like?* Nope. Marriage is an expectation, not an aspiration.

So, I take Charlie's hand. We can make a family. A good one. Love is something that imperfect people cultivate together. Commitment first, then love.

We race into the courthouse. Charlie notices that I'm still shivering and rubs my bare arms, draping his jacket over me, just like he once loaned me his soft gray sweatshirt at our debate tournaments. He's wearing a dark blue blazer, button-down shirt and red tie, brown oxfords, and a matching belt. I clump along in thrift store heels that are half a size too big. I couldn't find a strapless bra in time, so I'm wearing a regular bra with the straps tucked into the sides, and my pregnant breasts keep popping out, like two resilient Whac-A-Moles. Every couple of feet I trip in my heels and every couple more, I hike up my bra. The woman at the front desk looks up and smiles when she sees us together.

"Marriage?" She points in the direction of the stairwell with a pen. "Second floor, third office on the right."

We hand over my driver's license and Charlie's passport; he doesn't know how to drive since he was born and raised in New York City. Charlie comments that it's harder to get a fishing license than a marriage license and we giggle at this joke. The woman asks me if I want to keep my last name. I remember Mr. Lyon saying once that paperwork becomes confusing for kids whose parents have different last names.

"Nah. Let's get rid of it."

"You sure? You don't want to keep it as your middle name or something?"

"Less letters to spell."

I feel only relief as I imagine what it will be like to pick up the phone and make a doctor's appointment with the last name "Jones." I tell myself that I am a practical person—I don't anticipate the acute sense of loss I'll feel in the upcoming years. As I rewrite my identity in my husband's name, I don't think twice. We pay twenty-five dollars. The woman at the counter prints out our gold marriage certificate, displaying our two names united by one larger one: Dr. Bob S. Lyon, MD.

A year from now, I watch a Sunday school teacher draw a triangle on a chalkboard to illustrate the components of an ideal marriage: the husband and wife are two points united by God, the third. The lesson is that spouses cannot support each other alone, but when both pray and draw strength from God, they can forge a stable relationship.

Instead of God, we have Mr. Lyon.

At age twenty, I am even younger than Amma was when she got married. I joke about this, tell Amma I beat her to the punch, and she smiles cryptically. She won't tell me this at the time—she won't say anything to undermine the life I appear to have chosen—but she didn't want to get married so young. She had hoped to pursue her doctorate in biochemistry, but by the time she turned twenty-four, her father had lost patience. He let her complete her master's degree and she should have been satisfied with that. Despite Amma's initial reluctance to get married, it worked out well for her. To this day, Amma and Nanna have one of those precious relationships built on equal parts mutual support and good-natured teasing. But it's not what she wanted for her daughter. She wanted me to enjoy the luxury of time.

At this point, I only know of Amma's marriage as a success story—one that she recounted to me and my friends when we were teenagers as she prepared us warm cups of chai. I had absorbed this origin story into my DNA—like our family's own real-life *Pride and Prejudice*.

Her older sister was married first. My uncle drove by on his scooter every morning, far out of his way, just to wave to my aunt as she stood on her terrace, until he asked for her hand in marriage several months later. When it was Amma's turn, men traveled for miles to see her. She wore black saris for these visits, fussed with her food, and refused to make eye contact with her suitors. When Amma tells this story, she imitates her mother, smiling, laughing, adjusting her sari, and listing all the foods Amma could cook to the men and their families: "Vankaya kura, bendakai kura. All these dishes my daughter knows."

Amma had never touched a stove in her life. In spite of her uninterest, marriage proposals kept coming and she summarily rejected all of them. By the time she rejected Nanna, her father was furious. Nanna had such an impressive résumé, was studying in America, and came from a good family. Amma relented and agreed to meet Nanna once more but called in backup: she biked all the way to the nearest pay phone in her village and begged her older sister and brother-in-law to come rescue her.

"I was so rude." Amma smiles when she tells the story. "I asked him all these difficult questions, like how much money he makes. But he was so sweet. He answered all of them! He said, 'Right now I make this much, but I am hoping to make this much money in few years time.' My sister and brother-in-law kept walking past the room to give me a thumbs-up and make sure everything was okay."

Nanna would enter the room as she was narrating and make a joke about how he was tricked into getting a wife who couldn't cook and they'd laugh, smile coyly at each other, and segue into the story about the first time Amma tried to cook rice on the stove for Nanna's graduate school friends.

When I was in high school, everyone wanted to hear what arranged marriages were "really like," and I always leaned in, defending the institution. What had always been ordinary to me was a novelty to my classmates. When they scoffed and gasped at the injustice of the system, I was ready with personal anecdotes and those statistics on American divorce rates. Love, I argued, is the insane way to decide who to spend your life with. People marry for all sorts of reasons: money, status, convenience. Deferring to your parents' recommendation is hardly the craziest. My classmates would then ask if I was going to have an arranged marriage. I'd grin and reply, *Are you out of your mind? Of course not. But it works.*

Eliza and I once wrote down our predictions for where we would all end up in ten years, sealed it in an envelope, and buried it in my backyard. Married and pregnant at twenty was never on our list—like, not at all. I feel a pang when I think of her, partly because I miss her, partly from jealousy. I've heard her life is unfolding according to plan; she's living with Melanie, well on her way to that PhD in art history. She still reaches out occasionally, but—well, I'm in a car heading toward Mr. Lyon's house and she's not.

Barbara has been bugging me about wedding details all week. (It's only been one week since we told my parents about the pregnancy and decided to do this.) Color choices, nail salons, cake flavors. I told her as politely and appreciatively as I could that I don't care. No, I don't need my hair done. (I spent five minutes in the bathroom with a flat iron and still my bangs won't stay down.) No, the color scheme doesn't matter to me. (She asked the color of my dress and hung up a few streamers to match.) She decorated the pool house for me and Charlie. Tacky heart ornaments on each of the doorknobs. A cheese tray she bought from Walmart.

When we return to Mr. Lyon's house, he's in that same living room where I first met him, surrounded by those same pictures of his grandkids next to the tiny statue of Jesus. My parents sit on the same couch they did when Mr. Lyon first told them he could change our lives. Barbara's daughter, Noel, sits on the other couch with her two-year-old son. It's my first time meeting them. Charlie's parents aren't here because he still hasn't told them. I've protested repeatedly about this and asked, *When are we supposed to tell them?* After *we're married*? Mr. Lyon laughed and said, *You know, sometime before the kid turns eighteen.* When I've tried to press further, Mr. Lyon said most guys would have been out the door by now. I should let Charlie go at his own pace.

Mr. Lyon stands, clears his throat, and says words I won't remember. He asks if we had vows. We don't. Though I usually don't pass up a chance to write, I've never heard of wedding vows. Mr. Lyon hands us a sheet of paper titled "True Happiness Marriage Vows" and suggests we read it to each other. He suggests we read it ourselves first, so we know what we are promising each other, but we're already here. I read the vows out loud—something about sharing everything we own and always doing our best to love each other and learn. I pass the paper to Charlie, and he reads the same words back to me. Mr. Lyon says we can exchange rings and we laugh that we didn't have time to get any. Rings, like many other elements of this makeshift wedding, are not part of my heritage; Amma wears a *mangalasutram,* the traditional wedding necklace, a string of black beads with one gold disk provided by her family and one provided by her husband's. If I'm being honest, I want a ring to mark me as a married woman. Something to display my commitment and stave off questions from people like my hairstylist, but I tell myself that I am low maintenance. Sure, I am the kind of person who can get married without rings and a proposal.

Amma, Nanna, Charlie, and I take turns in the "photobooth" Barbara created—a picture frame she hot glued with blue plastic flowers—while her daughter takes pictures on her phone. Mr. Lyon sits on a stool at his kitchen counter while the rest of us stand around, eating cake on paper plates. He signs our marriage certificate.

"Congratulations, you two." His eyes crinkle.

We ride home in the back of my parents' minivan, like kids being driven back from soccer practice.

When I return to work the day after my wedding, Manuel, my manager at Express, takes me aside and says, "A little birdie told me a rumor."

He pulls my left hand away from my side and stares at my empty ring finger.

"Wait. Did you get married or not?"

"Yes," I say. "But it's complicated."

That week, one of my cousins calls to announce her engagement and invite me to her wedding. After I offer my congratulations, I drop my own news: I unfortunately can't make it because I got married, am pregnant, and am due the month of her wedding.

"Oh!" she says. "Oh, wow! Can I ask—was this planned?"

"Yes," I say emphatically. "I want this baby."

In less than a year, Charlie will graduate from college and apply to jobs in New York and San Francisco. We'll blend into whatever city we land in, and no one will count the number of months between my child's birthday and our wedding anymore. My cousin's wedding will be a day of joy and community—but I won't be there. In fact, she and I won't keep in touch after this conversation. It has been a year and a half since Mr. Lyon told me I had nothing to lose, and I believed him, but the people I once cared about are no longer present at my milestones. I push away these feelings and focus on the fact that I now have a husband and will soon have a child. I focus on the family I've gained instead of the family I've lost.

PART III

THE ROLE OF A WOMAN

Fwd: Twice is Nice
Barbara Lyon to Veena Dinavahi
Thu, Jan 17, 2013,10:13 PM

Hi, Little Mama,

So, do ALL your wishes come true as fast as this one? Bob told me that you recently said you had decided what you want to be when you grow up—a wife and mother. Then, BAM! Your wish comes true.

Here are some things I have learned:

1. People forget. Pretty soon it will be a year from now, then five years from now, and your baby will be a big boy and going to kindergarten while his two siblings are waiting their turn. I know. I have it all planned out. No one who you think cares now will remember.
2. If you don't have friends who have babies, I have two daughters who have just started their families. They would love to meet you.
3. Write things down that you're thinking of, so they are not in your head and you can revisit them later, and you don't need to talk with Charlie about these things as you think them. Men freak out. They all do. No matter their age.
4. When I look at your life the past year, or whatever, you were lost and confused and in pain, handled that one step at a time, and without wasting any time you are now at the step where you are going to have a baby. Well, it's perfectly timed as far as your recovery goes—meaning it couldn't have happened a month earlier. Sounds to me like this really could be "right on time."
5. Now you have to be nice to Charlie, because he's your man and men are needy. Women will be your nurturers more than any man. So, if you have women to talk with you, great, and if you need women to

talk to, I will be happy to hook you up. No kidding. I have nice girl children to talk/email/Skype/whatever to talk with.

DO NOT overdo it with thinking, shopping, or anything. It's wasted time and money and energy. Just one step at a time. Take pictures. Have fun.

Let me know if I can help.

Love,
Barbara

17

January to March 2014

The baby books describe the hunger cry as a dull, repetitive, *waa-waa* sound, but four-month-old Cleo has only one volume—tortured—and it throbs through every inch of my brain. All five-hundred square feet of our New York City apartment is overrun by primary colors and musical toys: a baby swing, Exersaucer, a changing table. The building is full of young professionals, with hallways full of gaudy chandeliers and black-and-white damask wallpaper. Cleo is the only baby in it. Charlie picked the apartment. New York was always Charlie's dream—not mine. Charlie is working in consulting and Bob says it's simple: you move to the location where your spouse's job is.

Around the same time that we relocate, Venkat moves to Brooklyn. Years from now, when I'm no longer speaking to Mr. Lyon, Venkat will tell me that his roommates had asked him when his sister got married and he wasn't sure. *What do you mean you're not sure? You didn't go to the wedding?* Venkat scratched his head. There was no wedding invite and no registry, so he assumed we must have had a courthouse marriage. When he tells his roommates that I had a baby, they ask him when, and he is not sure. *Dude, how can you not know your niece's birthday?* He feels dumb during these moments, but I don't even notice the potholes in our relationship. We live in the same city, but that's all we have in common.

Sometimes it doesn't even feel like the same city; he's living in an up-and-coming neighborhood with five international roommates and partying every weekend, whereas I hardly leave my apartment and I've never even stepped inside a bar. When we do meet up (roughly once a year) we have nothing to talk about.

In the first couple months of marriage, before Cleo erupted into our lives, I had moments of disorientation. You know when you wake up in someone else's house and can't quite remember how you got there? I'd wake up as a regular college student, survey myself in the mirror, and wonder why I looked slightly fat.

Oh! I was pregnant. Oh my god. I was married.

I'd tug on Charlie's arm as if imparting new information.

"Yes . . . ?"

"No, like, we're *MARRIED*. Why are we married?? You didn't choose to marry me. You didn't even propose! You've never even asked me out on a date!"

These conversations bewildered Charlie. "Of course I chose to marry you. I signed the paper."

His response agitated me further and he'd wind up on the phone with Mr. Lyon. Then he'd get down on one knee with a paper ring, smiling, certain that he'd cracked the code.

"What the hell is wrong with you! This is not how it works! We don't even have wedding bands!"

We went through several iterations of this scene before Mr. Lyon told me my pregnancy hormones were clouding my judgment and could I please take it easy on Charlie. I stopped bringing it up. Yes, of course we chose to get married.

In our flex-studio apartment in the financial district of Manhattan, the day begins at 5:30 a.m. Charlie buttons his blue Brooks Brothers shirt, laces his brown oxfords, and fastens his matching work belt—all gifts from his mother. Just a few months before Cleo was born, he finally informed his parents about our marriage and daughter. I wasn't there for the conversations. They hide whatever shock they might have experienced for fear of being removed from his life. Sometimes his mother will ask me how her son could have neglected to invite her to his wedding, and I think about Mr. Lyon's living room, and I don't know how to explain to her that it doesn't qualify as a "wedding" per se. Instead, I shrug and tell her what Mr. Lyon told me: Charlie was scared. And I don't understand it either.

At 5:45 a.m., he wakes me to tie his red silk tie. He doesn't know how. The only changes wrought by marriage are that I now do Charlie's laundry and keep a Google Doc list of foods he does not like: seafood, heavy cream, coconut, red meat, mayonnaise, and so on.

By 6:00 a.m. he rides down the elevator, and, without us, his family, he's inconspicuous among the other young professionals—he blends in with the guys in cashmere scarves and shiny black shoes that click against the lobby floor. I don't have this kind of privilege—I stay home with my daughter, so I stand out from the girls my age, with their camel-colored coats, designer bags, and marketing careers. At 7:00 a.m. sharp, Cleo wakes up screaming. She is my first child, so I assume all children wake from sleep in this way. I pull Cleo to my breast. Feed baby. Change diaper. Put down baby to wash hands. Pick up screaming baby. Promise to wash hands more. Wonder how truly compatible motherhood and hygiene can be. Wonder what it was like five months ago when I could simply walk out the front door when I chose. Sing to Cleo, quietly, to calm her, but by 7:00 a.m., the halls of the crowded apartment building are deserted. The only evidence of life is a noise complaint I receive from a neighbor, a scribbled note on a piece of paper slipped under my door.

At 8:00 a.m., I dress my doll. Slip little pink socks over her little pink toes. Select the sweater with the teddy bear and coax it over her disproportionately large head, gently, so as to minimize the protests. She is sturdier now, but I still treat her as though she might break. I can't move past the memory of being handed this little creature for the first time, feeling nothing but exhaustion, as the nurse barks, *Don't you know how to hold a baby?* Shaking my head, because my own daughter was the first newborn I'd ever seen, smelled, or touched. Amma visited me in the hospital hours after I gave birth and cradled my daughter perfectly in her arms, glowing and whispering, *Support the head.* I watched with trepidation, wondering if my own face would ever glow like that, and if the child in her arms really came out of me because I was expecting something a bit more, I don't know, brown . . . ?

Charlie was still at college when they sent me home from the hospital, just me, my breasts, and this child, and I collapsed on the floor of our apartment and screamed, That's it? How do I keep her alive? It was like the first time I learned to drive—how I expected the car to sort of know where to go, to stay within the lane lines on the highway, but in reality the power to wield the vehicle was in my hands. Then Amma came over, gently rubbed my back, and told me to breathe, told me she felt the same way when she gave birth to my brother; she was there for me, she was not going anywhere. But only a few months later, Amma and Nanna moved to San Francisco for Nanna's new job, and though Charlie promised that he would apply for jobs there, I'm beginning to think he never did. Their presence is replaced by my burning need to prove myself, because even though my family keeps their concerns to themselves, I know the odds are against me. My grandmother calls Nanna every month to ask if I'm divorced yet.

At 10:00 a.m. (Is anyone counting? Where did 9 a.m. go?), I make a grocery list even though I made a grocery list and weekly meal plan yesterday. The plodding rhythm of the hours makes it difficult to recall my days of being a temperamental teenager that already feel so far in the past. Motherhood feels as satisfying in the sinews as it does exhausting. My existential questions melt away in the depth of my daughter's eyes.

Today's grocery list consists of all the things that I forgot to buy yesterday: parsley, limes, heavy cream. They're things I can live without, but I glance around the tiny living space cluttered with baby toys and decide that parsley will add zest to tonight's dinner. Realize I'm not dressed and decide this does not matter as I zip myself into a big North Face jacket that masks my pajamas and transforms me into a puffy green marshmallow. Realize I haven't brushed my teeth. Brush, quickly. Grab a slice of wheat bread from the kitchen counter, baby still glued to my hip, and fold the entire thing into my mouth, chewing and swallowing in one motion. The baby permanently attached to my right hip gazes intently from the bread in my hand to the grotesque up and down movement of my jaws masticating, as if to ask, "Are these the healthy eating habits you are modeling for me, Mom?"

I ascribe some emotion to my baby's unresponsiveness; perhaps she wryly notes the hypocrisy of adults. I wonder what it will be like when those pristine pink lips are bigger, when they can move of their own volition and form words. What will this human being choose to say? What will be her favorite color? How will she love? Her ripe round eyes feel so new yet somehow so old, and the suspense kills me, like having to wait eighteen years to open Santa's best surprise. Of course, I wasn't raised with Santa, but I look at my daughter and think that if I believed in magic, it would have felt like this.

Buckle baby into the stroller and ride the elevator downstairs, alone. Wave at Hector, the doorman, the only person I see today whose name I know. I like Hector. Push the stroller along the pedestrian bridge over the West Side Highway and note that I forgot my gloves as the winter wind bites into my knuckles and cars rush past underneath. A woman clips past and scowls at me with the remark, *Where's her hat?* and then adds, *It's cold out,* as if my knuckles are not already screaming this information. I duck down and pretend to rummage through the diaper bag until she passes. I packed three hats: the pink stretchy one from the hospital, a Winnie-the-Pooh one with ears, and a white one with an embroidered duck. These are treasures Amma, Charlie, and I collected at yard sales in the months before Cleo arrived, handing quarters to mothers with toddlers hanging on their legs, fingering their ephemera with respect, and wondering what they would look like on my own child's head.

I didn't imagine, then, the amount of time I'd spend warming my baby's ears with my own freezing fingers because I didn't consider that she might hate hats and bows and anything rough or scratchy, and if I attempt to put one on her head, it will end up on the New York City streets two and a half seconds later. This will continue to earn me dirty looks and comments from strangers, but even as I feign forgetfulness, I cannot help but admire this small woman telling me so early on that she will not be trifled with.

I catch sight of my reflection in the store window and frown as I enter. My hollow eyes dredge up memories, stories of women who let themselves go post-marriage, stories of husbands who lost interest. Maybe Amma told me these stories, maybe my aunts. I add personal grooming to my list of resolutions, alongside hand washing and healthy eating. I attempt to drag my fingers through my rat's nest of hair, but they are too blistered with cold and I give up halfway, instead breathing into my hands, rubbing them together, and cupping my baby's small, frigid ears to transfer heat. I feel awkward, still, talking to a baby, but she looks up at me with such concern that I debate with her which parsley looks the least wilted. I load everything into the undercarriage of the stroller.

As I turn the block to my apartment, an attractive man in a hard hat accosts me, probably from the construction site next door. He jogs backward to keep up with me and my newly adopted New York City walking pace, asking if I'd like to get coffee sometime. I force a half smile and flash my wedding band—a cheap, modest thing that I bought for myself (I didn't want to be high-maintenance by asking why Charlie wouldn't buy me one). I tip my hand toward the stroller. "I'm married and have a . . . kid."

The man pauses and is left several paces behind me, processing. "OH! Oh, that's your kid? I apologize. I thought you were the nanny. Have a nice day!"

I catch another glimpse of my reflection in the revolving glass door and wonder when the postpartum baby fat will leave my cheeks, so I'll look old enough to be a mother, instead of like a sixteen-year-old brown girl watching some rich New Yorker's white baby. I wonder what the man could have possibly seen in me and pray fervently that my husband sees it still. I rush for the elevator bay and jab the buttons but before the elevator arrives, Hector calls out, *What, no hat for the baby?*

I've always loved words, but I stare between Hector and the arriving elevator, unable to cobble them together, to fashion any kind of tool out of them. Mom brain is real, according to every baby book I've consumed. Instead, I select the awkward laugh and sigh in relief as I step into the elevator. Groceries are filed away, heat is cranked up, and I begin the process of stripping the baby: first sweater, then pants, fresh diaper. I save the grocery bill in a drawer so that tomorrow I can try out that other market downtown and see which one has cheaper soy sauce. Shake my head with disbelief that a box of Raisin Nut Bran can really cost seven dollars.

Walk into the bedroom and attempt to swaddle my daughter with the adorable muslin swaddling blankets my father-in-law gave me. My husband gets home at nine, after Cleo is in bed. He sniffs dinner and reminds me that he doesn't eat cream-based sauces. I wonder if I should have spent the time showering, napping, or putting away clean laundry instead. I select the perfect size Tupperware to pack away an untouched dinner because now that I finally have time to eat, I find I'm not hungry. Selecting the perfect size Tupperware is my superpower and I return to the living room to share the joke with my husband, but he had a hard day at work with an angry boss and so I commiserate, wondering what it would be like to have a mean boss, or a career of my own. I forget to tell the joke about the Tupperware. I don't want to bother him, yet I can't help but ask if anyone at work knows that he's married or has a child yet. He mumbles and shakes his head, his ring finger still bare. It's been a full year since we got married in Mr. Lyon's living room but barely anyone in his life knows Cleo and I exist.

I walk into the kitchen for a glass of water and to conceal my dejection and hear faint snoring coming from the other room. My husband has fallen asleep on the floor, next to the baby gym. I rouse him gently, lead him to bed, and tuck him in, holding his cleft chin with the tips of my fingers briefly, trying to remember to tell him the joke about my Tupperware superpower tomorrow. I set a glass of water at his bedside and then collapse next to him, steeling myself for the 11 p.m. and 4 a.m. feeds, when Cleo will wake, screaming, and I'll rush to her before she wakes the neighbors. Sounds of laughter from the bar outside drift in through the window, evidence of friends and coworkers huddled under heat lamps, but I'll be alone in bed in an empty apartment building by morning.

18

April 25, 2014

Mr. Lyon sits at the front of an overcrowded conference room in a San Diego Hilton, wearing his typical plaid shirt, blue jeans, and, of course, just his socks. He kicked off his sneakers hours ago. A line of two hundred adults from all walks of life stand at the foot of the stage—flight attendants, police officers, social workers. Notably, these people don't belong to one singular gender, race, or sexuality—his followers are diverse. They've given up their lunch hour for the opportunity. He's on a dark brown couch in the middle of the stage. In his lap is a seventy-year-old man, bawling like a baby and clutching that plaid shirt by the fistful. Someone hands Mr. Lyon a box of tissues. He grabs several and dabs at the man's tears with the corner of a single tissue, the gesture as delicate as the fabric of the tissue itself.

Caroline, a school teacher from Dallas who I've been taking calls from, stands next to me and raises her eyebrows at the scene.

"This part is still so weird to me."

"It *is,* right?" I whisper.

You can't say this to just anyone in the True Happiness community. Some of them get worked up.

Mr. Lyon has been telling stories about me for three years now—

during interventions, on conference calls, at seminars. He tells little anecdotes of times my husband and I successfully communicate with each other instead of reverting to passive aggression. I am his greatest achievement. I've known about my role in his larger True Happiness narrative, but at the seminar in San Diego, I finally realize that Laura from Alaska and Will from Utah and Charlene from Texas are not merely names that get announced on conference calls but actual, real human beings, who happen to have a detailed knowledge of my life. When I walk in, everyone knows who I am. Strangers will start telling me a lesson Mr. Lyon taught them, and thirty seconds into the conversation, I'll recognize an intimate scene from my own life—a joke that Charlie made while we were brushing our teeth the other night and how we navigated conflict with humor. They'll pause, seeing the startled expression on my face, and say, *Wait, was this you and Charlie? That's my favorite blog post of Bob's!* I'll smile sheepishly and nod.

Our marriage sounds like a happy one when other people describe it, but I've tried to leave more than once. Charlie still hasn't told his coworkers that he is married or has a child. He didn't even want to come to the hospital when I was in labor. Cleo is now seven months old and not much has changed. I know he's embarrassed to have a family so young, but I wish he would just cut me and Cleo loose instead of keeping us in his back pocket without fully committing. It's as if we've been blotted out of existence. Nobody knows me in New York. If I were to die, it would be my mom who would notice first after I'd fail to answer her Skype calls—not the doorman, my in-laws, any of my faceless neighbors.

Time and again I try to tell Charlie that our marriage isn't working for me. He cries and begs me to stay, just like he did when we were dating in college, but now instead of eating gummy sharks, he calls Mr. Lyon. During these three-way calls, it becomes clear that I only want to leave because I am mentally unstable. My mind fogs over during these conversations and I can never remember the actual words that were said, only a feeling that I was in the wrong.

Last month I finally realized, *I have to act before I talk to Charlie and Mr. Lyon—before the fog sets in*. I packed a suitcase while he was sleeping, called Amma, told her I was coming to stay and bringing Cleo. She sounded worried and confused but said we'd get through it. Then she called back and said that I've displayed a long-standing pattern of running away from my problems and she could not support me abandoning my husband. Sounds familiar, right? But I wasn't in the headspace to notice that these phrases must have come straight from Mr. Lyon. So I hung up the phone and walked the city streets at night, with a suitcase and my baby in a stroller, wondering what options I had left. I might have been able to get a hotel room, but for how long? Mr. Lyon always said separate bank accounts were the prelude to divorce, and Charlie's money had never felt like mine. So that night, I went home, unpacked the suitcase, and fixed my husband's tie before he went to work the next morning.

Everyone in True Happiness is so convinced that Charlie and I are the perfect couple that I wonder if they're right. Other people would kill to have my life—hasn't that always been the case?—and I am ashamed that I still don't know how to be grateful for it. It's scary to think that without Charlie and Mr. Lyon, I wouldn't be able to tell which state of mind is fog and which is clarity.

Barbara has also begun to help me identify my problematic behaviors. The first day of the seminar I show up in a miniskirt, like the one I wore to my first intervention, and she eyes me up and down.

"It would be difficult to focus on loving someone while you're dressed like that. It would be too distracting for you and for them," she remarks.

I switch to skinny jeans.

"Those look pretty tight. Don't you want to be comfortable?"

I switch to a loose, floor-length maxi dress.

"Every time we get dressed, we are sending a message about who we are. This is certainly more appropriate than your previous choices, but you are trying to attract attention to yourself. And that's okay. That could be what you want people to know about you."

This is not what I want. Once, not long after Charlie and I got married, some guy chased me down the length of the mall to ask for my phone number and I called Barbara, panicked. She told me that we're always giving people signals about how we want to be treated, that there must have been something in the way I was dressed to give him the impression that his behavior was okay. I thought so, too, but I was wearing my big, red Bath & Body Works apron.

"Maybe you were wearing makeup or something, I don't know. But something about you told him that was okay."

I realized I'd been wearing bright red lipstick. Since then, I've completely stopped wearing makeup. I don't brush my hair any more than I absolutely need to. I try to wear loose, baggy clothing, but my whole wardrobe is bright colors and ruffles and skin. I tried to tell Barbara once that I just enjoy fashion, but she nodded and said, "Mmm. And why do you think that is?" in that really frustrating tone of hers. I genuinely thought fashion was a hobby of mine—I've binge-watched stylist YouTube channels since high school—but I am lucky to have Barbara to point out that my outfit choices are another symptom of my manipulative nature. My clothing is risqué, and excessive risk-taking is one of the symptoms of borderline personality disorder. I must be attention seeking.

Barbara gives me marriage advice now. Things like: write down everything you want from your husband and pick maybe two out of ten things to discuss so he doesn't feel overwhelmed. His job is providing for his family and my job is managing the home, so it serves no one if I complain about laundry or dishes. When your husband asks for sex, the answer is always yes. Some of her tips are hard to follow but I'm glad I have her guiding me; I'm twenty-one, I don't have any married friends I can ask for advice, and I never want to hear about my parents' sex lives—even though by the time I got to college, Amma had grown open-minded enough to surreptitiously leave a copy of the book *I ♥ Female Orgasm* on my bed.

Just one year ago I would have gagged at Barbara's idea of marriage as anti-feminist. It's hard to believe I was so selfish, but then again, I was raised with a very different example; Amma worked full-time and completed her second master's degree while Venkat and I were young. After learning about True Happiness, one of her greatest regrets in life has become the fact that she didn't spend more time with us. Now, we all know the purpose of life is to be loved, loving, and responsible.

I just don't know how to prove to Barbara that I'm trying. Each subsequent day I slip, like a greased turkey, further out of her graces.

When I return home after the seminar, I get a job offer from a Michael Kors store in Maryland. They kept my résumé on file from when I applied years ago. I want to ask them to transfer my application to New York, but Charlie says if I take a minimum wage job, we'll lose money after paying for childcare and taxes on two incomes. Again, I think about going back to school. Amma says she'd move to Virginia with me to watch Cleo. Then Mr. Lyon asks if I expect to keep my baby away from her father for the first two years of her life. Obviously, no, that is not what I want for her.

Mr. Lyon sends me more True Happiness participants to take calls from. Instead of sending me teenage girls and suburban moms, he sends me Lynn, a woman who has just been fired from her third job in three weeks, who screams at me over the phone about something someone did to her in the parking lot and then gushes about her two rescue dogs and tells me she wants to be a full-time dog trainer one day. Mr. Lyon sends me Arun, an Indian man who is convinced he is in love with me. Not ask-you-out-on-a-date type of love but picking-out-names-for-our-future-children kind of love. Mr. Lyon says this is normal and I'm just meant to guide Arun through his feelings. This explanation doesn't make the calls any less stressful. I slip the phrase "my husband" into conversation as often as I can and try to keep it light. Mr. Lyon then sends me Logan, a woman who transitioned to a man who then transitioned back after she met Mr. Lyon. Her stutter flares up when she tells me that she wishes she met Bob before she started hormone therapy, before her voice dropped. She was living in her parents' basement at the time.

I've got a roster of about ten people, some who call daily, some several times a week, and I've started hiding from my phone. When I tell Mr. Lyon it's getting stressful, he says I don't have to take their calls if I don't want to and then I feel dumb because "no" has never felt like a real option. He tells me that one of the people on my roster has borderline personality disorder.

"Not in the way you're borderline," he says. "You've actually grown. She's borderline as in she's one of the most unstable people I know—way beyond help. In all the years I've known her, she's never made any progress. I've given up on her. I sent her to you because it would be good practice for *you*."

I sour when his "unconditional love" does not seem to include everyone. I double down on my calls with this particular caller, because if even Mr. Lyon has given up on these people, who will believe in them?

Mr. Lyon tells me I could be the face of his company, one day. "You have a real talent for this. You're young, smart, and—I hate that this matters—but you're pretty."

While Mr. Lyon is preparing me to take over his company, Barbara is stalling from even certifying me as a coach. She says it's a maturity thing and, "We'll know it when we see it." I ask Mr. Lyon, "Does Barbara not like me?" and he says, "Correct. She doesn't like you. It's her problem, not yours." But he also says I have to work with her to get certified. Several years later, when Bob finally picks a new favorite (some young woman from the UK) and Barbara hates the new girl more than she ever hated me, I'll finally realize that I'm not the problem. Barbara hates all of Bob's chosen ones. After all, Bob was Barbara's coach when they first met. She was his first disciple—his first favorite.

The next time I ask Barbara what my next steps are, Bob scolds me for "cornering her" and "bullying her" into certifying me. Barbara takes away my conference call as punishment.

"If she finds out," he says, "I'll deny ever saying this, but start your own call and don't tell her. You're ready."

Outwardly, he has to support his wife. But off the record, he says that when he first met Barbara, she appeared to be "unusually willing to learn." Since then, however, her learning has slowed. I grow uncomfortable when Bob's compliments to me are coupled with insults to his wife and wonder if his marriage is truly healthy. I try to shake off my discomfort by telling myself that Bob is just being honest because he trusts me. Still, when the feeling of being the Ping-Pong ball stuck in the middle of their marriage overwhelms me, I finally stop taking calls.

Many of my friends from home are training to be high school teachers now. I learn about their lives through the rare moments I log into Facebook and come across their pictures on my feed: Ava Grace celebrating her twenty-first birthday at a hookah bar in a reflective onesie, Eliza and Melanie throwing college graduation caps into the air, Veronica moving in with a new boyfriend. Who are they trying to impress? I hover over the three dots next to their names and click "unfriend." The term feels melodramatic; I just don't know what we'd talk about if you put us in a room together. Facebook says, "Remember this day four years ago?" above a picture of me and Eliza at senior prom. I have three friend requests from True Happiness people: Stuart from Encinitas, Selma from the Bay Area, and Kate from Phoenix. I accept all of them. I only log into Facebook now to post on the True Happiness pages. True Happiness for Parents. True Happiness for Wise Men and Women. True Happiness Book Study Groups.

*

The next seminar I attend is months later, in Phoenix. After the first day, I hang out in Mr. Lyon's room with a group of coaches, listening to his stories.

"Sometimes people will say, 'True Happiness is a cult.'" He laughs.

I've never heard this before, but the idea is immediately ludicrous. What would he stand to gain? Money? He made more as an eye surgeon.

"I tell 'em, if it's a cult that makes me a better person, sign me up!"

I laugh along with him. In all the time I've known him, what are the things Mr. Lyon has encouraged me to do? Apologize to my parents when I'm rude? Communicate with my husband more kindly? Feel grateful for my daughter? The idea that there could be a nefarious element to personal growth is silly. The fact of the matter is Mr. Lyon sometimes tells people things they don't want to hear. People are arrogant and closed-minded, and they make excuses to ignore Mr. Lyon so that they can continue in the comfort of their selfishness rather than take up the gargantuan task of enacting real change. I would do *anything* to never again feel the way I felt staring down that empty bottle of Tylenol. And I haven't felt that way in years—he helps me and it works.

Toward the end of the seminar, I get a call from a woman named Glen who I've been taking calls from for a month. She has three PhDs and seven siblings, and we get along famously. Her intervention is scheduled for next week.

"Veena"—she hesitates—"one of my friends looked up True Happiness on the Internet . . . and I think it's a cult. Like, an *actual* cult."

I laugh. "If it's a cult that makes me a better person, sign me up!"

She tries to say something more, but I cut her off. In the brief silence my conviction solidifies. I won't google "True Happiness Company" until after I file a lawsuit against Bob five years from now. Then, reading the posts about him on a discussion forum, I'll think back to

Glen and wonder what she would have said had I let her speak. But in the moment, she doesn't press further.

"Okay, Veena," she says. "It has been nice getting to know you."

Months later I return to that familiar living room in Georgia, except this time, I'm the one sitting where Enid once sat, at the window, taking notes. A wealthy New York divorcée sits on the couch and I'm the one Mr. Lyon points to and says, "When I met Veena, she was a wreck. Attempting suicide, not a single stable relationship in her life. Now she's happily married and the mother of a beautiful daughter. I can help you, like I helped her."

19

April 2014

The way the missionaries wind up in my apartment feels like happenstance. The day they arrive, the doorman calls, confused. He says that two people who call themselves “sisters” are here to see me.

“You want me to send them up? You sure? I can get rid of them for you.”

I have to tell Hector three times that, yes, it is okay for them to come up. When the missionaries reach my floor, I understand his confusion. At my door stand two teenage girls: a tall blonde with side bangs and a name tag that says Sister Alrich, and a brunette at least two heads shorter with a name tag that says Sister Sampson. Both wear unflattering calf-length skirts and clunky black shoes with messenger bags slung across their shoulders. Sister Alrich gives me a friendly smile and Sister Sampson gives me her best attempt at one.

I invite them into the apartment. Besides my mom and my mother-in-law, they are the first visitors I’ve had. No one has seen me in this space—no friends from high school nor friends of Charlie’s. When we first moved here, I assumed we’d have a built in-network, returning to Charlie’s hometown, but as far as I know, even he hasn’t met up with any of his old friends.

When the sisters sit down, the tone of the apartment shifts, as if they brought their own air with them, one cleaner and fresher than exhaust-clogged New York City air.

"We wanted to start off by asking what you know about Jesus Christ."

I know the first twenty stanzas of the Bhagavad Gita by heart from the summer that Venkat and I stayed with our cousins in Ohio and our uncle woke us up at six every morning to recite it for two hours. I can tell you the exact lessons Krishna taught Arjuna on the battlefield—but my knowledge of Jesus?

"Um, I know that he died on a cross," I offer, bouncing Cleo on my hip.

I did believe in God once, when I was younger and didn't know any better. Hindu icons were ubiquitous in our home, as if Amma's gods might disappear if she did not keep them close at hand: on top of the oven, in kitchen cabinets, on my parents' nightstands, on family room ledges. Some were solid gold, some gold plated, all twenty-four carat, some no bigger than my thumb, some larger than my head, some bedazzled with various gems and crystals, and all with way more arms than seemed necessary. Whenever my childhood friend Kate came over, she'd ask, *Why do they have so many arms?* while squinting her eyes and tilting her head, as if that would reduce the number of appendages.

I started relaying these questions to Amma (*Why do they need that many arms? Can't they put one thing down before picking something else up?*) and Amma would laugh and explain that they didn't really have that many arms—they were symbolic. One hand held a book to represent knowledge, necessary in conjunction with love for the betterment of mankind. Another held *japa mala,* prayer beads, to signify union with God. The other two hands held a veena (my namesake), a musical instrument, to suggest that the seeker must tune his mind and intellect to live in harmony with the world. All the elements had to come together to achieve happiness and spiritual enlightenment. Amma's philosophy—that religion should not be taken too literally but used as a means of finding inner peace—satisfied me for a while. But by adolescence I was picking apart the mythology and pointing out problematic scriptures.

"We'd like to start by telling you the parable of the lost sheep." Sister Alrich unlatches her messenger bag and takes out a pamphlet with a picture of a bearded man in a white robe holding a lamb.

My expectations are low. As an adult, organized religion strikes me as a security blanket for people uncomfortable with gray areas in life.

"If you were a shepherd and you had a hundred sheep and one sheep went missing, would you go look for that missing sheep?"

"Um, no?"

"Jesus will always go look for that single lost sheep. Do you know why?"

I shake my head.

"Because the ninety-nine sheep, they have each other. They're going to be okay. That lost sheep has no one."

My reaction to this parable surprises me more than anyone else. The sensation that follows is devoid of thought. But in this city full of people, by some miracle, someone has noticed me. My body goes cold, like someone has poured ice water over my head, and it takes me a minute to realize that my face is wet. You'd think I would have run out of tears by now.

"We are the sheep. Jesus finds us. He returns us to safety every time."

I nod and rub my sleeve against my face. Because I remember what it was like to walk down my childhood street, knocking on doors for any reason not to swallow sixteen pills of Tylenol or scrolling through my phone contacts on my college bed, searching for any reason not to do it again. Because I remember what it felt like to be in the hospital a second time, but this time, to not have to scroll through my contacts, to know exactly where to go. To the man who has answered every one of my calls, who has cared for me and comforted me while I am needy and desperate and stubborn and arrogant and annoying, who has never let me tell him thank you and made me feel like I am a gift instead of a burden. I was lost and He found me.

Believe me, I did not plan on having a sudden religious rebirth. Barbara's daughter, Noel, sent the missionaries to me based on a misunderstanding. Back when Barbara still liked me, she said I needed mom friends and introduced me to her daughter, Noel. Even though Noel lives in Phoenix, we started talking on the phone almost every day about diaper rash, teething, and nasal aspirators—things I can't talk about with other twenty-one-year-olds. The only time I met her in person was at my wedding when she took pictures for Charlie and me on her cell phone.

During one of our calls, Noel mentioned going to church and I asked which church, not thinking anything of it, and instead of delivering the elevator pitch I expected, she launched into the history of Joseph Smith and how he uncovered one of the missing books of the Bible that was buried in upstate New York. I only understood every third word that came out of her mouth, so I feigned polite interest. The next day she told me that she filled out an online form to send missionaries to my apartment. She misinterpreted my curiosity as interest and I let it slide rather than correct her. No one else was coming by the apartment anyway.

"*Who* is coming over?" Charlie looked at me askance when I told him.

As a young couple living in downtown Manhattan, we were not exactly the target demographic: me, a twenty-one-year-old Hindu-raised atheist, and him, a twenty-year-old atheist Jew. But I was not going to be the one to tell the Christian lady to please keep her missionaries to herself.

"I guess do whatever you want as long as I don't have to talk to them," Charlie conceded.

*

On another one of our calls, I asked Noel what it was like having Mr. Lyon as a stepdad, and Noel called him a miracle worker. She also called him "Dad" and said he saved her life.

"Isn't it weird," I asked, "hearing all of these strangers call your stepdad 'daddy'?"

"No," she answered unequivocally. "He really treats everyone he sees like his own kids. Dad is the most brilliant man I know."

And she was right. Anytime I had a question—about roommates, parenting, relationships, or the general purpose of life—he always had an answer. He didn't even pause before delivering thoughtful, incisive wisdom I'd never heard before—from all my years in therapy, from philosophy books, from any number of wise friends. I asked Mr. Lyon, *How do you know all this stuff?* and *Where do you get all the energy to talk to people all day?*, and after months of cagey answers he finally said, "You really want to know? I don't make it up, sweetie. I'm just not that smart. I get these answers through prayer."

In the three years that I'd known him, this was the first time he'd mentioned religion and it caught me off guard. He used generic words like "divine inspiration" and "spirituality," but then he sent me to a Christian website that was almost as grating as his own. I grimaced and changed the subject, but anytime I tried to avoid a suggestion of Mr. Lyon's, we went through some version of this conversation: *Try it my way and if you hate it, you can always go back to doing things your way. But we already know your way doesn't work.* And if I still didn't follow his advice: *Have I ever lied to you? Have I ever led you astray?*

So, I told myself not to be cynical and closed-minded and now I'm crying in front of these two teenage girls with name tags, unable to explain the transformation occurring inside me. Now, everything Mr. Lyon has been preaching feels plausible—like there could be another father, one like him, but more perfect and all-encompassing. The sisters hand me a small black Book of Mormon with tissue-thin pages. They leave me with an invitation to attend church on Sunday.

I take the uptown express train and get off at West Fourteenth Street, 40 percent sure that I got off at the right stop. This is one of my first times taking the subway, though we moved to the city in February, and it's now April. I pick up Cleo's stroller and climb the grimy stairs with her, blinking when I make it to street level and spin several one-eighties until I orient myself. I walk confidently in one direction, realize I'm going the wrong way, cross the street to feel less stupid, and head north again. Tucked away between rows of brownstones is an unremarkable gray building with a plaque above it that reads:

CHURCH OF JESUS CHRIST OF LATTER-DAY SAINTS

VISITORS WELCOME

The church's main room is unassuming. No stained glass or gaudy crosses, just rows of wooden pews and a stage, where an older lady is playing the organ. The murmur of polite conversation braids into the organ music. The sisters had informed me that women typically wear skirts or dresses, and men typically wear suits, so I was expecting something akin to *Little House on the Prairie*. Instead, beautiful blond women in bright lipsticks and equally bright heels smile at me, with teeth so white it's like staring down thirty-two tiny headlights in each face. I meet mothers completing master's degrees at Columbia University through night classes, refined investment bankers, an opera singer, a food blogger, a woman who works at Yves Saint Laurent and looks like she stepped into church directly out of a magazine. No one asks my age or looks at me strangely for having a child. In fact, everyone seems to have three or four small children in tow, all dressed in matching slacks and bows. Women as young as me have husbands on their arms. A blond woman in fuchsia heels and cherry lipstick introduces herself as Eden and I immediately feel connected to her. A small crowd of warm, open faces gathers around me, offering their names, warm handshakes, and warm questions about my day and my life. I'm experiencing the most human interaction I've had since becoming a mother seven months ago. I look around at the faces, equal parts exhilarated and overwhelmed. Among these people, I start to feel like I can finally start fresh, without the baggage of my past.

Cleo and I settle into a pew next to a kind-looking couple—a young woman of color with a white husband, like me—and we crack open green hymn books and sing. Even though I've never heard the songs before, the feeling of sitting amid a congregation singing in unison stirs something in me: I begin to understand that look of peace on Amma's face when she prays every morning. We listen to several people speak for the first hour and the themes resonate with those I've been taught in True Happiness: how to be a better person, how to admit when you are wrong, what it means to know we are loved unconditionally by a Heavenly Father. I realize that much of Mr. Lyon's teachings over the past three years have been extrapolated from the basic tenets of the Mormon doctrine. And it's comforting to know he has not been inventing all these principles on his own.

The service is three hours long and I had intentionally brought Cleo to have an excuse to leave after the first hour, but it turns out there is nothing I'd rather do with my time than discuss how to be a better person with other people who share that goal. During the second hour, adults separate from children for Sunday school, though Cleo stays with me because she is too young. During the third hour, men and women separate for individual classes. I remain riveted to the end, listening to these thoughtful, intelligent women debate the finer points of Scripture. Disagreement is encouraged and everyone engages in a healthy discussion about motherhood and service. The last time I had an intellectual discussion with someone who wasn't Mr. Lyon was a full year and a half ago, before I dropped out of college. The whole experience feels like a shot of adrenaline to my atrophied brain.

I leave with an entirely transformed understanding of what it means to be religious, several invitations to family dinners, and a promise to return the following week. Mr. Lyon is immensely proud of me when I tell him I attended church because, out of all religions in the world, he says True Happiness most closely aligns with Mormonism. He follows up our phone call with an email filled with specific Scriptures I now recognize from church.

"The sisters came over," I report to Noel.

"Great! When should I book my flight for your baptism?"

I hesitate. Everything about the church feels like the intuitive next step alongside Mr. Lyon's teachings, and I plan on attending as long as it feels good, but baptism has not been on my radar. I don't even know what it signifies. "Maybe wait until they ask me if I want to be baptized . . . ?"

It doesn't take long. Three weeks after I meet them, the sisters ask if I am prepared to be baptized into the Church of Jesus Christ of Latter-Day Saints. I think about how Mr. Lyon says skepticism is lazy, that it takes real courage and emotional vulnerability to actually *try*. That if I want to be happy in a way I've never experienced, I have to be willing to do things I've never done. I could sit in the apartment all day while my daughter chews on Sophie the Giraffe and I could poke intellectual holes in every organized religion. But happiness and peace have found me in the most unexpected places: in strange living rooms and nondescript chapels. Amma has always told me that different religions are paths to the same God, so I latch on to this inner calm and allow it to quiet the questions I should be asking myself about doctrine and culture. I don't deeply consider the differences between my mother's makeshift shrines and the building on Fifteenth Street. Even though I never envisioned myself making small talk with a roomful of white-toothed Christian women, I am nothing if not adaptable, and if there is a chance that this structure can focus and amplify my joy in life—well, you already know my answer.

I say yes. They ask if I am willing to practice abstinence. I'm already married and faithful. They ask if I will pay 10 percent of my income to the church. I don't have an income. They ask if I will commit to follow the Word of Wisdom, which means giving up tea, coffee, and alcohol. I haven't been drinking since college, but out of everything they ask, the one thing that gives me pause is the thought of relinquishing Amma's chai. It's a fundamental tenet of our relationship—watching her as she grates ginger, tosses in loose tea, and realizes too late that the pot is boiling over on the stove. Something in my chest kicks back against this, to preserve my memories of Amma gossiping with her sisters on sleeper trains, aggressively swatting flies, and chasing after *chaiwalas,* the skinny men carrying large steel tankards of the aromatic tea on their shoulders, walking through the train, calling, "Chai . . . chai . . . tea . . . chai . . . hot, hot chai," dispensing the burning liquid into paper cups at ten rupees apiece. After giving up my last name, giving up proximity to my parents, and giving up my education, being asked to give up chai feels like too much.

The sisters repeat their question while looking at me eagerly and I remember that Mr. Lyon has never led me astray. He would never suggest I do this if there wasn't a good reason, if it wasn't worth the cost. I make a face, but I say, "Yeah, okay." I can always change my mind later; saying yes to missionaries is hardly a binding contract.

Amma's open-mindedness regarding different religions does not hold water when I tell her I am converting to Mormonism. It is another one of those conversations where Amma looks like she has something to say but, after a pause, Nanna says, "Whatever brings you peace, *amilli*. We will support you." As far as I know, their questions end there. I don't know that Amma calls Bob and demands to know why I am joining the church. His answer is curt: Veena needs the socialization. Amma can think of a million other ways to socialize, but his tone of voice has a bite to it that discourages further discussion. Above all, her priority is supporting her daughter. So though she declines to attend my baptism, she otherwise swallows her objections.

*

When I tell Venkat about my conversion, he is certain I am joking. But my friends from church come over and they respectfully refer to my parents as Mr. and Mrs. Dinavahi. They roll up their sleeves and wash the dishes I've let pile up in the sink and they bring over dinner when I am exhausted. They engage in conversation about the stock market, and when we move from the West to the East Side of the city, they hand carry our television across town because it doesn't fit in the U-Haul with the rest of our furniture. They're too *nice* for anyone to take real issue with, so ultimately even Charlie stops cracking jokes.

The sisters ask if I have anyone in mind to perform my baptism (any male member of the church is qualified) and a week later, Mr. Lyon hobbles into the chapel basement. He seems somehow larger out in public in his suit and tie; I'm accustomed to seeing him in the privacy of his living room. He has a magnetism that draws my congregation toward him. They've heard so much about him from the talks I've started giving in church. The man who I used to describe as "a sort of therapist" has become "the man who brought me to the church" and now "the man who saved my life." Mr. Lyon answers questions politely but glances back at me and winks. We are the only two people in a room full of noise. His presence makes it less painful that my own parents and brother are not here.

Rows of folding chairs are set up in front of a baptismal font in the church basement. The font looks like a small version of a dolphin tank in an aquarium, with stairs leading down into a basin of water, enclosed on one side with plexiglass so onlookers can watch. I sit in the front row of folding chairs, with Charlie on one side, Mr. Lyon on the other. The ceremony begins with a hymn about following in the footsteps of our fathers. My voice falters at this line, unable to escape the conclusion that I am not following the footsteps of my ancestors. My forefathers' bare feet walked the cool marble floors of Hindu temples. My father's knees bent in front of Hindu idols, hands clasped in prayer, eyes closed, mouth repeating words in Sanskrit. My feet clatter through the church in bright, impractical stilettos, and I no longer kneel before my parents' gods.

Mr. Lyon's baritone voice booms beside me and I remind myself that I have a new father now. I am following in His footsteps. The sister missionaries lead me into a bathroom and hand me a boxy white jumpsuit to change into. I open the door directly into the font and climb down toward Mr. Lyon in his whites. The water is waist high and cold. The jumpsuit clings to my skin as I push through the water and into his arms. One hand is placed behind my head, the other held high at a 90-degree angle. I grasp his arm as I've been shown.

"Veena Jones, having been commissioned of Jesus Christ, I baptize you in the name of the Father, and of the Son, and of the Holy Ghost. Amen."

His hands move me swiftly back and under the surface of the water until I am completely submerged for two seconds. I thought I was prepared, but I arise sputtering and wiping wet hair out of my face. The Hindi idols, the incense, the Sanskrit verses are washed away, replaced by my new family watching in awe from their folding chairs. Vibrant saris are replaced by knee-length tea dresses, button-down shirts, tweed blazers, and slacks. I rise, shivering and cleansed, and change back into my five-dollar thrift store dress. My friends gather around me afterward, asking how it felt.

"Wet," I answer honestly.

Mr. Lyon and Charlie comment on how grimy the baptismal font was and ask if I noticed.

I did not. All I noticed was the strength of the hands holding me.

20

2015 *to* 2016

Women of God can never be like women of the world. The world has enough women who are tough; we need women who are tender. There are enough women who are coarse; we need women who are kind. There are enough women who are rude; we need women who are refined. We have enough women of fame and fortune; we need more women of faith. We have enough greed; we need more goodness. We have enough vanity; we need more virtue. We have enough popularity; we need more purity.

—MARGARET D. NADAULD,
Young Women, general president, "The Joy of Womanhood"

The structure and rules of the Mormon Church ensconce me like a weighted blanket. Go to church every Sunday. Create a Family Home Evening lesson every Monday. Make a casserole for a family who just had a baby. Always wear religious garments underneath your clothing. Men, provide for your family. Women, bear and raise children.

I used to hate Sundays. The threat of Monday looms on the horizon while the memory of Saturday reminds you of how good the weekend can be. Now, Sunday is my favorite day. You drink a thimble of water, and all your sins are washed away. All the mistakes you've made, the wrongs you've committed, they're all wiped clean. And don't your mistakes feel suffocating at times? Isn't life one long series of moments you'd rewrite if you could?

I've always been good at following rules, and, despite the physical toll on my body, I become pregnant again when Cleo turns two. I vomit ten to twelve times a day and collapse with dehydration. Nothing tastes as good as ice chips when I wind up in the ER—except the sacrament on Sundays.

This pregnancy is something we plan and anticipate with the joy that is meant to precede parenthood. Even though Charlie has not gotten baptized, mere proximity to Mormonism has changed him. He attends church with me sometimes and befriends proud Christian fathers who also work in consulting but who do not define themselves by their careers. Three years in, Charlie finally starts telling people he is married. He puts a picture of Cleo on his desk at work and tells his coworkers about milestones she crosses. He buys himself a wedding band and starts wearing it. Against all odds, we have made it. Those two scared teenagers from two years ago have transformed into a proper family.

Instead of feeling trapped in our one-bedroom apartment, I walk to the Union Square farmers market with my fleet of fellow Mormon stay-at-home moms and their double strollers. We laugh at passing comments about the "mommy brigade," stop for the free cupcake of the day at Georgetown Cupcake in SoHo, and beg our children to take potty breaks. Motherhood is teaching Cleo the individual names of each shape of pasta: rotini, spaghetti, elbow, tortellini. It is watching her stoop to literally smell the roses next to a shit-smeared sidewalk and marveling at her sense of wonder. She is the answer to that one-word question I asked the ceramic sink in the girls' bathroom of upstairs G Hall after Sarah Rose died—the question I asked myself in the psych ward, in my college dorm, and so many times since: *Why?*

Her. All of it, for her.

Even though Charlie will never join the church, we decide to name our second child Mary. Mother of God. He likes the sound of "Mary" and loves the effect the church has had on me.

As soon as I acclimate to New York, Charlie accepts a job at a firm in the suburbs of Connecticut and we move to the same town where we spent our first Thanksgiving together. Much like Severna Park, there are a lot of white people and there is nothing to do at night. In important ways, though, this town is different: the kids here, apparently satisfied with their backyard pools and tennis courts, do not kill themselves. There is a complacency woven into the fabric of this town that is new to me.

When we pull up to our new apartment in a U-Haul, I wait until Charlie gets out, and instead of calling Bob, I call Nanna. I cry that we've traded in the people of New York City for the deer of Connecticut. Nanna tells me to take a deep breath. He and Amma will visit. Had I called Bob, he would have reminded me that I'm borderline and cannot trust my reaction to the move. I still mostly believe him when he says happiness is a mindset unrelated to physical circumstances. But the older I get, the more stable, the more it seems like our surroundings *can* impact mental health. When I was a kid, I was in a shitty situation: surrounded by suicide, feeling disconnected from my support system, and lacking effective coping skills. Now, as much as I dislike this town, I am an adult, I'll make friends in church, and I have a clear role and purpose. I've spent years retraining my thought patterns to redirect and reframe negative thoughts. I can make this work.

The school system in this suburb is also great, much like the schools in Severna Park. Cleo—who so recently attended a New York City preschool class, which, yes, cost the price of a black-market organ but was incredibly diverse—has been deposited into a predominantly white preschool. Time passes, but it feels sudden when my daughter comes home telling me she's embarrassed of being Indian. I gape and pump Bollywood music through the kitchen with more urgency after that, pausing every now and then to ask some variation of *Isn't this great?* Her eyes are skeptical. I've never really cared about heritage before, but now, seeing my daughter reject it so openly makes me wonder what I've lost.

Nanna calls Bamma, my paternal grandmother, to announce my second pregnancy.

"Ah! Veena . . . is *EXPECTING*," Nanna yells into the phone.

"Eh??" The connection is bad and Bamma's hearing aids are acting up.

I'm in California visiting my parents; the pregnancy nausea has become too severe for me to care for Cleo on my own. I'm on the strongest anti-nausea medications typically reserved for chemo patients and even that doesn't work.

Nanna tries again. "VEENAAAA . . . is EXPECTING."

A click of her tongue indicates that she heard the second time. "Too bad." She sighs. "Oh well. They're not divorced yet?"

I stalk out of the room, fuming. Nanna follows me into the family room and sets a gentle hand on my shoulder.

"To understand Bamma's reaction," he says, "you have to understand her past."

I have never heard Bamma's history before. Her mother died with she was eight and she was beaten by her stepmother. She was forbidden to pursue an education, but she wouldn't accept that. She went on a hunger strike until her relatives allowed her to complete high school. Married off before she could finish her undergraduate studies, Bamma became a young mother of three boys. Then her husband died of a heart attack when Nanna, the oldest, was eight. This is the only part of the story I've heard before. Bamma refused to accept money from her rich relatives, knowing they would force her sons to work as servants. Instead, she worked full-time and went back to school until she was finally able to become a physics teacher.

Nanna wipes away a tear as he finishes the story. My whole life, I have only known this woman to lurch by my bedroom, telling me to drink milk for strong bones or complain about the degradation of Indian culture. A single ten-minute conversation has completely transformed the way I think of my grandmother, my father, and my own identity.

"Are you kidding?" I ask. My newfound admiration for Bamma and empathy for Nanna is briefly overridden by the fact that I've never been able to know my grandmother this way, that yet again my family's history has been censored and siloed. "Why didn't you tell me this when I was in school studying to be a physics professor?"

Nanna shrugs. "I don't know why I didn't tell you. She's happy for you, Veena. She just knows what it is to be dependent on someone else. She's worried you never finished your degree because she knows education means having options."

All this time I've been interpreting her behavior as condescension when, with the appropriate context, it turns out she has been trying to care for me in her own way.

After hearing about my grandmother's past, I insist on bringing the girls to another cousin's wedding, even though I've never really liked that cousin before. We return to Connecticut with henna on our hands, and one day, Cleo comes home from kindergarten, trying to scrub the henna off. She scrubs so hard I worry her hands might bleed and finally, I broach the idea of moving back to the city, to a place where differences are celebrated. But of course, nothing is worth making my husband commute. The only times I speak to Bob now are when Charlie insists on a three-way call—usually because I've asked for something he doesn't want to give. But I have nothing to complain about in my daily life. I've heard my parents speak about close family members and friends who have been beaten by their husbands—not badly enough to be hospitalized, but badly enough for my parents to speak about them with concern—and those women expected to work things out. I'll learn to be happy here. When I feel sad—which happens less and less often these days—I push my daughter endlessly on the swings. The first buds of spring sprout, the last leaf crumples and falls, the first snow dusts the ground, and still, I push Cleo on the playground swings into each new season.

The next time my parents visit, Amma puts on a pot of chai and prepares three cups, handing one cup to Nanna and pausing as she gets to me.

"Oh. Oops. I forgot." She pours my cup down the sink.

I start trying to talk to Cleo in Telugu, but it is late in the day. The only words she knows are: *ammamma, tata,* and *akka:* maternal grandmother, grandfather, and older sister because I forgot the word for "little sister." The conjugations are marbles in my mouth. Cleo calls me "mom." Marbles, lodged in the throat. I stop every three seconds for a vocabulary word I've forgotten. I want to drink the ocean through a straw. Amma and Nanna sit next to me on the couch, sipping their steaming cups, but the distance between us feels much farther. Nanna sings a Hindi song in his deep baritone.

"Veena, the poetry in this song is so beautiful. The man is singing to God: take all my wealth, take all my fame, even my youth, but give me back the season of my childhood."

When my second daughter, Mary, is born, I give her the middle name "Adavi," half of Bamma's maiden name. It means "forest" but still, all I see are trees.

Another Sunday comes and I cannot wait to wash away the week. Heavenly Father has a plan for me. Even if that plan involves changing more diapers than I'd like. Cleo sits next to me in the pew, tugs on a lock of brown hair and says that she wants to be blond. I cannot hear the still small voice of the Holy Spirit over the shattering of my heart as I watch the seeds of self-hatred sprout in my child. I'm not supposed to use the name of the Lord in vain, but, God, I hate it here.

The next time I take the sacrament, I cannot help but wonder if it's washing away more than just my sins.

21

2017

"How many of you believe in agency?" I ask. I'm standing before a classroom full of teenage girls and a handful of other leaders in my weekly lesson as Young Women's teacher. At the start of every meeting, we stand and recite in unison a statement about preparing to strengthen home and family—not quite the teaching I had in mind when I was studying physics, but in a way it's more rewarding. I'm teaching practical principles of happiness to young people who need them. Everything I've learned from Bob over the past six years coalesces here, in the church.

When I ask who believes in agency—a sacred principle of the church—every hand in the room goes up. I pick up a fork I brought with me and walk toward the loudest, most popular girl in the room whose attention is currently divided between her best friend and her phone.

"Hold still," I instruct and raise the fork, as if about to bring it down into her thigh. Hannah shrieks and jumps away from me. The entire room falls silent.

"Why did you move?" I ask quietly.

"Because you were about to stick a fork in my leg!"

"But I'm your church leader. You know I wouldn't hurt you. Why didn't you choose to trust me?"

"I was scared!"

"Right." I point at her. "You were scared."

I cross the room and write on the whiteboard: *To kindness, to knowledge, we make promises only; pain we obey.—Marcel Proust*. "If Hannah had tried harder, could she have followed my instructions?" I put away the fork. "No! The choice to remain still technically existed, but there was no way Hannah could have made that choice in that moment. How many of you still believe in agency?"

A couple of confused hands waver in the air.

"What I am telling you"—I soften my voice—"is that the mistakes you have made in your life are *not* your fault."

A couple girls start crying silently, guilt shucked off their faces. Their expressions remind me of myself the first time Bob said my mistakes were a reaction to pain. The other leaders exchange bewildered glances; they've been raised in the church their entire lives, but I'm not following any lesson plan they know of. I'm speaking in a language only the girls understand.

"Does that mean we can do whatever we want? Julia?"

Julia shakes her head. "Christ still asks us to love one another."

"Exactly. And we can only be happy if we love one another. The reason I'm telling you this is so that you don't feel guilty for the times you mess up. All we can do is keep trying our best. The atonement makes up for the rest."

By the end of the evening, girls are weeping in my arms and leaders are cornering me, telling me I need to inform them of my lessons ahead of time so they can all participate. All the pain I have survived is worth it now, to pass on the compassion Bob has shown me.

I am still riding the spiritual high when I get home. Amma is visiting from the West Coast to spend time with her grandchildren, but I breeze past her to share the moment with someone else.

Bob and I rarely speak about my mental health since I've become a mother. Instead, I call him when I have a spiritual moment that I know only he will understand. He sends me conference talks about motherhood. We quote specific Scriptures to each other, and he tells me that he has conversations with me that he's never been able to have with anyone else in his entire sixty-some years of life. I'm only twenty-four, but I tell him the feeling is mutual. I've debated the smartest kids from the most elite Ivy League schools, and I've never met anyone as smart as him. I've never encountered another person who understood me so immediately and without explanation.

When I get on the Skype call, his large round face bends into a smile. He's in the La-Z-Boy in his office, the spot where he always takes calls. The harsh lighting shows his hand on his chest. That means I'm supposed to put my hand on my chest and remember his hand pressing down on me. I always ignore it until he calls me out.

"That's incredible, sweetie. Do you know what a difference you could have made in those girls' lives?"

I beam and awkwardly pat my chest with my hand. "But I think I freaked out the Young Women's president. I don't want her to feel threatened by me."

"Oh, you're just using them, sweetie." Mr. Lyon grins.

My brain stutters. "I, what? Who? I was trying to fulfill my calling."

"You," Mr. Lyon enunciates, "were using the young women like toys. You get a feeling of power from using them."

My ears and forehead burn, and I try to breathe through it. I don't know why I get so upset when I hear from Mr. Lyon lately. When I first met him, our conversations always gave me a sense of purpose and comfort when I was depressed. I'm now happier than I've ever been, but our communication leaves me agitated. I try to remind myself that anger is wrong.

"If you were truly loving them, you wouldn't be concerned about the leaders' reactions. You would just do the right thing. You know how you can identify a trailblazer? He's the one with all the arrows in his back. Look at what they did to Jesus for trying to love people. You think he had time to care about what people thought of him?"

Mr. Lyon's tone loses its soft caress, but there's no noticeable change in his expressionless face—just a feeling of coldness. Sensing my resistance, he presses further. "If you'd been loving, you wouldn't feel this excited. Sure, you'd be pleased, but it would be a calm feeling of satisfaction."

He pats his chest. I don't blink or speak or move. Mr. Lyon sighs. "When you fight me like this, there's no point in talking further. Text me or send me an email telling me what you've learned when you're ready to listen."

Skype clicks off and I curl up on the floor and scream into the carpet. I relive each moment of the evening for any sign, any hint of my fanatical arrogance. I replay every sentence I said, posture I took, facial expression or article of clothing I wore, searching for how I can be wrong. I want to be happy, not right.

Amma knocks on my door to check if I am okay. She steps into my room, cradling Mary. I say something about how annoyed I am at Mr. Lyon.

"You still talk to him?" she asks. She and Nanna have only ever been in sporadic contact with him. "You don't need him, you know. He's not right about everything."

My annoyance turns to anger as I pace the room. She and Nanna were the ones who forced me to talk to him in the first place. Maybe Amma expected me to "take the good and leave the bad" with Mr. Lyon's teachings—like she did—but I've had his voice in my head for so many years that I no longer know who I am without him.

"He's doing this for me," I say. "I'm borderline, remember? I can't tell when I'm wrong!"

She furrows her brow and squints at me. "What's borderline?"

"Borderline personality disorder," I huff. "You know this."

Amma's head snaps to attention. "Who told you this, Veena? Did Bob say that?" she asks. "You don't have any personality disorder. We had you tested, remember?"

What would she know, anyway? Mothers always think the best of their children. "If you can't help me see how I'm wrong," I snap, "then you're not helping me!"

Amma rocks Mary gently in her arms, at a loss for words, until she finally backs out of my room. I lie down on my floor mattress and squish my face into my pillow.

I regain enough composure to text another True Happiness girl named Penelope asking if she can Skype. She's my age and Bob introduced us via email last week, saying only: "You two should know each other. Have fun." Penelope then reached out with: "Hello fellow 'freak.'" Apparently, that is the term Bob uses to describe people eager to learn and grow quickly. I know nothing of her except that she also met Bob through her mother and that she has been living in Japan for several years. It's only my second time speaking with her, but people in True Happiness understand and value honesty in a way the average person doesn't, so there's no small talk on these calls; you immediately state how you've been wrong so that the other person can accept all of you, complete with all your flaws.

Penelope answers Skype. Her head is full of perfectly refined curls, and she has a beauty mark near her lip that looks like it specifically chose that spot for the most elegant impact. Her voice is soft and soothing. Everything about her is arranged and presentable. Her apartment is as tasteful as her cardigan, which I somehow already know is merino wool. My face is covered in snot.

"This was the one time I was certain my motivations were pure," I cry. "If this isn't love, I give up. I am never talking to that man again."

"Awww. You're really terrible, aren't you?" she teases softly. "Sucking all those young women dry, like a vampire bat." She flaps her arms.

I laugh with her at the absurdity of it all and honk into a tissue.

"Veena, you're incredible. I didn't have a single adult who was there for me the way you are there for these girls. The fact that you even listen to them about their lives without judging or criticizing them is huge."

"You think Mr. Lyon is wrong?"

Her soft curls bounce slightly as she shakes her head. "I think you might be overreacting to what Daddy said."

I wince at the word. The fact that I still insist on calling him "Mr. Lyon" has become my quirk and the way everyone recognizes me on conference calls—though I stopped logging onto them regularly years ago, somewhere between having my first and second child. It's harder to replace "Daddy" with "father figure" in my head when everyone uses the word so carelessly and earnestly. I don't know Penelope well, but she strikes me as supremely composed—the opposite of my current condition. And if she is so comfortable calling him "Daddy," I again wonder if there is something wrong with me. Maybe I have deep-seated trust issues, and this is another aspect of being borderline.

"You think so? He sounded mean."

"No! It doesn't sound mean to me at all. He said you, like everyone else, have some mixed motivations. That's all. If it were me, I'd text him how I was wrong."

I call several other people in True Happiness, and everyone confirms what Penelope told me: I'm overreacting. Since I am not reckless enough to assume that I am correct and every single one of them is wrong, I play back the night again, slower, in more excruciating detail and plan out apologies to—who? The other leaders? The Young Women? My True Happiness network invites me to explore why I am fighting Bob so much in the first place. Why am I so invested in this idea that I am a good person? I don't know why I am like this, honestly, but I can do better.

I haven't worked out the details of my mistake, so I will have to keep the apologies general-purpose and vague.

I'm sorry, I text Bob.

No need to be sorry. What did you learn?

Not to worry about other people's reactions. My motivations aren't as pure as I think.

I love ya, kid. You're amazing.

The next time Penelope emails me, her new email address has "Lyon" in it.

Penelope Lyon to Veena Dinavahi

Sat., Apr. 1, 2017, 4:35 p.m.

Hey, Veena,

You've been on my mind quite a bit recently. I've been wanted to share what's been going on in my life. . . .

I started talking with John—Daddy's youngest son—around the time we Skyped last, and then just a few weeks later I moved out to Salt Lake to try living there and practice being partners. Two months later we got engaged, started living together, and then just said screw the whole wedding thing and went down to the courthouse last Monday and got married. We're on a sort of honeymoon at Daddy's now. It's all been incredible and crazy and fast.

I'm at Daddy's till Thursday the 6th. Really any time between then and now I could talk. I'm up between 8 a.m. and 8 p.m. EST. I know it can't be easy making time with two little ones, so you can just Skype message, email, or text me whenever you find a spare minute if that's easier.

22

March 23, 2017

It's my birthday and, for the first time in our relationship, my husband, the pragmatist, has brought me flowers. I rummage through the kitchen cabinets, searching for a vase until I realize we don't own one. Instead, I peel the roses out of their plastic, arrange them in the blender of the Vitamix, and place it back in the center of the kitchen island. Charlie hugs me as I stand back to admire them.

I like the idea of being a pragmatist—the jeans and T-shirt girl next door who doesn't know what day her anniversary falls on. I like the idea so much that every time someone asks me what day I got married, I shrug and reply, "around Valentine's Day." It drives my mother-in-law nuts trying to figure out which day to send a card.

It's February 18. I got married on February 18.

As much as I admire that woman—the one who can sleep through her birthday and overlook Valentine's Day without so much as a recriminating glance toward her spouse—I've never been her. In the time that Charlie and I have been together, special occasions have not gone well. But we've both grown. Tonight, Charlie made dinner plans in the city and surprised me with tickets to a Broadway show. Amma is in town to watch the kids.

"We should leave soon to make our reservation," Charlie says, glancing at his phone.

I'm not used to having him home early. He's been staying later at work with a coworker he promises is just a friend. Not that I have anything to complain about; I'm about to find out that Penelope moved back to the States to marry Bob's only single son—and she's about to find out he's a closeted alcoholic. We Skype every day.

I'm so lucky to have Charlie. He plants a kiss on my cheek, and I rush into the bedroom to change and find pants in four different sizes but none that fit. My body keeps changing with each pregnancy, and I don't have many clothes left now that I've given away 80 percent of my wardrobe to meet the modesty standards of the church. I squeeze and suck in and eye myself suspiciously in the mirror, calculating how to optimize dressing up for my one night out of the year and find an outfit Charlie will like. I settle on a pink silk blouse and faux leather overalls that almost fit, but sort of stick around the legs and make an awful chafing sound when my thighs rub against each other.

"Ready, honey?" Charlie calls.

"Almost!"

Five-month-old Mary cries in the next room and my breasts swell. Milk seeps into my nursing bra. Between potty training Cleo and breastfeeding Mary, I haven't had a full night's sleep in months. Cleo has started coming home from Sunday school, talking about how many children she will have when she grows up and gets married. And as much as I'm grateful for the opportunity to be a stay-at-home mom, Cleo's dreams for the future worry me. I want more for my daughters than I want for myself.

I survey my outfit in the mirror. The milk stains are covered (mostly) by the overalls and I groan in anticipation of the dry-cleaning charge. It's a shirt Charlie bought me on one of those birthdays when he was really trying. He didn't realize that mothers and silk don't play well together. I don't like the shirt, but I wear it now, fully prepared to pretend to love it because I love him.

I open the bedroom door and Charlie stands in the doorway, looking me up and down with a slight grimace.

"You hate it," I say.

Charlie grins. "It's, um, not your best look."

I stand still and watch him, his gray V-neck T-shirt and dark skinny jeans framing his lean, newly muscular body, untouched by the creation of our family. Charlie is training for a marathon and ran five miles with his coworker today. I've been advised to discontinue exercise and consume more calories to boost the quality of my breast milk. Charlie goes to work, to a job he loves, where he speaks to adult humans, while I spend my days picking soggy macaroni out of the apartment's inconceivably carpeted dining area and pretending to be the boat from *Moana* while my girls sit on me and steer. A nurse mentioned the possibility that I might have postpartum depression, but after my experience with two involuntary hospitalizations, I lied on the questionnaires at the doctor's office. It's a ten-question screening. *I have looked forward to things with enjoyment:* As much as I ever did. *I have blamed myself unnecessarily when things went wrong:* Almost never. The word "unnecessarily" gives me pause. It is usually my fault when things go wrong.

I look at my husband a second longer and then unbuckle my overalls and toss my silk shirt on the floor.

"I give up."

"Wha—wait, hang on, sweetie."

I strip down to my underwear and gesture to my body, the enlarged breasts, the pattern of stretch marks and perpendicular scars across my stomach and thighs, the hips that protest against every pair of pants I own.

"*This?* This is all I have right now."

"Whoa, Veena, slow down." Charlie scoops up my face in his large, knobby hands and squishes his nose against mine. "Veena, I love you. I love you so much, and I love all of this." His hand rubs my leg toward my waist, and I begin to soften like butter when it's left out of the fridge.

"You are so beautiful, and I don't care what you wear."

"But you do." I pout. "You did."

Charlie shrugs. "I don't know why I said that. It was a stupid thing to say. But we really should get going if we want to make it." He pulls his phone out of his back pocket and glances at the time again.

The anticipation of finally getting to leave this apartment is so overwhelming that my excitement has morphed into tension. I leaf through the closet and tug on my hair in frustration. "I can't do this."

I stomp over to our bed—still just a mattress on the floor—and disappear beneath the covers. My breasts are now two warm, pulsating rocks, engorged from the one feed I skipped earlier in the day. They burn and leak openly now. I don't recognize my body or this life in the suburbs. I wonder where Venkat is now. He sold all his possessions and set off to travel the world. The last time he visited he asked how my writing was going, and if I wanted to be a stay-at-home mom, but I haven't been honest with my brother in years. I don't even know if I've been honest with myself.

I lie there, listening. Charlie on the phone with his mother, Amma feeding the girls as they sing and babble, the sound of Charlie logging into Skype, then, the emergence of an unmistakable voice.

I jump into the bathroom and lock myself in, back against the door. I slide to the floor with quick, shallow breaths, wondering why I feel so agitated every time I hear Mr. Lyon's voice. Sometimes I go through my text history and delete all my texts from him, but I don't know why. The backs of my thighs touch cold bathroom tile. I don't bother with the light. If I sit in the dark, maybe Charlie won't notice I'm in the bathroom. Maybe everyone will have exceptionally strong bladders tonight and no one will need the restroom and I can evade Mr. Lyon until morning. He only wants to help. I want to do better. I want to be good, to appreciate Charlie's birthday gift to me, but I am so tired. I put my ear to the floor and hear the faint, garbled sound of Charlie on the video call, filling in the story's blanks: Charlie did everything he could to please me, I'm never satisfied, I overreacted again, I picked another fight, I am ungrateful. It is the same story he tells Mr. Lyon every time I ask to go back to school, to move to New York—it is the same story he told on New Year's day back in 2012, when I didn't want to get out of bed and Charlie called the cops.

My stomach is a handful of worms. It's all true. Mr. Lyon is always right. Mentally, I review a list of the times when Mr. Lyon helped me, unflattering parts of me he revealed to help me improve myself. I hear the deep rumble of his voice again. I trace the pattern of ugly, sluglike scars on my thighs, the perpendicular groups of threes. The cuts I made at age fifteen were so shallow that they weren't meant to scar. I had no idea how they would look on my thighs a decade later, two steps into motherhood. I lean my head against the bathroom door and close my eyes.

It's my twenty-fifth birthday.

The scars on my stomach have been warped into stretch marks by my pregnancies. They're hidden by the religious garments I'm meant to wear under my clothing at all times, so no one sees them anymore. I remember Mr. Lyon once said that cutting is all about control: That's why they always cut in straight lines. I haven't cut myself since I was a teenager, but somehow this sentence in my memory enrages me, his incessant explanations of my life, my choices, my thoughts, my motivations.

I pull back the vanity mirror and rummage through the medicine cabinet in the dark until I find a razor blade. I slice swiftly and diagonally across my left arm, still not deep enough to do any damage but enough to release some of the anger, rain evaporating to steam on hot pavement. The blade reveals white flesh underneath, quickly filling to red.

Charlie knocks on the door. "Honey? Can I come in?"

"Go away."

I wrap myself in the plush purple bathrobe hanging on the back of the door and cut several more times. I bend down, knees to tile, and pray the only words I can muster: *Help. Heavenly Father, help.* The lock clicks open. We have hard habits in our marriage; I lock doors and Charlie opens them. He finds me there, kneeling on the bathroom floor, pries open my fingers and takes the razor blade out of my hands. Silently he pushes up my sleeve and stares at my work. My husband stands, flicks on the lights and dabs away the excess blood with a tissue, whispering to himself, "No, no, no." He retrieves a box of Band-Aids from the medicine cabinet, gingerly selects the appropriate sizes and places them over me. He rests his hand there and looks up at me finally, with wet eyes.

"Veena," he says. "Veena."

What have I done to my husband? To all the people I love?

"Will you please talk to Mr. Lyon?"

I shake my head.

"Please, Veena." Charlie tilts his head back and with his fingertips wipes the tears from his eyes. "I hate to see you in pain like this. I want to help but I don't know how. I'm not qualified."

"He's mean," I mumble.

Charlie half chuckles. "I know it is hard for you to listen to him sometimes, but we need him. He cares about you *so* much. I care about you so much."

Charlie applies a slight upward pressure to my elbow and I rise, allowing him to lead me like an invalid back to the bedroom, back to our mattress on the floor. He tucks me in, folding the blanket in and around my arms and legs. His tears fall on my face as he plants a kiss on my forehead. I grasp his shirt and hold him close to me, breathing him in. Charlie leaves the room, promising to be right back, and returns holding a laptop with Mr. Lyon's round, pink, smiling face on it, eyes crinkled at the edges. The open laptop is placed in front of my face. Mr. Lyon grins and chews the inside of his cheek. I peek out from under the blanket, hair matted into my face with snot and tears, steeling myself for what will follow.

"Ohhh. Is that my little sweetie? I would just kiss your sweet little face all over if I were there right now."

"See?" Charlie smiles from behind the screen. "He loves you."

I cry with relief. I was so silly to doubt them. I make a mental note to defer to Charlie's judgment when I can't trust my own. "Why do I still feel this way, Mr. Lyon?" I cry. "I've done everything you told me to."

Mr. Lyon puts his hand on his chest. "Oh, honey. I am so sorry. I didn't give you what you need. Oops. Oh, well." He shrugs. "We'll just fix it now."

"Wha—what does that mean?" My muscles tighten. This is the only time I'll ever hear him say sorry. Not knowing why he's apologizing makes me nervous. I want to be punished for my behavior. His tenderness scares me more than his anger.

"You understand the principles perfectly—you just need to FEEL it more. You come down here and we'll take care of everything. Okay? What does that tell you?"

"That you love me," I answer mechanically.

"You bet I do. Like crazy."

Mr. Lyon checks his calendar and squeezes me into his first opening in April. He asks me to intern for someone else's intervention but tells me to arrive earlier so he and I can have an entire day together.

"We'll do whatever it takes, honey," he says. "If that means stripping down naked, that's what we'll do. If it means sticking beans up our noses, that's what we'll do. Just survive these next few weeks. Don't think. Don't have any serious conversations without me."

I catch myself before spiraling into catastrophic thoughts about what he means. In our last email exchange, he told me that my thinking gets in the way.

"And try to be nice to Charlie, okay?" Mr. Lyon winks at me and I duck behind the blanket.

"I know," I wail. "I was crazy."

"Hey, hey—no shame, okay? Who isn't crazy?" His brown eyes glint with mirth and compassion. "Just remember that Charlie is trying to help. And if he asks you to talk to me"—Mr. Lyon belly laughs—"just nod, honey. You can't tell when your own hair is on fire. He can. See you soon. Love ya."

He waves goodbye and Charlie shuts the laptop, beaming at me. "I really do just want to help."

We hear Mary crying from the other room and Charlie places our dark-eyed baby next to me. I unsnap my nursing bra, wincing as she latches on to my nipple and drains it. Mary's breath is warm on my chest and her soft, round body nestles into my curves. Cleo scampers into the room and straddles me with her slender, three-year-old legs, clad in a footed fleece onesie. Pink with green frogs. She rubs her nose into my shoulder and drops *Little Quack's Bedtime* on my face, asking me to read her a story. Charlie laughs and removes it with the reminder, "No books on Mommy's face!" Cleo giggles. Mary breaks off and fixes her large round eyes on Cleo, milk dribbling down her chin. I pull my family in tight. I cannot afford these relapses, not with these two tiny women relying on me, their four eyes drinking in my every move.

Whatever it takes, I'll do better.

Charlie surprises me by opening the maroon leather-bound Scriptures I keep at my bedside and reading from the Book of Mormon, Second Nephi.

"'And when I desire to rejoice, my heart groaneth because of my sins; nevertheless, I know in whom I have trusted.'"

Learning

Veena Jones to Bob Lyon

Sat, Mar 11, 2017, 2:13 PM

To Bob Lyon

This is what I learned, Daddy: I think and think and think and all I want and need is to feel.

Bob Lyon to Veena Jones

Sat, Mar 11, 2017, 4:52 PM

Bless you, my sweet daughter.

Yeah, you just need to feel.

We didn't finish the healing, so the thinking gets in the way.

I love you,
Your daddy

23

April 26, 2017

"We'll do whatever it takes to get you to happy. If that means stripping down naked, then that's what we'll do. If it means sticking beans up our noses, that's what we'll do."

I tell myself this is just Mr. Lyon's odd manner of speaking, but it's the third time he's said these exact words: twice in the last half hour and once on Skype, before I even got on the plane to come see him.

We're in his pool house this time. It's a gravel path away from the main house. Mr. Lyon laid down the gravel; he loves getting his hands dirty. Chopping wood, pouring concrete. He can talk for hours about the exquisite pleasure of splitting a log with a termite nest, complete with gestures and sound effects. At night, it gets so dark that you have to carry a floodlight to go anywhere, and the frogs get so loud that you can't sleep, only lie on the bed and hope. It's the middle of the day now, though.

The pool house is a glorified bathroom and shower, a long narrow room with a bed tucked away behind an oddly shaped corner at the far end and a small wooden table with a single chair at the other. Barbara always keeps the cabinet above stocked with the same foods: packets of dry oatmeal, coffee and tea, protein bars, PopCorners. There's a mini-fridge on the floor and a fresh case of bottled water next to it. Tile flooring—though not much of it—presumably in case anyone actually uses the pool. Barbara says it's too much work for the rare occasions the grandkids visit and, besides, they have the lake in the back. In the few times I've been here, I've only seen the pool covered.

I sit on top of the covers and the bed sags several inches under Mr. Lyon's weight as he lowers himself next to me with a grunt of exertion. After his total knee replacements, he's not as limber as he once was. All those days playing tennis, he says, he didn't feel a thing. Now he does. He lets out a sigh and says, almost to himself, "Yeah, you have had just about enough experience being miserable." Even though he just came in, his plaid shirt and undershirt are soaked through with sweat. He has a condition. He reaches up to fiddle with the thermostat. "If my shirt bothers you, just let me know and I can go change it. I really don't mind. It drives Barbara crazy."

It always bothers me, and I always insist it doesn't.

"Oh, I'm sorry I didn't give you what you needed all these years." Mr. Lyon swings his legs onto the bed and pulls my face into his wet chest. "And, well, I'm also not sorry because I was just doin' the best I could. Yeah, you just need more, honey. Deeper."

As he says this last word, he places his hand on my chest and presses down hard, to the point where it's difficult for me to breathe.

"What does that mean?" I ask loudly, trying to pull away without looking like I'm pulling away. "The past six years don't count for anything? All this time I've known you?" I married Charlie. I joined the church. I've stayed home to care for my children. I've followed all his instructions.

Mr. Lyon smooths out the wrinkles on my forehead with his thick, rough fingers, calloused from all the yard work. He whispers that I shouldn't worry about the past, that I should trust him. Don't think, he tells me. His face is right in mine. All I can see are his eyes, the sharp lines of his face. A bead of sweat rolls off his nose onto mine.

My body stiffens as I try to relax it.

The bed we're on is the same bed that Charlie and I shared after Bob married us in his living room, when Barbara had decorated the pool house for us, adorned all the doorknobs with tiny hearts and left a cheese platter with a sweet note on the table. That was four years ago, back when she still liked me.

"Do you see how you're pulling away? It's so subconscious you don't even notice it. You still don't trust me." Mr. Lyon strokes my hair and kisses my nose as he says this.

I did notice. I hoped he wouldn't. I feel a pang of guilt that, after all this time, I still don't appreciate him. I've attended so many seminars and interventions, seen so many people dying to have the attention from him that I do, people who eagerly jump into his lap and call him "Daddy," and I can't. I just can't.

He reaches out and rubs his thick finger across my lips. "Do you feel how stiff you are? Here, feel mine." He grabs my hand and moves my fingers across his thin and dry lips. With my fingers in his mouth he garbles, "They're like gummy worms. No tension whatsoever."

I smile politely. "Okay, so what do I do? I don't want to keep feeling this way. I'd like to feel relaxed."

Mr. Lyon nods. "Slow down, honey. You're always in a rush. We'll get there. Right now, you just have to trust me. That's all. Once you trust one person completely, you're free. Before you get to that point of complete vulnerability, it's terrifying. You're scared and scared and scared and when you finally reach past that to a point of complete trusting, you reach an island of calm where no one can hurt you. You become invincible."

I laughed at the word "terrifying." "I am definitely scared."

Mr. Lyon rubs my arm and kisses my nose. "Yep. You always are, kid—more so than most. That's what we need to get past. You always want to fight. You always want to think your way out of everything. Can't think your way out of this one."

I wince. Am I that bad?

"Ready to change things?"

"Yes. I want to be happy."

"Okay. So—without thinking, take off all your clothes."

As he says this, he gestures for me to stand and disrobe.

I recoil. My head surges and my body feels hot all over. *This isn't real. This is not happening.* I choose my next words clearly and carefully.

"FUCK. YOU."

I'm on the corner of the bed, as far away from Mr. Lyon as I can be without standing. There's been a misunderstanding. I've misheard what he asked me to do. So much of our relationship is contingent upon me reframing his behavior, focusing on his intent rather than his actual words. *He means well.*

He sighs heavily and shrugs his shoulders. "Everyone is different. For some people trusting looks like jumping in the lake. For others it's going for a ride on the ATV. Some people can just do it by talking."

"Great," I snap. "Let's go jump in the lake." I can't swim, but drowning out there can't be worse than this.

Mr. Lyon's usually impassive face belies his disappointment. "I wish there were another way, sweetie, but this is what it's going to take for you. Some people are more resistant than others. I'm just willing to do whatever it takes to help you, honey. Most people can't do this without getting confused, and I'm just willing to help."

I laugh maniacally. "You're . . . you're willing to help me? I have done EVERY. SINGLE. THING. you have asked me to do for the past six years. EVERYTHING!" I scream. "And guess what? *None of it helped.* And now"—I can't stop laughing—"now, I'm supposed to take off my clothes and that will cure me? This is EXACTLY where I was scared this whole thing would lead."

Mr. Lyon sits up with considerable effort next to me on the side of the bed. We don't look at each other. Or at least, I don't look at him to see where he is looking. My eyes fixate on the tan tile floor and my mind rakes over every memory of the pool house. Every time I interned. Every time I went for a retreat. My wedding.

"I am your daddy, honey. You're my little sweetie."

"You . . ." I breathe. "You . . . are not my father. No father would ask his daughter to do this."

"Not at this age, no. But you're not—how old are you now? Twenty-five?—you're not twenty-five years old in my arms. Emotionally you are just a little newborn baby. *My* baby. I'm crazy about you, kid. Did you ever hold one of your girls completely naked when they were born in the hospital? Skin to skin? No diaper or anything?"

I tuck my head between my knees and hold it down with my hands. A dull pulsating roar in my ears. *This is not real.*

"Yes," I say finally. "I love that moment."

"That's how I feel about you, honey. You're my little baby. You are not the first person I've done this with."

I bark out another strained laugh without picking up my head. "And—what?—they just listened?"

"Stood up and immediately stripped down, no questions asked. She knew she was in trouble. She was headed down a path that did not go anywhere and she knew she needed a change."

"Who?" I demand.

"I won't tell you her name now, but maybe later. I've done this with plenty of people, sweetie. I held a woman who was sixty-five years old, had been sexually abused by every single man in her life—dad, brother, uncles, boyfriends, everyone—and I held her naked and she said it was the first time she had ever felt clean in her life. You need to feel completely vulnerable with someone who has no ill intentions."

At this, I look up. I hadn't put a term to what was happening: "sexual abuse." Now that Mr. Lyon has said these words out loud, the term seems all the more distant and unlikely. This can't be it. I'm overreacting. This is a thing I do, as someone who is borderline.

"Well . . ." I say slowly, "I wouldn't trust my own judgment since I've never been . . . abused, but I guess . . . she would know. She would be able to feel it immediately if you wanted something from her."

"I don't want anything from you. I'm just willing to do whatever it takes to help you. It's not about the clothes. It's about you not being able to hide anymore."

"Does . . . Barbara know?" I don't know if this question is okay to ask or not. Mr. Lyon doesn't actually yell; it just seems like yelling to other people.

"No one else has the guts to ask me that. No, not yet. Barbara just . . . takes a little bit more time. When she's ready, I'll tell her. You should have seen her the first time I held someone in my lap."

Mr. Lyon's eyes widen, and he shakes his head in mirth.

I push back onto the bed and curl up in a ball, rocking slightly back and forth.

Mr. Lyon continues talking and pausing, but only bits of it come through.

"If you don't listen to me, honey, everything will be like it was when you first met me. When you were nineteen and depressed and had absolutely no hope in the world—except now you have a husband and two children to provide for and they will absolutely suck you dry. You won't be able to provide for them. You *will* be dead—physically or not."

I rock back and forth.

"Gotta make a choice, honey. No choice is death."

I already made my choice.

"I know you, sweetie, and pretty soon you're going to get to a place where I can't reach you. I'm trying to help, but I'm not going to push you to do this. It has to be your choice." Mr. Lyon clears his throat and wipes his eyes. "Hate to leave you like this, sweetie, but I'll be in the house if you decide you're ready to listen."

He slips his socked feet into his enormous black Crocs and fiddles with the doorknob. That door is a stubborn one and only closes when you slam it so hard the whole pool house shakes. I sit, unmoving now, pulling my legs into my body as tight as I can while the slamming door resounds through the pool house and the walls wobble.

My jeans suffocate my legs even though I purposely chose a loose pair for the trip. Every article of clothing in my carry-on was meticulously selected to look unremarkable, to pass Barbara's scrutiny. For this trip I packed three white T-shirts, one pair of blue jeans, and a set of exercise clothes, but no one was meant to see me in those. My face is bare and unkempt. I've stopped wearing makeup entirely. I didn't bring so much as a hairbrush. I open Uber and check the prices to the Atlanta airport. It's an hour and a half away and $150 but I would pay any amount of money to leave. I request a ride but cancel it five minutes later.

I don't know how long I sit curled on the bed, but when I get up, I can't stop walking. I walk back and forth along the side of the bed, frantically calling Charlie. I don't realize I'm crying until I hear my voice aloud. My face is wet but I can't tell if it's Mr. Lyon's sweat or my tears.

"Charlie. Charlie. Charlie. I can't stay here. He's lost his mind. He's crazy. He's fucking insane. I—I can't do what he's asking. I'm going to come home. I'm coming home now."

Charlie is at work, fresh out of a meeting. "Hold on. Slow down, sweetie. You mean Mr. Lyon?"

I nod, without realizing Charlie can't see me. His voice is a sweet saturation of concern, tension, and distress. "Yes. I need to come home."

"I don't know what is happening right now," Charlie says, "but I know Mr. Lyon has always helped us in the past."

I want him to *ask* outright what is happening, but he doesn't. Even if he asked, I don't know how I'd answer.

"He's always been there for us. I know it must be so hard for you. And I will still love you if you come now."

I collapse on the bed, phone to my ear. There's a subtext to his words; he knows my tendency to overreact.

But he doesn't know. He doesn't *know*.

"Veena . . . ? Honey . . . ?" The timidity in his voice snakes into my lungs and solidifies. Mr. Lyon is right: I can't take care of my husband alone. I can't handle my daughters, the three-year-old or the six-month-old, on my own. I throw my phone across the room, gasping. The dull roar pulses again through my ears and I tuck my head back between my knees to keep the room from tilting. Blue and white spots appear and disappear in my vision, and I squeeze my eyes shut.

When reality persists, I decide to drown myself in the lake behind the house. Everything will be like it was when I was nineteen. I can't return to my family without Mr. Lyon's support and I won't . . . well, I won't. And then I imagine Charlie alone in an apartment with my two young girls. Mary crying and throwing food off her high chair onto that stupidly carpeted dining area. Cleo throwing a temper tantrum about shoes being the wrong color. Charlie hiding behind a locked bedroom door, crying.

I hear a faint buzz across the room and pick my phone up off the floor.

> If you're going to be this difficult, there is no further point in you being here. Barbara will help you arrange for a taxi back to the airport.

A knock at the door immediately follows the text and I feel a flash of panic. Charlie must have texted Mr. Lyon and told him I want to leave. I knew I shouldn't have told him. How am I dressed? Are my jeans okay? Is my T-shirt see-through?

Another knock followed with a "Hellooooo?" in Barbara's saccharine voice.

I text him back frantically: Is it too late?

I snatch open the door and hastily cross my arms in front of my chest, wondering how much Barbara will hate me now. From her perspective I am proving to be the spoiled child she knows I am, wasting her husband's time with another tantrum. I wonder: Would she hate me more or less if she knew?

"Hi!" she says with an enthusiastic lack of emotion—the kind of politeness that says *I'm a good person, so I'm going to thinly veil the fact that I hate you.*

"Bob asked me to help you prepare. What do you need? Do you need help calling a taxi? Or an Uber? Have you booked a flight yet?" Her eyes are bright, her mouth unamused.

I gape and watch her mouth thin further into annoyance with each passing second. As she is about to speak, both of our phones buzz at the same time. She pulls hers out of her back pocket and puts on the red spectacles she wears on a chain around her neck to read it.

"Aha! Okay. I am not supposed to be here. Pretend I was never here."

I stand in front of the slamming door as she leaves. I crumple to the floor and clutch my phone with both hands, rechecking Uber prices, requesting a ride and then canceling it over and over. I reconsider the lake and pray.

I watch Mr. Lyon walk toward me, through the window of the pool house, ambling down the path with his awkward, goose-like gait, both feet splayed outward. If I am ready to die, maybe I can be ready to do what he's asking. Maybe I can live. Maybe I am wrong. Maybe Mr. Lyon really is like a dad and I am being too stubborn to see that, even though everyone else can. Two sharp, quiet knocks at the door. "Come in," I croak.

He thrusts open the door and slams it shut behind him in one swift motion. He crosses the room and closes the window blinds with several awkward jerks because the blinds are caught on the curtain rods. The self-awareness of this one gesture curdles all my reasoning and rationalizations into nausea and shame. Mr. Lyon seats himself on the bed, still not making eye contact, and clears his throat to pave the way for one of his monologues.

"Barbara said"—his voice cracks and I notice that he is crying—"Barbara said, 'You look like someone just died.' And I did. That's how it felt. I truly mourn when people choose not to listen. Just as if they'd died." He pulls out a handkerchief and blows his nose loudly and messily, before sticking it back in his breast pocket. "When you texted me, 'Is it too late?' I'm thinkin', for you, honey? Never. It wouldn't have been too late if you'd gotten in a cab and gone halfway to Marietta."

He reaches over and squeezes my thigh with one hand while wiping tears from his eyes with the other. He chews the side of his lip and smiles, admiring me with the look of a mother who has just given birth. He asks me what made me change my mind.

"Charlie," I whisper. "I want to be the wife he deserves."

I know this is my calling in life—to be better for my husband and children—but I'm constantly weighed down with guilt that I don't love Charlie like I should. Maybe this will finally fix me. I will do this for my husband—who followed me to Georgia without question, who built a family with me and inspired our daughter's first laugh with a game of peekaboo on her first Christmas.

Mr. Lyon shrugs. "Whatever it takes to get you on the path to happiness, kid."

"So," I say brusquely, "I had this realization while you were gone that I actually trust you completely and just need to go jump in the lake, learn how to use a chain saw, and ride an ATV. Then I'll be all healed." I grin, but Mr. Lyon shakes his head slowly. "No?" I whisper. "It was worth a shot."

"You're stalling, kid."

"Of course I'm stalling."

"I've got all day, kid. But you don't. You gotta make a change or you're screwed."

I stand with the wobbly legs of a newborn goat. "So just . . ." I gesture down the sides of my body.

Mr. Lyon nods. "Just." He imitates my gesture.

I make a comment about not having my religious garments on. The white undershirt and shorts are supposed to be on my skin at all times, day or night, a symbol of the covenants I've made with the Lord, a literal and metaphorical protection from the evils of the world. The garments have four symbols on them: one on each breast, one on the navel, and one on the right knee. A square for the justice and fairness of our Heavenly Father. The compass to represent the North Star. The collar to show that his yoke is easy and his burden light. Strength in the navel and marrow in the bone. Every knee shall bow and every tongue confess that Jesus is the Christ.

I didn't pack them because I didn't have clean laundry, but that explanation is beginning to feel inadequate.

"How—how do I tell the difference between right and wrong?" I ask.

"The Holy Spirit will testify."

"I don't feel the Spirit with me now, Mr. Lyon."

"Ah, you can't feel the Spirit when you're scared. Until you're not scared anymore, trust me." He smiles tenderly, showing off the slight gap between his two front teeth. He's sweating again.

"That makes sense, because I am really scared."

"Honey, in the six years that you've known me, have I ever done anything to hurt you? Have I ever led you astray?"

I search the face of this man who saved my life, while he mops it with the other side of his handkerchief. I want to say yes, that he has hurt my feelings, that he has misled me, but those times don't count. His memory isn't what it once was, and my feelings were hurt only because I refused to listen when he was gentle. I give an imperceptible shake of the head. Of course he hasn't led me astray.

My face is wet again as I peel off my jeans and step confusedly out of the tight ankle part. I pull my shirt off over my head and cower at the foot of the bed, weeping openly now, sucking in breath after breath and trying to cover as much of myself as I can manage with my arms, like twigs trying to hide a tree.

Mr. Lyon shakes his head. "Not enough. Everything has to come off."

"How . . . is this not sexual? Can you explain it again?"

I comply with his instructions and hide underneath the covers on the opposite side of the bed.

"Honey, if this were sexual, it would be awful. Like pouring gasoline over ice cream. Why would I do that?"

"I—I keep having flashes where I picture this from an outside perspective and think 'Oh shit! I'm crazy!' and then I have to talk myself back."

"I understand, honey. No judgment. Out there"—he points aggressively at the closed window and another wave of sickness comes over me—"is the crazy world. In here is the sane world."

In the darkness of the pool house, I close my eyes and think of the Scripture: *For the word of Lord is truth, and whatsoever is truth is light.* Mr. Lyon pulls me closer toward him and draws back the covers. Eyes still glued shut, I plead, "Can we be done now? I did it, right? We're done? I conquered my fear?"

Mr. Lyon begins working his hands up and down my body. "Oh no, honey. We're just getting started. This won't work until you *enjoy* yourself." I bite back more tears as I lie next to him under the covers. "Hang on, sweetie. I'll just text Charlie to let him know that everything is okay because he was freaking out for a bit there." He turns his body over toward the nightstand in several effortful twists, reminiscent of a beached whale. He reaches for his phone on the nightstand and speaks as he types, "Cancel making plans for Veena return . . . We're . . . having . . . fun."

How is Veena doing? She texted me asking to come.

I spent 3 hours with her last night period Then 3 hours with her this morning. We were really trying to make a breakthrough in her being vulnerable, which is exactly the problem that she has refused to face all alone. She turns opportunities for vulnerability into intellectual jokes.

I wish I could help her. As you know, she cut herself a month ago, about the time that she blew up at you for making some innocent comment about what she was wearing on her birthday.

She is becoming increasingly annoyed at pretty much everything, including Cleo and you. I really tried to help her. But she did what you've seen many times. She shut down completely and curled up into a ball. There was nothing I could do to reach her after that.

Now Barbara is going to help her find a shuttle and Away Home.

Is there anything I should do? I know how important this was to her before she left.

I spoke to her on the phone and let her know how special she is to me.

You hold on for a bit. We might be able to resurrect this

Ok

Cancel making plans for Veena return. We're having fun.

PART IV

GRAY AREAS

24

2017 to 2018

I have this neighbor, Dave, who wakes up each morning and deliberates where to plant shrubs to optimize the water runoff in his yard. Bob talks about people like Dave all the time, how they may have a well-drained backyard, but for better or for worse they will never do anything truly wild because their focus is limited to observing rain after it falls. These people would never join True Happiness. Mr. Lyon says they wouldn't have the courage to do what I did. And that's okay for Dave. It's not like Mr. Lyon judges Dave. There have been times in my life where I have craved a plodding normalcy, this ability to look one step ahead instead of feeling the weight of every possible future pressing down on me at every moment. To survey a backyard and have that be the extent of my concern. But Mr. Lyon says I am meant for more than that. For a life pursuing answers to hard questions, so the hope of any kind of ordinariness is far out of reach. Now, the thought of a life spent planting and replanting shrubs makes me want to rip my skin off with my teeth. It's not for me.

I return home from the weekend at Bob's with a glow. My eyes and my smile are unnaturally wide, but I keep this grin plastered on my face because I can't risk unbottling the feelings underneath. I have to be healed now because, if not, what was it all for?

When we moved to Connecticut, my husband deliberated for months over which couch to buy, and it baffled me, the idea that a couch could consume so much of his mental energy when he's never deliberated so carefully about the trajectory of his life. Down or synthetic filling. L-shaped or U-shaped. Leather or pleather. I could never live with his priorities because twenty-five years ago my life happened, but six years ago, with Mr. Lyon's help, I *decided* it would continue happening. I chose life in a way most people never get to do. Ever since then, I've come to analyze life like my husband analyzes the couch selection at Restoration Hardware. Excitement or stability in a relationship. Permissive or authoritative parenting. Religion or atheism. Because if I am signing up for this bizarre, brief existence, I might as well do it right. Thoroughly. Put me in the Garden of Eden and I am going straight for the apple tree. And, yes, sometimes this desire, this need to know things at their deepest level, this willingness to do *anything* in order to find out confuses and scares me. Sometimes it lands me in strange pool houses doing things I never planned on because *what if*? What if I'm wrong? What if I really am crazy? And I have only this one life to fix it.

Maybe my life doesn't look anything like I thought it would when I was a kid and everyone asked that impossible question, "What do you want to be when you grow up?" and I said painter, then singer, writer, lawyer, professor. I never said wife, mother, Mormon; but it is an openness to experience, to different value systems that has landed me here, in this homogenous town with this beautiful family.

This life is the outfit I tried on at the store, told myself I could return later, but my great-aunt has an entire closet of cocktail dresses, new with the tags on, of things she told herself she could always return later. The season of cocktail parties has long set on her, but still, she tells herself that these are decisions she can undo if she wants, if she just finds the receipts, which are around here somewhere. Well, anyway, I'm here, the outfit is cute—no, it's *stunning*. These children, this husband, that house. I'm wearing it now, so it has to be.

The whole time in the pool house, I was terrified Bob would also remove his clothes, but he never did. I try my hardest to box away what did happen but I'm still overcome by this feeling that I've done something wrong but necessary and the fear that my husband will leave me once he finds out. Before I left, Bob said, "I'm not going to tell you what to do, but I can tell you that you won't like the results if you tell Charlie." He always speaks that way. He's just *describing my choices*. Choice A is sunshine and rainbows. Choice B is eternal doom and hellfire rained upon all my loved ones and their puppies. Choice A, of course, is his way.

This time, I pick B. I can't keep it in. Secrets, to me, are like the flesh-eating scarabs in *The Mummy*—and with a secret of this magnitude, I am Imhotep, scratching at the inside of his sealed coffin.

I take Charlie into our bedroom and sit him down. "Mr. Lyon told me not to tell you but, screw him. I'm not keeping secrets from my husband."

"Okay . . ." Charlie bites his fingernails and stares at the bedding.

"Mr. Lyon held me . . . completely naked. That's why I wanted to come home." It's not a whisper but I say it in the lowest voice I can manage. I don't offer details for many reasons, but none of them matter because Charlie will never ask for details. *Just like a baby,* I tell myself. *He held me just like a newborn baby.*

Charlie's eyes bulge and he pulls his head back. "That's . . . not normal."

When he says, "That's not normal," my brain hears, "You're not normal," and from there it is an easy leap to "You are disgusting." Ever since I felt Bob's hands on me, it has taken all my energy to push down an overwhelming revulsion. I can't stand myself, and the look on Charlie's face brings my self-loathing bubbling to the surface: he can't stand me either. Whatever happened in the pool house has left me besmirched and my husband won't want me anymore. I did it all for him, but he'll hate me for it. It doesn't fully make sense, how allowing that to happen could benefit my family, but I called Bob back into the pool house for Charlie. So that I could be an unconditionally loving wife and mother. So I could give and give and give without ever needing anything in return.

Charlie quickly recalculates, seeing the look on my face. "But I can see how that would be helpful. I mean, it clearly helped. I can see how happy you are now."

And I am happy. It *did* work. It had to mean something. It all has to be leading somewhere. It worked so well that even my husband can see that I'm happy and healed and now I have the energy to care for my family like never before.

And yet, I feel like I've swallowed canola oil every time I think or talk about it, so I change the subject quickly.

Minutes later, Charlie jokes, "Maybe I just need to be held naked, too."

"That is *NOT* funny!" I shout.

"Okay, okay, calm down. I'm sorry."

"I feel so uncomfortable about the whole situation and I never want to talk about it again," I say. "I just needed to tell you because I can't live with secrets in my marriage."

But, it turns out, I do want to talk about it again. Next week. Next month. Two months from now. The more time passes, the more the specifics cloud over like frosted glass. I bring it up in the kitchen, at bedtime, on the weekends.

"The holding thing," I say. "It feels wrong. It's making me feel bad."

Charlie looks up from whatever he is doing at the time—checking the mail or clipping his toenails—and he smiles with compassion. "I love you, sweetie, and I think you're using this as an excuse to distance yourself from Mr. Lyon."

"Really? Would you have undressed if he asked you to?"

Charlie turns back to his toenails. "I don't know. I wasn't there."

"Exactly," I mutter, but I let it slide.

When Charlie and I have sex now, he does certain things that make my head swell with rage. Though I don't consciously remember the details of what happened in the pool house, the memory is imprinted on my body. When Charlie bites my lip or caresses me in a way that feels uncomfortably familiar, I have an almost irrepressible urge to bite down on him—hard. Anywhere. A lip, a hand, more sensitive spots—until I draw blood. But I can't articulate why I'm having this reaction. I lie in bed, shaking afterward, wondering what is wrong with me that I want to do bodily harm to my husband.

I become pregnant again when Mary is nine months old. Imagine that your house is burning and instead of reaching for an extinguisher or calling the fire department, you show up with a tank of gasoline and an armful of kindling. On purpose. People say pregnancies last nine months but they're actually ten. For a third time, I'm unable to keep down food or fluids. Imagine throwing up eight times a day from New Year's to Halloween. But surely, it is worth it, to fulfill Heavenly Father's plan for me.

Around the same time, I become obsessed with trying to figure out who else Bob has held. I call people in True Happiness and drop as many hints as I can. No one bites. When I have the urge to call Bob, I call Penelope instead. She shows me the new cross-stitch she is working on and fills me in on how Bob has her hand-feeding his son Antabuse every morning and drug testing him at night. She found needles in his backpack when he came home from work. I try very hard not to be critical of her husband in these conversations, but he does not make it easy. Toward the end of the call, Penelope finally tells me that Bob has held her naked—but she assures me the experience was healing and transformative. I cannot believe we are referring to the same events.

I watch the #MeToo movement come and go with skepticism. (*That many women? Really?*) In the back of my mind, I have this sensation that I could say I've experienced something similar—but I don't want to be attention seeking. My experience is not the same at all. Equating my situation to theirs would be diminishing their trauma.

The next time Penelope calls, she tells me her husband screamed at her for taking away his car keys while he was drunk (something Bob instructed her to do), but the story has a happy ending: later that evening he wrote her an apology letter and slipped it under her door. Penelope beams as she unfolds it and shows it to me over Skype. *Isn't he adorable?* It looks like something a five-year-old scrawled with a piece of crayon he found under the back seat of the car, and it says something stupid like "I love you. Sorry." I hold my tongue and try to be happy for her. Before hanging up, Penelope mentions that she has started to feel worse about "the holding thing." But she doesn't want to overreact. My distress is entirely mollified by this confirmation that her perceptions align with mine. I'm not alone.

Almost a full year passes before rumors start circulating in the True Happiness community that Bob holds people naked. My name doesn't come up, but I am terrified that someone will discover what I have done. Penelope finally talks to Bob directly.

"He was so sweet, not at all how I was expecting," she reports. "He said that he made a mistake. That he is bipolar, and he was in one of his manic states. He told Barbara about it, and he's now calling everyone he held and apologizing.

"Just talk to him," she urges me. "You'll feel so much better."

Charlie supports Penelope's suggestion. He supports anything to repair my relationship with Bob. It is the last thing I want to do, but it's been almost a year since the pool house and maybe it is time to move on.

I glance at the clock every fifteen seconds so I can avoid being too early or too late and cry as soon as his familiar face appears on my computer screen.

"The holding stuff"—I sob—"feels wrong."

"Ohhh, honey," he says, patting his chest. "I didn't mean to scare you," he whispers. "I didn't mean to scare you."

I've spent so much of my life crying, but this sobbing feels uglier. "I was scared you'd tell me I'm overreacting."

"You did the right thing talking to me about it. There ain't nothin' I won't listen to, you hear me? Nothin'."

I nod. It's not true, but I nod.

He starts telling me about the koi pond he built in his backyard, about how he spent all weekend cleaning it out with a machine that has the horsepower of a car. He's wrangling this enormous hose into the bottom of the pond to suck out all the fish shit and the motor is going—he can hear it going like crazy—but nothing is being sucked into the machine. He goes to take a look at it, and you know what the problem was the whole time? There was a kink in the hose. No matter how hard it sucked, nothing was going to happen because the kink needed to be straightened out.

"Just like you, honey. You just had a kink that needed straightening out."

I struggle to process what he is saying.

"Don't let something like this come between us, okay? Otherwise, it will create distance between us and that distance will grow until it can't be bridged."

Downstairs after the call, Charlie smiles at me. "All better?" he asks.

I smile and nod. Nothing feels better.

Bob told Penelope she was the last one on his list. Does he think I can't handle it if he admits it was a mistake? Penelope said he told Barbara about everyone he held, but somehow, I know he did not tell her my name. He never apologized, and more than anything that happened in the pool house, this is what I fixate on. An apology would mean that what happened was wrong and that how I feel is right. If I could have this confirmation that I am not crazy, I think I could forgive him for anything. But instead, I got, "You just had a kink that needed straightening out." Which means that I was broken, and he fixed me and what happened was right?

I want the words "I'm sorry" rubbed into me like a salve. I need them. The burning will abate. I'll be able to kiss my husband again without wanting to rip into him with teeth.

I think.

25

2018

My unborn child starts falling further off his growth chart at every ultrasound. I'm presented with a multitude of questions that I'm unprepared to answer. Do I agree to an amniocentesis for genetic screening? Is the risk of miscarriage acceptable to me? Do I want to abort the pregnancy? Between my husband and Mr. Lyon, I haven't made any major decisions on my own since I was nineteen. When my life was the only thing at stake, I didn't mind deferring to other people's judgments. But now that there is a tiny person inside me, developing at a stunted rate, suddenly my choices matter in a way they never have before. I tried not to complain in previous pregnancies, but now I'm no longer willing to bet against my instincts. This time in my doctor's office, I actually ask for something: I explain that I've been unable to keep down fluids and ask for an IV.

My doctor, another old white man, looks me up and down and says, "If you were vomiting that much, you'd be dead."

I know how I look, as a brown twenty-six-year-old stay-at-home mom, pregnant with her third kid. Cleo and Mary are running around the office, getting into drawers they shouldn't be because I don't have childcare. (Charlie says we can't afford any right now.) I can surmise what this doctor thinks of me.

"Do you remember," I ask, "when I gave birth to Mary?"

The doctor is confused.

I called the doctor in between contractions and sounded as calm as if I were booking a hair appointment. He told me to wait until the contractions were regular and Charlie told me to come snuggle him in the meantime—while I was fully in labor, screaming and banging on the wall in pain. Amma heard me from the other room. It was the evening of Cleo's third birthday party and Amma hesitantly suggested we go to the hospital. The contractions never became regular, and I waited so long that I arrived fully dilated, threw up in the hospital parking lot, and gave birth five minutes later with no anesthesia.

"No one wants you to wait that long this time—"

"That's not my point," I cut him off. It's been years since I interrupted someone (it's an unloving thing to do—not very True Happiness), but it feels good. Love is not going to usher my child safely into this world. Medical care will. "I am telling you"—I lean forward in the examination chair so that he backs away slightly—"that I have an incredibly high pain tolerance. I am not exaggerating," I enunciate. "I am telling you I cannot keep down fluids. What I need you to do is call back the nurse and have her administer an IV for me. Now, please."

It has become easy to think of myself as weak, crumpled on the bathroom floor, but as I say it out loud, I know that I am not. I have the grit of a punching bag.

"No one said that you were exaggerating!"

I sit back in the chair and do not bother pointing out that he implied exactly that. This time, my needs will be met.

The nurse comes back and reports that my urine has ketones—incontrovertible evidence that I am on the verge of dehydration. That my perceptions are accurate. My doctor mentions the word "hyperemesis" in passing and it is the first time I find out that my condition has a medical term associated with it, that I could have been receiving biweekly IVs for all three pregnancies if anyone had stopped and taken my symptoms seriously.

Betting on—and asserting—my own judgment has paid off: I've successfully advocated for the needs of my unborn child, and I am filled with relief. I can't yet consider that, maybe, I should have been betting on me this whole time.

After a difficult, protracted labor with Pitocin and no pain medication, Hugo is born with the distinctive Dinavahi windshield wiper eyelashes and soft hair covering his translucent skin. I told myself that once my son was born, he'd be okay. He'd eat. He'd gain weight. We just made small babies. But when Hugo comes out full-term, he is so small he hardly seems human. Five pounds, six ounces. Smaller than Cleo's plastic baby dolls. I hold him on my bare chest, skin to skin underneath my hospital gown for the briefest moment before he is taken from me and sent to the NICU for low birth weight and fluid in the lungs. He looks even tinier placed inside a sterile Isolette.

Hugo reminds me of a sloth I saw once in Costa Rica. My family went there on vacation when I was a kid. It hung upside down on a vine and attempted one step. Just one. It reached out with a front paw that looked like one of those metal claws in a toy machine—absurdly impractical for the purpose of actually grasping anything. The sloth swiped, painfully slowly, at the bit of vine ahead. The vine slipped through its hand. It tried again. Slipped again. I watched for several more attempts before growing restless and, like the sloth, giving up.

My son's grasp on life is like that.

Hugo does not eat, uncertain what to do with my breast. Milk dribbles down the side of his perfect pink mouth. He falls asleep. I tickle his toes. Rub his back. I have a long list of maneuvers to wake him, but none of them work. You might think people have some built-in instinct for survival, that they will fight against death, but not babies, not this little. They are born into life briefly, but life has not yet been fully born into them. They can slip out of your hands and into death easily, like slick bars of soap.

My maternal grandmother intimately knew of the tenuous existence of babies. I was in high school the first time I heard her story. She knitted all day—doilies, hats, coasters—babbling to whoever would sit still long enough to listen. Nobody had the patience to pay attention to her when she was married off at sixteen, and even fewer people had the patience since she had aged. Her teeth were a set of dentures that perpetually sat in a dirty glass on her bedside table. She never wore them because they itched, and she didn't speak English, so her stories were a garble of gums and Telugu words I had forgotten. I knitted next to her and perked up when she said the word "son."

"Wait, Ammamma. You had a son?"

She held up three bony fingers. I was sixteen years old and it was the first time I had ever heard of my three uncles who died before I was born. The oldest drowned in a well trying to teach himself how to swim as a teenager.

"What happened to the two babies, Ammamma?"

My grandmother adjusted her sari over her loose, dangling breasts. "How do you say in English? When the babies become yellower and yellower?"

I supplied the answer, aghast: "Jaundice."

"Ah. Yes. That. Of course, we didn't know at the time."

While I live near some of the finest hospitals in the country, I feel as helpless as Ammamma, not knowing what unseen forces are incapacitating my child's body. I tell myself I'm not going to let my son go the way of my grandmother's babies, to recede from life into memory, but one month later, Hugo is still not eating.

We're driving to my cousin's wedding in Ohio, while Amma and I sit in the back with all three of my children. I've spent the past five weeks watching Hugo grow sallow and limp, five weeks watching him fall off his growth curve and listening to the pediatrician say, "Aw, sounds stressful," in response. Five weeks of watching him push every bottle out of his mouth with a tired tongue, until I grew so desperate that I tried to feed him with a syringe, but he vomited it all up.

On the way to Ohio, Hugo spikes a fever. I pull out my phone to text Bob but stop. The last time I reached out to him, Bob told me that Hugo could die an early death if I wasn't more loving to my husband, that even babies can sense the lack of love in a household. I don't need to be chastised for being unloving. I need actionable medical advice. I text a friend from church who used to be a nurse instead.

He's under three months. Fever could mean sepsis. You need to take him to a hospital now.

I falter at the text.

"I think I should take Hugo to the hospital," I call out from the back seat.

The *Lord of the Rings* soundtrack is playing. Cleo is asking Amma for a story. Mary is fussing. Nanna and Charlie are discussing the stock market.

"The hospital?" Charlie asks. "It's just a fever. We'll be late to the wedding if we stop."

"C'mon, Veena," Nanna says. "Kids get sick. This is not a big deal."

I call the on-call pediatrician and fight to be heard over the noise of the car. She echoes the advice; Hugo needs the hospital.

"Can you turn off the music please? The doctor said he should go to the hospital."

"Veena, really?" Charlie groans.

"Veena," Amma starts to say, but I have reached my limit of people wielding my name like a pacifier.

"PULL. OVER. NOW."

The car is silent and Cleo is staring at me because anger is wrong. I have one hand on Hugo's clammy forehead, the other gripping the seat in front of me. They can think I am crazy. They can think that my perceptions fail to align with some objective reality. All I can think is: *What does a baby look like right before it dies?*

Charlie drops Hugo and me off at the curb of the Cleveland Children's Hospital Emergency Room and everyone else continues to the wedding.

The ER nurses triage Hugo in quick, quiet alarm. It takes eight hours and five nurses to pierce one of his collapsing dehydrated veins for the IV. Cameras are stuck in every orifice. Barium is poured down his throat. X-rays are taken. No one knows what is wrong, but the doctor confirms that on a good day, Hugo is consuming less than half the calories he requires. I miss the first wedding ceremony, the main event, and the reception, and my son is diagnosed with "failure to thrive."

Nanna visits us in the hospital and cries as he holds his grandson. "I'm so sorry, Veena. I should have listened to you. I should have listened to you." He can't stop saying this.

It no longer matters to me who listens. Trusting myself has saved my son's life.

Our hospital stay lasts a week—long after Charlie has driven home with Amma, Nanna, and the girls. We are discharged with a feeding tube that I have to thread through my son's nose every time he sneezes it up. The days pass slowly but the months pass quickly. Hugo turns four, five, then six months old. He has a team of doctors, in specialties I've never even heard of, and they suspect some underlying condition. His medical problems require a slew of surgeries—to correct his crossed eyes, to implant a feeding tube directly into his stomach, to lower an undescended testicle. Sometimes when I'm waiting for Hugo to wake up from anesthesia, a doctor will ask hesitantly, *Is there a father in the picture?* and I have to say, *Yes, my* husband *is hard at work to provide us with this incredible health insurance.* Amma hasn't visited me in months because of some fight we had that I can't remember.

Charlie says it's time for us to stop renting apartments and buy a house. Something about interest rates that I don't understand. He picks a gorgeous one, with a backyard the size of a football field. First floor master bedroom with a heated bathroom floor and two shower heads. Three fireplaces, two gas and one traditional. I do a double take at the price tag but he says we can afford it. Courtesy of his recent promotion at work. In this five-thousand-square-foot house, Hugo and I are shackled to a feeding pump I roll around on an IV pole. I don't sleep because his feeds run for an hour and a half every three hours. I need to hear him breathing at night. The rhythm of motherhood is syncopated now; start Hugo's tube feed, change Mary's diaper, clean up Hugo's projectile vomit, run the feed again, pick up Cleo from preschool.

On the way home from the grocery store one night, I see Charlie running on the side of the street with his coworker when he told me he was working late. Five-year-old Cleo asks, "Mommy, who is Daddy with?" And I tell her, "Just a friend, sweetie."

I again float the idea of childcare and Charlie says we can't afford it. I haven't seen his pay stub or the balance of his trust fund that footed our down payment, so this could be true, but assuming a rate of twenty dollars an hour—no, let's assume thirty dollars with wiggle room—the three-thousand-dollar treadmill he just purchased for the exercise room and the two-thousand-dollar grill for the patio would equate to 166 hours of childcare. One hundred sixty six hours of sleep or hygiene. I smile innocently at him when I say these numbers out loud, and, when he looks surprised that I can do simple math, I remind him that I took multivariable calculus when I was fifteen. The look of surprise on his face tells me that he has actually forgotten.

Caring for my children is starting to remind me exactly who I am.

26

November 2018

I wish I could tell you that after fighting for my son's life, I realized I didn't need Bob and I never doubted my own judgments again. In reality, I was brought to the verge of a mental breakdown over apple picking, of all things.

Charlie's mom and sister came to visit and we all decided to go apple picking—the one benefit of Connecticut living. But while I was putting Mary and Hugo down for their naps, Charlie took his family and Cleo to the orchard and left me at home with the babies. He'd done the same thing last year. I logged onto a True Happiness Skype call and explained how upset I felt; I hadn't been able to leave the house in months.

Penelope's mom was on the call and she said: "It seems to me that Charlie is doing his best to care about you and that blaming him only makes you feel victimized and trapped."

One of the men on the call cleared his throat—a man I'd taken calls from years ago, when his adult daughter wouldn't speak to him. "Let's focus on how you can be a better wife and mother. What's one thing you can say to Charlie to show him how much you care about him?" I hung up and screamed. It echoed through the magnificent house with its hardwood floors and woke up the babies.

Who do you call when your house is empty and you ache to be understood because there's so little of you left that you might disappear if no one remembers to look at you and really *see*? You can scroll through your phone, but it doesn't matter how many people smile and wave when they see you at church, or how many mothers in your daughter's kindergarten class have suggested playdates, or what time zone your brother is living in these days. When it really comes down to it, there has only ever been one person you can ask: Can you talk?

All I wanted was fresh air.

> Of course they don't understand you like I do. Call me. It's been too long.

The more grounded I become in the reality of dirty diapers and the more medical terms I learn for my son's endless surgeries (left orchiopexy, strabismus correction, G tube placement), the less I think of Bob—and the more I think of Amma. We made up after our fight, and she offered to visit whenever I need help. In contrast, his turns of phrase that felt so wise to me when I was nineteen now strike me as trite and oversimplified. Ever since the pool house, he has felt like a stranger to me. I only called him once, in that moment of apple picking–induced weakness, but once was enough to reopen the door. By the time Penelope begged me to sign up for a retreat so we could meet each other in person for the first time, I relented. Retreats are a new type of event he's been experimenting with: capped at twelve people, held in his home, at some midpoint in both intensity and cost between an intervention and a seminar. Penelope and I have been talking on the phone every day for more than a year. Seeing her was the only thing that could motivate me to return to Georgia.

She arrived late last night. I was in the basement guest quarters when she walked in wearing a cashmere cardigan and high-waisted mom jeans, her fingers wrapped around a Red Bull. I squealed, jumped up, and squeezed her around the middle. We pulled back and examined each other as everyone else in the room watched.

"You're so dainty!" I exclaimed.

"You're so tiny!" she said.

After she settled in, four of us piled back into her car—Penelope, me, a twenty-three-year-old from the UK named Clara, and a twenty-nine-year-old piano teacher named Noah who lived in Connecticut. Noah wore a low ponytail and thick-framed glasses that accentuated his already intense look. Charlie and I have known him and his girlfriend for years, ever since Noah contacted me after finding Bob's website. He and Charlie bonded over their love of Magic: The Gathering. He even babysat Cleo once. Together, the four of us are the youngest people in True Happiness.

We howled to Adele as we drove. Penelope put on a song she wanted me to hear. Soft piano was pierced by a voice that filled the car like cool water. I stuck my hand out of the window into the balmy Georgia air as we crossed the railroad tracks near Bob's house. We stopped at Walmart and took a picture of Clara holding a ten-pound bag of ground meat. Penelope and I bought matching llama sweaters. We drove to the downtown strip, a cobblestoned street with pubs and hip restaurants like every other American downtown. Feeling like schoolchildren, we ducked into an arcade, played Skee-Ball, and left with candy in our pockets.

I didn't want to come upstairs this morning. While Penelope fixed her curls with one of her fifty beauty products I stood in the bathroom and groaned that I didn't want to go to group.

"Then don't," she said.

"I . . . can I do that?"

She shrugged. "He always tells the same dumb stories every time anyway."

Still, some sense of obligation propelled me upstairs, but now, back in the ugly living room, I'm already regretting it. I'm sitting next to Noah while Bob is on the couch across from us, holding Clara. Bob is in the middle of some idiotic story about how Clara slapped him when the two of them were alone this morning, and he didn't react.

"She's in pain." He shrugs. "Okay. What do we do about it?"

The moral of this story is supposed to be that he loves Clara enough not to be irritated that she slapped him, but it doesn't make any sense. People *should* react when slapped. Before I can organize my thoughts, Clara lets out an abrupt, bloodcurdling scream. I jump. No one else flinches, and I scan the room thinking, *This cannot be normal. Someone screams, and no one reacts?* It's meant to be just another "expression of pain," but nothing that is happening makes any sense. Bob continues talking as if nothing has happened, but I scan Clara's face. Do I ask her what's wrong? Everyone in the room remains fixated on Bob, hanging on his every word. Clara's state of mind does not seem to be a concern. Eventually, she stands up and takes a seat next to me on the floor. She smiles as if everything is fine, but I keep wondering what would make her scream like that.

Bob looks at me and says, "You. You need more."

He always singles me out like this. The woman next to him squirms disappointedly, and he pats her on the leg saying, "Don't worry, we'll get to you. There's plenty of time."

I stand, stiff and gangly, and lower onto his lap, wishing I were anywhere else. At least I'm wearing jeans. He puts one thick arm around my thighs, the other around my back. He pulls me in close, nose-to-nose, and I try to look past him as his eyes bore into me. I quip about the awful print of Siamese cats on the wall to get him to look away. It doesn't work.

"You're talking a lot," he says, his breath on mine.

"It's funny that out of everyone here," I whisper so only he can hear me, "I've known you the longest and I trust you the least."

Sometimes he tells me that I was a girl when I met him and I've since grown into a woman.

I launch into a story about Hugo's doctors until he puts a finger to my lips. "Shhh. Don't think."

My eyes can't avoid his anymore.

I could have been downstairs laughing with Penelope while she does her hair, but instead I'm in Mr. Lyon's lap, being held like a baby while he entertains everyone else in the room. He holds me like this, pressed up against his chest, for another fifteen minutes until someone else gets impatient, tugs on his jeans, and says, "Daddy, can I have a turn?"

Finally, I am released.

During our lunch break, Penelope, Noah, Clara, and I share a box of Bojangles chicken and biscuits on the dock by the lake. I pass around the box of grease and sip on a sweet tea the size of my head.

"You know that story he told earlier?" Clara asks, declining a piece of fried chicken. "I didn't actually slap him. I tore his shirt and one of his buttons popped off. When he didn't yell at me, I said, 'No one's ever cared about me more than a button.'" Clara is lying down, in a cropped white T-shirt and a pair of jeans that looks like it was made for her body, with embroidered roses climbing down her pockets.

The sweet tea in my throat sours.

"Well, you know what he always says," Penelope chimes in. "It's not the physical details of the story that matter but the point of the story."

This explanation, which always felt sufficient, now feels woefully inadequate. I've known Bob to tell the occasional lie. But the fact that he told us Clara slapped him instead of telling us she ripped his shirt feels deliberate. He didn't want people to wonder what else happened while they were alone. The wild look on her face and her earlier scream suddenly make sense.

"I need to stop being scared of him," Clara says.

"He's a scary person." I laugh. All eyes rivet to me and I know I've said the wrong thing.

After the awkward silence that follows, Clara says gently, "No, it's me. I need to stop blaming him and making excuses."

Bob recently helped her get out of an abusive eight-year relationship, so I understand her loyalty to him. Noah and Penelope nod their heads.

"I know what you mean," Noah says. "It can be hard to focus on the ways we're wrong."

I don't argue further. But if something is off in her relationship with Bob, *he* must be the one at fault. Not the sweet twenty-three-year-old in front of me. If she is scared, it's because Bob has done something to frighten her.

Penelope hums. I wait until Clara and Noah wander off through the grounds before speaking again.

"She's been through it, too," I whisper. I haven't stopped thinking about the pool house.

"Who? Clara?" Penelope furrows her brow, wiping crumbs off her pants. "I don't think so. She would have told me."

I lay back and watch geese fly overhead. "She has."

Later, we head to the pool house and flop down on the bed. Noah says something about how it feels good to be back here, but I mutter, locking eyes with Penelope, that it gives me anxiety.

"I know what you mean," she says under her breath.

"What? What are you guys talking about?" Noah asks.

"All the memories," I say before changing the topic.

We head back to the basement of the main house. Penelope and Noah drift into a conversation about the phonetic alphabet while Penelope prepares miso soup and talks about the eight years she lived in Japan, before she came back to the United States and married Bob's son.

*

For the last day of the retreat, Penelope and I skip most of group. She's right; Bob tells the same stories every time and we've heard them all. I've always felt like a kid around Bob, but this time, with a friend to validate my experience and with Amma and three children waiting for me at home, I finally feel like an adult. Bob's home feels like a dollhouse I've outgrown, the participants seem like caricatures, and I can't wait to leave.

Everything feels not quite right but not wrong enough.

27

February 2019

After the retreat, I cannot stop thinking about Clara's scream. I've stopped contacting Bob, but still, my life is tap water that doesn't taste right.

I keep bringing it up during my conversations with Penelope. There's something about the whole situation that doesn't add up. We dig up one of Bob's old videos, an early interview with Oprah. He's out of sync with her the entire time. Oprah makes a joke, and Bob is so overeager that he doesn't even wait for the laughter to die down before launching into another fervent explanation about the power of unconditional love. She tries to make the occasional quip, but Bob talks over her, bent on getting out the sentences he's planned beforehand. His inability to read social cues unsettles me. Is this the man I've admired, whose advice I've accepted without question for years? The video is decades old. Maybe he's learned in the time since. Maybe he's not good at interviews.

Penelope's husband, John, begins talking to us about his dad's younger years. Bob once made his kids shoot a cat that was living on the roof of their house. John starts telling us stories of the specific things his dad did after shooting up with heroin. Come to think of it, why had my parents ever taken me to see a therapist who'd been addicted to narcotics for twelve years? How did that seem like a good idea?

And when Bob said Hugo could die an early death if I wasn't more loving—how could anyone say something so cruel to a mother? But then I remember some of the achingly sweet things he's said to me over the years, his poignant insight into my character, his ability to complete my thoughts before I can, and I again feel bewildered trying to form a coherent picture of this man.

Penelope calls more often. She keeps feeling worse about what happened. We try to piece together how Bob's help was so effective. Our lives had been nightmares and Bob had saved us. Right?

"I think it basically boils down to the idea of unconditional love," Penelope says.

"Is it that? Do we really think the answer to happiness is being loved, loving, and responsible?"

Quiet. "Vulnerability plays a big part."

"Which Brené Brown has already figured out with actual research. . . ." I point out.

"And without all Bob's unnecessary craziness."

Further quiet.

"What does Bob actually *add*?"

The question hangs uncomfortably in the air.

Penelope texts me later. She needs to talk. She's been having a harder time talking to her mom lately; Penelope's mom used to be a social worker—until she became more deeply involved in True Happiness. Sometimes Penelope can't even hold a conversation with her own mother because she sounds so irritatingly similar to Bob.

"Is that what I sound like?" she asks me. "Do we *all* sound like him?"

Right now, she sounds strained, tired, and confused. She sounds how I've felt for the past eight years, as I've scoured the True Happiness community for even a single person who will admit that Bob is not right about everything. But whenever I've pointed out my concerns, I've been met with a brick wall of Bob's aphorisms: *You're only upset when you're fighting the truth. Skepticism is lazy. Doubt your doubts before you doubt your faith.* Now that Penelope finally shares her own misgivings, it gives me permission to fully explore my doubts—and it doesn't feel good.

"Veena, I think it's so much worse than we thought," she starts. "I feel like I'm coming out of a fog. The only other time I've felt this way is when I got out of an abusive relationship. Why do I feel this way now?"

I pace the length of my bed, stomach already sinking.

"I don't understand what happened to my life. I was living in Japan. . . . It's been my dream to live in Japan since I was a kid. And I'd been living there for eight years, I met Bob, and then suddenly I moved back to the States? And married this alcoholic? The second time I met him? I didn't want this, Veena. I don't think I chose this."

The past eight years dance in my mind and reorganize themselves into a picture my stomach cannot yet accept. Fragments from that phone conversation I had with a woman I'd been taking calls from (was her name Glen?) come rushing back: *My friend looked up True Happiness on the Internet . . . and I think it's a cult. Like an* actual *cult.*

I let out a shriek and punch my bedroom wall. It hurts my hand more than it hurts the wall. There is no satisfying hole, just a crack in the drywall next to the fireplace. I wish I could break something the way my mind feels like it is breaking now. My knuckles are raw, but I wish they hurt more to distract me from the thoughts I have to face next. I collapse to the floor.

*

There is no way to capture the moment you realize your reality is warped because, in that moment, conscious thought dies. There is only sensation. First, a crumpling. A heat, flushed quickly away by a chill. Pervaded by the watery feeling of slipping. Thoughts struggle to be born here but are crushed like new grass under the sneaker soles of playing children. When thought finally and impetuously elbows its way back into your mind, it is not complicated or nuanced. It is a single, visceral word: *no*. This word disperses throughout your system, passed like oxygen between blood vessels, delivered to your extremities. It catches like a grain of sand in your veins. You need this word that badly. Once administered, it will render you healed.

The feeling I describe is cognitive dissonance. The first time I met him, Bob asked me if I knew the term. I defined it for him: holding two contradictory beliefs at the same time. He said that one term described my entire life, and he was right. The key to moving forward is deciding which belief comes out on top.

"Veena?" Penelope asks. Her voice sounds small in my phone. "Are you okay?"

"Oh, God," I groan. My body goes rigid to soft to limp. "It's a cult. We've been in a cult." I tuck my head into my chest and shut my eyes to stop the room from spinning.

Penelope groans, and I feel the same realization rotate through her.

"Holy fuck."

That "no" pulses gently, like an open wound. Gradually it transforms into a "yes." Yes, I am seeing clearly. Yes, this really is my life. Yes, I can unfold myself, stand, take one step, then another in the same world I have always lived in, and yet one that is entirely new to me.

After a silence in which our pasts narrow to a single point, we both reach for our computers to google "signs of a cult." At least that is what I type in.

"'One: The leader is the ultimate authority. If you're not allowed to criticize your leader . . . you're probably in a cult,'" Penelope reads.

"Check," I say.

"'Two: The group suppresses skepticism. Three: The group delegitimizes former members.'"

"Check. Check."

"'The group is paranoid about the outside world, relies on shame cycles, leader is above the law.' Yes, to all of those."

I find the article she is reading from: "Ten Signs You're Probably in a Cult." "'Seven: The group uses "thought reform" methods. If your serious questions are answered with clichés, you're probably in a cult.' Ugh, Penelope."

A wave of nausea overcomes me and I have to stop reading and curl back up on the floor until it passes. It is worse than falling for a QVC ad or a multi-level marketing scheme to sell boxed knives. All the information is *there,* all the signs are *there*—hell, I'd even been *told* it was a cult, and still, here I am, waking up from the Matrix eight years later. Suddenly I am nineteen again and bewildered that the three small children in the next room are mine.

Penelope continues: "'Eight: The group is elitist. If your group is the solution for all the world's problems, you're probably in a cult. Nine: There is no financial transparency. Ten: The group performs secret rites. . . .'"

Penelope and I both sit in silence until she starts describing exactly what Bob did to her in the pool house. Our experiences are not identical, but they are similar enough that scenes and images flood back, and I feel physically ill. She asks me: *Did he do this to you? Did he do that?* Yes, yes, no. I don't know how we manage to end the conversation because once we hang up, I feel adrift in some private world.

*

"Hey, I thought I heard something," Charlie says, walking into the room. He stops when he notices the crack in the wall and stares. "Did you . . . punch the wall?"

I nod and reach for him. "Charlie"—I gasp—"I think we were in a cult. True Happiness is cult."

"Oh." He stops and goes silent for several seconds. Then he cocks his head and says, "Yeah, that makes sense."

After just reassessing my entire adult life, Charlie's nonreaction feels like it will shatter my sense of reality entirely. "What? What do you mean, 'That makes sense'? Did you know?"

"Of course I didn't know," he says simply. "But it makes sense."

His lack of response shocks me more than the fact that I was in a cult. My husband attended one of the best boarding schools in the country and has worked at some of the top consulting firms in the world. Yet he sat in this man's lap, and isn't expressing any signs of surprise. Bob, at least, makes some kind of perverted sense. The signs have been there all along. But Charlie? I don't recognize my husband.

"We called him *daddy,* Charlie."

He smiles wryly. "Yeah, that was a little weird now that you say it."

He walks me to bed. All my questions about the cult have taken a back seat to my questions about Charlie. I am too stunned to ask any of them. He tucks me into bed understandingly.

"You can rest. We'll talk about you punching the wall later."

I stay in bed for most of the day.

It takes two weeks for me to work up the guts to tell my parents. They come to visit, pass by my room, and comment on how much time I'm spending in bed. I'm still in shock and cannot tell where my skin ends and where the sheets begin. Amma says something about my children asking for me and I know I should go to them, but I have just woken from a dream state, and I am still grappling with the fact that they exist.

I stop Amma in the kitchen one day and tell her. I don't remember the words I use.

She freezes and stares at me for a moment.

"But . . . you fought him off, right?"

My stomach sinks as I begin to realize the difficulty I will have in conveying the depth and force of his manipulative influence to anyone. If my own mother cannot understand, who will? "No, Amma," I answer.

"How? Why?" Her voice is soft and confused. "I don't understand. You let him? Why didn't you fight him off?" She tells me about a time she physically fought off and blackmailed a family friend to avoid being raped.

I don't know how to answer.

"I said no." I start crying and Amma hugs me, alarmed. "I tried to say no."

But inside, I am already wondering if Bob was right, if there is something wrong and broken with me, because how could I have allowed this to happen?

Several days later, I tell Nanna. He nods, tears welling in his eyes, and says under his breath, *That fucker.* He hugs me, unable to speak.

He gives me a wide berth for a day or so and then says, *Okay, things happen, time to move on.*

Part of me feels like Mr. Lyon is the only one who would understand, and I don't know what to do with this feeling. I have to resist the urge to call and ask him to help me.

Months will pass before it finally occurs to me to google "True Happiness cult." Then, I'll read a series of anonymous discussion board posts ranging from 2014 to 2017. One of the posts asks for information regarding the organization:

> My uncle joined the group along with his wife. I've heard some pretty weird stuff about this group. Should I be concerned?

An anonymous response reads: Yes, you should be worried. I got pulled into all of this five years ago. Long sorry story short, I stopped speaking to all my friends and family and divorced my husband, which I bitterly regret.

The person mentions spending thousands of dollars on interventions during the lowest point of their life. I needed help but True Happiness wasn't the answer, the post reads. Attempting now to regain a sense of reality but it's really challenging. Let me know if you need more info.

Perhaps this person is right: True Happiness wasn't the answer. Nineteen-year-old me needed help, too.

28

March 2019

In the month that follows my realization that I was in a cult, I constantly break down in tears without warning. In parking lots. At grocery stores. At Party City buying supplies for my son's first birthday party. I run on the treadmill while blasting pop songs and pretending I am in a music video and then play the piano for two hours and then shower and then cry and lie down on the floor of the shower for an hour and then put on a full face of makeup, eat a slice of my son's leftover birthday cake, and wash all the makeup off. I shower a lot, scalding certain memories off my skin. I can't get clean. I spend too much money online shopping for miniskirts and bikinis—anything to expose the maximum amount of skin. As a member of the church, I'm not supposed to wear them, but I've missed the feeling of sunshine on my body. Then I worry about all the things I'm avoiding (the forms I need to fill out for my kids' schools, the doctors' appointments I need to schedule for my son, the home repairs that need taking care of), and then I drink a cherry Pepsi and stay up late journaling. I open and close my fridge ten times in five minutes, as if I'm Dorothy and clicking my heels will magically restock my fridge. I swallow a tall glass of water that I try to convince myself is dinner.

*

Penelope tells her husband about what happened in the pool house and John immediately supports her. He asks if she is okay, apologizes repeatedly for what his dad did, and cries with her for several hours. Afterward, he calls Bob on Skype and yells over and over, "You put your fucking fingers in my wife's vagina??" Bob denies everything and spends the entire call asking, "Are you recording this?"

I crave some kind of empathetic response from Charlie—some acknowledgment of what has happened—but one never comes. When I try to broach the fact that Charlie defended Bob for years after I told him about the pool house, he grows embarrassed and says, "Well, we were both brainwashed." He clings to this line, but it doesn't satisfy me. I apologize for introducing Charlie to Bob in the first place, but the more I replay the past, the more it strikes me that Charlie made sure not to get too involved with True Happiness. He never listened to the conference calls, went to seminars or retreats, or joined the church. In fact, after our marriage, his main interactions with True Happiness were making sure I stayed enmeshed in the community. When I try to raise the issue, however, Charlie's voice gets small, and the conversations end soon after that.

Penelope and I tell people in True Happiness. Or rather, Penelope does, while I continue to do my treadmill-shower-makeup routine. She sticks to the facts and doesn't use the word "cult." Less to argue with that way. *He did this. He did that.* People argue anyway. Bob tells people in the community we're making up stories because we are angry that we didn't get to take over his business. This rhetoric becomes less convincing when we speak with other women whom he also held naked—including Penelope's mother, a former social worker. She sits on Skype with Penelope, stunned, supportive, and apologetic.

"I've been trained to recognize this stuff," she says. "How did *I* fall for it?"

She emails Bob once to confront him, but after he denies everything he did to Penelope, she cuts off communication.

I slide between two realities now. In one reality, I am a girl who was once nominated most likely to succeed but whose entire adult life has been predicated upon a lie. Intellectually, I know this version of reality is true. But still I ooze into the other version, one where I am an ungrateful bitch who has turned her back on the one person who has been there for her through everything. A physical sensation accompanies this oscillation, like I am slipping through the floor and my limbs are jelly. I call Penelope frantically during these moments. *Am I crazy am I crazy am I crazy.*

"No," she says. "We're finally sane."

I wish there were some way to be certain.

"Someone who is genuinely loving doesn't go from helping people to putting his fingers inside young women."

That feels more certain.

I keep waiting for him to call. In those first months I am convinced he will call at any moment, and I will answer. He'll use that soothing tone of voice and say, *Sweetie, what's going on? You're in pain, honey, you're in pain.* I will agree with him and cry, and he will explain how I am mistaken, how he never would have used me like that. As soon as he calls, my conviction will dissipate, and I will fold back into him.

The fact that he never calls almost hurts more than the past eight years.

Penelope, three other women in the community, and I tell our bishops. *He probably shouldn't be baptizing people, right?* I let her do most of the talking and the thinking for both of us at this stage. We have separate calls with Bob's bishop, where we describe everything he did in detail. It is the first time I say these things out loud and I convulse, and my body goes cold to the point where it is hard to get words out. I feel like an idiot, but the bishop is kind. He believes us but ultimately there is nothing he can do: it is Bob's word against ours. It was chilling, the bishop tells us, sitting there and listening to Bob lie about everything. Still, he goes to church every Sunday. Continues baptizing people.

Separating myself from him is trying to separate the yolk from the white after the yolk has already been punctured. Each week I have some new revelation about another aspect of my life that he orchestrated: My decision to drop out of school. To have the baby. To get married. To join the church. Logan, one of the people I used to take calls from, reaches out and she tells me about specific scenarios Bob engineered, like the time he called her boss and got him to leave the floor wet so that Logan would fall and learn her lesson. She doesn't even live in the same state as Bob so she has no idea how he got hold of her manager's phone number. She laughs like a fever has broken at confirmation that she is not crazy.

Penelope and I call the police in Bob's town. They speak with slow, Southern drawls when they ask, "He asked you to do what, now?" They scratch their heads when they find out that Penelope and the other women didn't say no. She sends them the specific statute that we think Bob violated and offers to forward emails. The whole police department starts googling his YouTube videos, and he is a weird egg, they'll grant us that, but they spoke to him, and he says he didn't do it.

It will be a long time before I can touch the word "molested."

Somehow, we thought there would be consequences for his behavior.

I show up to church one day, crying partly out of emotional exhaustion, partly because in my gut I don't know if I genuinely believed a man from upstate New York named Joseph Smith had a divine revelation from God. This annoys me because, once I admit this, I am back to square one with all my existential questions about the meaning of life. When the patriarch sees me crying, he asks if I want to speak with him, and I nod. He is a leathery old man who often goes on long tangents about the brilliant people he has met in his lifetime just to tell me that I am more brilliant. He has sought my advice on how to approach the people he counsels more often than I've sought his. In the basement of the church, I try saying, "He brainwashed me" aloud for the first time and it sounds as absurd as you'd think.

The patriarch studies me in confusion. "That can't be true," he says.

And of course, it cannot be, because I am sitting next to him in this classroom, looking relatively composed in my maxi dress and my winged eyeliner, and the patriarch is telling me that in my talks at church, I've illustrated concepts from the Bible that, in his seventy years, he's never heard anyone articulate before.

"So, I can't believe that your choices weren't yours," he concludes.

"But . . . I let him touch me." I stare down at my hands as I say it.

He pauses. "Can I ask why that is bothering you so much?"

I don't know how to answer so I just repeat myself: "But I let him *touch* me."

"I assume you mean with your clothes on," he replies.

His response catches me so off guard that all I can do is balk, shake my head, and wish I could melt into the floor. For a second, he doesn't know what to say. Then: "Well, I don't believe you enjoyed that."

When I remain silent, he continues: "If that is the worst thing that has happened to you, I would get down on my knees and thank Heavenly Father."

There is some truth to what he says: I am alive. My children are alive. Plenty of people have survived worse. But now I'm starting to realize that the pain of others does not negate my own. I find it difficult to focus for the rest of the conversation. He says something about how this is not one of those sins I need to confess to the bishop. I exit the room disoriented and feeling worse than when I entered, but unable to pinpoint why.

I think I just want someone to see me the way I thought Bob did.

All my passcodes and PIN numbers are the month and year that I met him. At what point did I begin measuring my life in terms of Him? What benchmarks of my own do I have left?

If no one is willing to hold Bob accountable and stop him from molesting young women in the future, Penelope and I decide to file a civil suit to deter him. I call a Georgia-based lawyer to see if we have a case and begin telling him the story in fragments. "It wasn't anything overtly sexual. . . ." I trail off toward the end of this sentence, remembering the feel of his hands cupping my breasts, his teeth tugging on my lips, the tightness in his pants. I wonder what an objective observer would say if they had been there with me. Maybe the third person would describe those events as overtly sexual.

"I regret to inform you, Mrs. Jones, that I cannot take your case. There are several reasons. First, there's the waiver that he had you sign initially."

My head swims at this sentence. I was nineteen then, the day I sweetened my Earl Grey with ant poison instead of sugar. It doesn't make any kind of sense that my name on the line that many years ago could so drastically alter the course of my life, that it could affect a lawyer's willingness to take my case.

"And second, strange as it may sound to us, he is going to claim that holding people naked, this 'rebirthing' or what have you, is a legitimate form of therapy," continues the voice on the other end of the phone.

I hang up and sit on a bench in my kitchen, watching birds outside the window returning home after the winter. Blue jays, cardinals, finches. I boot up Hugo's feeding pump and carry him and his IV pole to the family room. Hugo squirms in my arms, his eyes occasionally crossing. The decorations from his first birthday party still hang in the dining room, deflated Mylar balloons marking what should have been a moment of relief and pride that we had made it thus far. I had worked all the stress of the past weeks into planning Hugo's party. Had turned the stairs into a mattress slide and built a tunnel out of cardboard boxes that blocked the door to the garage.

"I would describe it as very sexual," Penelope says when I call her after the conversation with the attorney. "He rubbed me in circles for like half an hour."

I frown at the floor and scratch my head. Yes. Of course, that was sexual. It was wrong. I get off the phone and write down an outline of my entire relationship with Bob and call the attorney back.

"I think," I stammer, "I think I downplay everything because I've been living inside his head for so long. Can I describe the whole thing to you?"

My body clenches into a ball. I pace. I sit on my bed. "I met him when I was nineteen. He forced me to call him every day by telling my parents to call the dean of students and get me kicked off campus if I didn't. He diagnosed me with borderline personality disorder even though he has no degree in psychology and no medical license. I met Charlie, and Bob engineered our relationship—he had Charlie call the cops on me and diagnosed me to the head psychologist at the hospital. I was going to get a physics degree and within a year of meeting him I had dropped out, gotten married, and become a stay-at-home mom. He told me not to get an abortion and married my husband and me in his living room. He baptized me into the Mormon church. Every time I wanted to go back to school, he told me I was seeking material things. He said I couldn't trust anyone but him. And when he held me . . . he didn't just hold me. He made me lie on top of him spread-eagle. And do mouth-to-mouth breathing with him and—"

My hands shake and I collapse to the side of the bed, unable to continue.

"Okay," comes the attorney's calm, measured voice. "In light of this new information, I have decided to take your case, Mrs. Jones."

"Thank you," I wheeze. "I'm sorry. I'm sorry."

"Please," he says, "you have nothing to apologize for. Even if we don't get any money out of him, sometimes you have to take a case just because it's the right thing to do. Let's get this creep."

I hide my face in my still trembling hands. *I am not crazy. I am not crazy. I am not crazy.* My body is hot, cold, flushed. I cannot stop shaking now that a sane professional agrees that what happened was wrong. That it was illegal. No matter the outcome of the lawsuit, this recognition of my reality from a stranger is all I need to begin trusting my own perceptions again.

At my attorney's request, I start digging through my thousands of emails from Bob for evidence, and each one induces nausea. Seeing our exchanges preserved word for word removes any lingering doubts I had about Bob's intentions. In the emails, he tells me clearly what to do at each juncture, ridicules and shames me for the ordinary mistakes of a teenager, and creates problems and presents himself as the only solution. In each subsequent response, I come back more contrite, small, and confused.

The physical violation is not what unravels me. It's the loss of life experience, the mental and emotional violation of having my young adulthood orchestrated by someone with undue influence over me. It's the friendships that disintegrated. The career paths unexplored. The opinions he replaced with his own. How close at hand the world had been, how many people lived beside me in New York City for years, how many people I would've befriended if I hadn't been rushing home to Skype a weird old man in Georgia.

I think about how often Bob used to tell the story of how we met, and I imagine how he tells the story now: *She refuses to take responsibility for her choices, and it's convenient for her to blame me. I tried to help her, but that's what people in pain do.* Doubt seeps in like an unpleasant smell. I am tempted to call him and apologize (I don't know for what). After being made to question my own judgments for so long, logic isn't enough to convince me that True Happiness is, in fact, a cult, that Bob's actions were wrong. I need outside confirmation. The more, the better.

When I google "True Happiness cult" again and come across more anonymous discussion board threads detailing other people's experiences in the community, I finally get that confirmation.

Any survivors out there who have left the 'True Happiness' cult? The post begins.

I hadn't thought of myself as a "survivor"—the term felt too melodramatic compared to salacious cult stories I'd seen depicted in Hollywood movies. But it comforts me to know that other people who share my experiences also find them emotionally traumatic.

Did I really lie like a baby in the arms of an adult? Am I the only one who did this naked? Did I really reject my own parents and accept a new 'daddy' who I believed would parent me properly because True Happiness told me that my parents didn't really love me and had raised me wrong? Did I actually believe that my new daddy had my best interests at heart? Did I really become Mormon after only a short time with the group, because "Mormonism aligns the most closely with True Happiness" (not connecting the dots that the True Happiness founder was a Mormon)?

I find myself asking the same questions. How had I—the physics and philosophy double major with loving parents, good friends, and every kind of privilege in life—fallen for a cult like that?

Did I really follow those written and verbal instructions to the letter?? Did I really believe that if I did not attend a True Happiness Group, listen to conference calls, watch the weekly Bob video chats, read the books over and over, go to all the programs and weekends, see my daddy weekly and keep having more and more interventions that I would not be able to cope, able to live? Did I really believe the suggestion that "We/I get to choose," every time I was told to do something, say something, believe something that was not my own values and ideas? Did I? Did I? Did I?

The patriarch may have believed my choices were my own; my attorney may not have understood the extent of Bob's influence until I described the graphic details; my own mother may have struggled to understand my experience; but reading this person's account, I finally start to feel sane.

Though we are not able to use the posts as evidence in the lawsuit because they are unverified, I am hardly bothered. Finally, finally, finally I am able to kick free of Bob's version of reality. *I am not the only one. Penelope and I are not the only ones.*

Sitting through church services becomes more difficult. Regardless of Bob's motivation in introducing me to the church, I've found comfort here, a community and structure that my children thrive in. I still badly want to be a good person, and listening to sacrament talks inspires me to live a principled life. The issue is: What principles am I absorbing? At first, I cannot tell the difference between official church-sanctioned doctrine and Bob's own personal dogma, loosely mixed with religious ideas he used for his own ends. But as the church's position becomes clearer to me, I still find too many ideas at odds with my beliefs. I start arguing with the Sunday school instructors about the role of women being restricted to the home. I argue with Young Women's leaders during their lessons on purity, when they say heterosexuality is the will of God. While I have outspoken liberal friends in the church, who vocally oppose the strictures they disagree with and raise difficult questions about the church's problematic past, ultimately, I decide the cost of staying is too high.

The decision to leave is not easy. Every fork in the road is paralyzing without someone else in my ear. I cannot yet articulate or prioritize my own desires. The only way I am able to start reclaiming my agency is by asking: What is best for my kids? Cleo comes home from primary lessons, talking about how to honor her parents, how to be kind to others, and how to know the difference between right and wrong. But she also continues talking about who she will marry and how many children she will have when she grows up. Hearing her regurgitate these patriarchal values becomes the deal-breaker. I leave the church to untether her dreams.

Not long after we leave, conversations about her future husband are replaced with discussions about the meaning of life and death if we no longer believe God is real. Looking into the caverns of my daughter's eyes, I'll wish I had some security to offer both of us, but instead I will say dumb things like, *Sometimes it is okay to not know*, and she'll roll her five-year-old eyes at me and say, *Okay but can you just tell me the answer to what happens when we die for real?* I'll worry for my daughter and doubt my decision, but with time, as we both acclimate to gray areas together, we will find a way forward. Nuance won't always feel so scary. The patriarch from church will still visit to check in on me and bring me clementines on occasion.

I begin to reach out to the people I have dropped along the way. Melanie. Eliza. The high school literature teacher who came to my baby shower. *Yeah, it's a weird story,* and I fill in the details of something they broadly already knew. *What concerned me was not that you were changing, but that you were turning away from everything that made Veena, Veena.* Transformations that are surreptitious and gradual to us can be painfully obvious to those who know us best. These conversations are stilted and uncomfortable, as I acclimate to a type of intimacy that does not swallow me whole. I apologize a lot and reach out to everyone I've ever given a copy of Bob's book to with an awkward, *Hey, listen.*

I remove everyone from True Happiness from my social media pages, watch my follower count dwindle and then slowly rise as I painstakingly repair relationships and forge new ones. I go over to the house of a fellow mom from Mary's preschool, sit on the stool in her kitchen, and tell her, *I think I was in a cult.* She nods, makes me a cup of tea, and tells me about a friend of hers who recently went through something similar when she realized the founder of her company was a narcissist and was embezzling money the whole time. She tells me that she always wanted to be friends with me, but I seemed closed off and—well, now she understands why. She also tells me where to get the good bagels in town.

It is through the little, unremarkable details—cups of tea and bagel recommendations—that I'll learn the world is a kinder place than Bob led me to believe. That there is room for me in it.

29

April 2019

Going back to therapy is the last thing I want to do. My first post-cult therapist is Jane, whose office is in yet another Connecticut suburb that resembles a J.Crew catalog. She's recommended to me by someone from church. Jane sits across from me in a blue velvet chair that looks like it wandered off, tipsy, in the middle of a dinner party and accidentally wound up in a therapist's office. She has bleached blond hair and bleached white teeth, each one as large and distinctive as my pinky fingernail, as opalescent as her globular pearl earrings. Jane charges me $250 an hour to listen to her aggressively cheery voice and she strikes me as the kind of person who has a much deeper understanding of blow-dryers than human nature.

It takes me halfway through the session to notice I've immediately reverted to my teenage habits of judging therapists.

And on the drive home, I realize for the first time that every one of my psychologists has been white. I don't see Jane again. My list of reasons for wanting to avoid therapy is as long as the list of therapists I've seen over the course of my life: The psychologist who asked if I thought suicide was the cool thing to do. The one who placed me on medical leave without informing me. The psychologist at the hospital who blindly accepted Bob's authority without bothering to verify his credentials at the word of my nineteen-year-old boyfriend. It was the incompetence of these psychologists that made Bob compelling by contrast. And now there's Jane, who, through no fault of her own, comes from a very different set of life experiences—one that I have trouble relating to.

But I am no longer a teenager and one of the benefits of adulthood is an appreciation for nuance. Yes, some mental health professionals did not meet my needs as a teenager, and some actively caused further harm. But that does not negate an entire field of research. Or the help I received from Mr. Carl and my high school psychologist and others along the way. Contrary to what Bob taught, I do not need a parental figure to understand all the minutiae of my personality. I need a professional who can help me weed out Bob's thoughts and opinions from my own, so I don't have to hear his voice in my head every time I meet a new friend or get dressed in the morning. I go back to therapy because I have three kids at home, and I cannot keep crying in parking lots.

After a couple of months of trying out therapists in attempts to find one who feels right for me, I go to Rebecca, a psychologist recommended by the kids' pediatrician. Initially, I try to redirect every conversation back to: *So, do you think he ever actually cared about me?* She tells me that people can contain multitudes. This answer may be satisfying if you find out your best friend stole your sweatshirt, but it's less satisfying if you're trying to untangle yourself from the influence of a cult leader.

Rebecca has the patience of a saint as she sits through session after session in which I agonize over every symptom of borderline personality disorder and try to convince her that I have it—and also that Bob is a well-intentioned but misguided old man.

"Just to recap, the man who gave you this diagnosis was an ophthalmologist, yes?" Rebecca asks.

I nod.

"Who surrendered his medical license only after admitting to a twelve-year-long addiction to narcotics?"

"Um, yes."

"And has absolutely no background in psychology or psychiatry whatsoever?"

"Correct."

"You've been diagnosed by multiple actual professionals and they all agreed that you had situational depression, right?"

"Well, yeah."

"And, this . . . man, he diagnosed you within hours of meeting you?"

Something begins to click.

"And he ended up molesting you?"

I nod, following her now. Her logic stacks up so neatly that I cannot argue with it. I've started reading books that describe grooming and I break out in chills sometimes seeing conversations I've had with Bob, almost word for word, played out in someone else's experience. That Bob understood me like no one else had before, that he didn't need ridiculous questionnaires or a background in psychology to see into my soul.

"But you still think that he's right and all the actual trained medical professionals who diagnosed you are wrong?"

I hesitate. "Maybe . . . *he* was wrong?" It's the first time I say it aloud.

She sighs compassionately. "Sweetie, he *manipulated* you."

I flinch at the word "sweetie." The most jarring part of returning to therapy is noticing all the similarities between what my therapist says and what I've heard from Bob over the years.

"He *used* this diagnosis to control you," she continues. "It may take time for you to see it, but he knew what he was doing."

It does take time. The official diagnosis I am given is PTSD. This time, I choose not to go down any rabbit holes of googling symptoms. Instead of hyperfixating on the label itself, day-to-day I focus on course correcting the hyperbolic thinking that Bob taught me, building confidence in my own decisions, and regrowing my faith in people.

Charlie starts staying later at work with the coworker he keeps insisting is a friend. Initially, I am determined to make the marriage work, regardless of the bizarre circumstances that united us. Without Bob as the unwanted third wheel in my marriage, I tell myself that Charlie and I will be stronger than ever; after this ordeal, my husband will finally support and believe me. After all, every concern I raised about Bob has been proven correct. Surely, now my husband will finally have to acknowledge that my perceptions are accurate and valid.

This is not how Charlie reacts. Instead, he insists more openly than ever that I am mentally unwell and need to be medicated. He raises the number of times I've tried to leave the marriage as evidence of my instability. He kept track and, on average, I tried to leave at least twice a year. Months ago, I would have believed Charlie. Now, it occurs to me that I simply didn't want to be with him. He calls from the parking lot at work to tell me he'll be home late again, but recently, all our conversations circle back to the time I punched the wall.

"Have you gotten diagnosed yet?" he asks.

"I told you my psychologist says I have PTSD."

"I think you need to be tested again," he insists. "You're unstable."

In the eight years we've been together, he's implied as much through his tone of voice, but this is the first time he's said it so plainly and coldly. I'm at a loss for words, struggling to make sense of his reaction. We've just realized that I was molested—that Charlie pushed me toward my abuser, defended him for years after knowing what he'd done, and tried to convince me that being molested was good for my mental health. Wouldn't any husband be horrified to hear that his wife had been sexually assaulted? Why doesn't Charlie even *care*?

"You have a personality disorder," he continues. "You need to be medicated."

My head swims. I've spent months coming to terms with the fact that Bob may not have cared about me. Finally, I start to wonder if I have been wrong about Charlie, too.

"Just to be clear," I say, "are you saying that you think Bob was right about me? Are you saying I'm overreacting?"

He doesn't hesitate before answering: "Yes."

I can hear the impatience in his voice to get back to whatever he was doing. I hate myself for crying again, but in this moment, I know that my husband has never really seen me. He's too invested in whatever reality is convenient for him; the reality that keeps me at home, cooking his dinners, folding his laundry in the way he likes, and not asking questions when he comes home late.

I rub my temples. "So, according to you, what would be the appropriate emotional response to everything I've experienced?"

"I don't know," he says, "but it's not yours. You are a danger to our kids in this state. You need to be medicated for their safety."

I stare out the window, looking over our beautiful football field–sized backyard as I clean up Hugo's projectile vomit, wondering if this conversation is real, if I heard him correctly. I've dedicated my whole life to my children. I've put my life on pause and given them everything, held Cleo through her nightmares, been there for Hugo every time he wakes up from anesthesia. Charlie is never home to help with the kids, is again refusing to provide childcare, and is now telling me I'm a danger to them? There is no winning in his paradigm. I cover the speaker of my phone so he cannot hear me cry.

Charlie says he has to get back to work; we'll have the conversation I want after I have "calmed down." But as I hang up the phone and restart Hugo's feeding pump, I realize that conversation is never coming. Because there will always be another behavior of mine to pathologize in order to avoid facing his own. Suddenly I know that no matter what roles he plays, I will be the one who gets called crazy. Who has the power to define what is "crazy"? Who gets to benchmark their experience as "sane"?

Our marriage ends unceremoniously one night when Charlie goes out with his coworker and doesn't come home. When he returns the next day, he lies down on our bed, face down, on a pillow while I sit across from him and ask, *So, is this it?* He shrugs and I hear a muffled, *I guess so.* From the boy who began dating me with effectively the same response, this end is fitting. He mentions that he thinks he may have Asperger's syndrome. I am not sure what to do with this information. Is it meant to explain certain things? Absolve him of others? I still don't have answers.

Of all the times I've tried to end our marriage, it ends, finally, when he decides it's over.

30

2019

As soon as Charlie moves out, my limbs feel light and the sky feels suddenly expansive. My parents move back to the East Coast to help me and the kids through the divorce. Nanna takes a job in Pennsylvania to be within driving distance, and they come to Connecticut often. One day when Venkat is visiting, Amma digs up old family photo albums and home videos that we all look through together. I flip through picture after picture of me smiling freely, with abandon. In a home video of my third birthday, I am calm, bright, and joyful while Venkat runs in and out of the frame screaming, "*FIREEEE! FIREEEE!*" after Nanna has lit three candles on a Carvel cake. Amma and Nanna try to calm him down, but he keeps running and yelling, undeterred.

"Wow." Venkat laughs as we watch. "Was I always that, uh, hyperactive?"

Amma nods, smiling. "Yeah, I forgot. You were a lot to deal with."

"Wait," I interject. "I thought I was the difficult one. You always told that story about how I wouldn't smile for the perfume ladies."

She turns, as if considering me for the first time. "Huh. You were actually the easy baby."

We scour the albums and finally find the picture where I wouldn't smile for the photographer. I am eight months old and Venkat is four years old and, sure enough, I am scowling while he is laughing. But it is a single picture out of hundreds. I wonder how many times that story must have been told and retold to crowd out the other, less dramatic moments of joy, how the expectations associated with the role of "good daughter" shaped my understanding of myself and informed my relationship to the world.

"Did I tell you guys," Amma starts, "about the time Venkat set the carpet on fire? Or the time he stuck a screw up his nose?"

Memory is a funny thing.

When I first attempted suicide, Amma and Nanna launched a coordinated siege to convince me to keep the Incident secret—or at least as secret as possible, considering how many people I'd already told.

"It will be much harder to get into college and get a job."

"People judge, Veena. They may be nice to your face, but they will gossip about you."

"Have you considered that people might be accepting and supportive?" I asked.

My parents scoffed in unison but collected themselves when they realized I was being serious.

"Hm. I don't think so, Veena," Nanna said gently.

When we went to India that summer, my cousins asked question after question about my high school boyfriend, but no one asked if I found life worth living.

I told my friends anyway. At my school, my situation was hardly unique; if anything, the suicide epidemic created a sense of solidarity among the students. My friends responded with the kind of concerned compassion that felt supportive without being overbearing. But their reaction didn't assuage Amma and Nanna's fears. When I was fifteen and trying to kill myself, they said: "Don't tell anyone." When I was twenty and unexpectedly pregnant: *Don't tell anyone.* Well, you can't hide a baby for that long. *Fine, but they don't need to know the details.* When I was twenty-one and baptized into Christianity: *You don't need to mention that to our family.* Every time I opened my mouth, my monologue came back covered in red marks, like that horrible linear algebra test I took in high school.

These days when I reveal my life through writing, I hear Amma's voice—not only because she's literally downstairs—but also because her wisdom and tales of caution have been burned so brightly into my mind that they've left afterimages. Her voice says the same thing she repeated to me growing up: Protect yourself. She was raised on the aphorism "Blood is thicker than water" and grew up in classrooms where you had to stand up while your grades were read aloud to the entire class. Every friend she had was a competitor. When I spoke of wanting to be searingly honest, to be unashamedly myself, fear ignited in her eyes. This is what you get when you transplant a person from one culture into another world. The immune system flares up in resistance to change. It is difficult to say whether the body is rejecting the organ, or the organ is rejecting the body, but, either way, the result is strife.

My mother just wanted her daughter to be safe. Now, as my own children discover pain for the first time, I understand Amma's impulse to shield me. I watch, helpless, the first time my kids stub their toes running barefoot down the driveway. When they burn their fingers on a baking sheet fresh out of the oven. And, ultimately, when their best friend no longer wants to play with them at recess. I think I have known heartbreak and pain in my life, but as I watch my six-year-old daughter slump off the school bus with a sag in her step and a droop in her shoulders, I realize anew that nothing can compare to the initial discovery that people can hurt us. Like my own mother, I swing into fixing mode: That girl doesn't know what she's missing, plenty of other fish in the sea, and all that. I have obviously forgotten what it means to be six (or human) because this does not assuage her agony. The expression on her face contorts further.

As much as my mother might wish security upon me, like I wish it upon my daughter, I know, too, that Amma has never shied away from risk or confined herself to societal norms. She railed against an early marriage, refused to learn how to cook, talked her way into jobs she was grossly underqualified to hold, and rose to the occasion every time. The women of my family do not play nice when asked to conform to expectations. We are simply unwilling to forgo a world of experience.

There is a story in the *Ramayana,* a Hindu sacred text, about Sita, wife of the god Rama. Sita; her husband, Rama; and her brother-in-law Lakshman were exiled in the wilderness for fourteen years. Ravana, king of the demons, was bent on kidnapping Sita. When Rama went out hunting, Lakshman drew an enchanted protective circle around Sita to keep her safe. The circle encompassed nothing but her feet and a small patch of grass. Sita got bored. She was lured out of Lakshman's protection by a beautiful golden deer who turned out to be Ravana's evil servant in disguise. And of course when Sita dared to stray outside the lines, she was kidnapped.

All my life people have drawn circles around me. They've justified these circles differently: It's for my safety, for my reputation, for my sanity, for my success. To make me happy, healthy, and unconditionally loving. To turn me into a good wife and mother. None of these reasons satisfy me any longer. I don't want to be safe; I want the golden deer. I want to eat the apple.

When I first began having doubts about my faith, I called up my former bishop and asked him what he would think if I left the church. He told me that the safest place to weather a storm is inside the boat. I never went back after that conversation.

I look again at my daughter, but really look this time, and I see a tiny, formidable person who deserves more than the circle of earth beneath her feet. She is owed the full breadth of human connection. My therapist is always suggesting I sit with emotions rather than trying to pass them off like a hot potato or correct them. I say to my child, *It must have felt awful when your friend didn't play with you.* There is a shift and release as she burrows her small, dark-haired head into my stomach.

My mother has stopped saying "Protect yourself." Though my pending divorce is even more scandalous than my suspiciously timed first pregnancy, she now places a hand on my shoulder and says, "We'll get through this." One day Amma catches me in the kitchen, while I am digging through the fridge, and squeezes me silently from behind. Lately, she spends her free time deep cleaning my bathroom, vacuuming the basement, and making me dinner.

"Amma?" I ask when she doesn't let go.

"I'm just so glad we have you back."

I turn to hug her face-to-face and lose track of how long we stand there.

"Never again," she says. "I'm never again going to let someone come between us like that."

She starts to rant about all the damage she has done to me, about how everything that happened was her fault—even my depression and suicide attempts. I cut her off.

"That was what Bob taught us, Amma," I say. "He made us believe that because it served him. You've always supported me. Even in taking me to see him, you were trying to support me when you didn't know how."

She quiets, but I don't think she believes me. Deep down, I think she still believes that I wanted to die because she wasn't good enough as a mother. As a mother myself—one who has also struggled to keep my son alive—I can only imagine the weight she carries. I don't know how to take it from her. It's hard for her to remember the times she chaperoned my school field trips, planned museum dates for the two of us, made chai for me and my friends, when it is so easy to diminish my childhood to that two-week stint in the psych ward. Amma and I will have this conversation repeatedly over the years, but I still don't know if she believes that my mental health struggles were not her fault.

Between the divorce, my three children, and the lawsuit, my time and attention is spread too thin and something has to give. Every communication from the lawyer reminds me of the events I have been trying to forget. Through his attorney, Bob claims he is broke and offers a settlement that is less than what my parents paid him for the first visit. If we keep going, it will escalate to a court trial and, realistically, I know I cannot preserve my mental health through that process. We settle the case and finally it feels like I can begin the life that was put on hold. Exploring my own desires still feels blinding, like staring at the sun, so I stay within the Venn diagram of what I might enjoy and what will also benefit my kids; I enroll in a child psychology class at the local community college.

One day, when I walk out of the YMCA with my children and my mother, Cleo points at geese in the sky, flying in typical V formation.

"Why are they together?" she asks, brushing unkempt hair out of her face.

"Why do people stick together?" I ask in response.

I've become allergic to reductive answers. Now, I am one of those annoying parents that responds to every question with a question. It drives Cleo nuts. She rolls her eyes and grumpily stomps the pavement. I point at her little sister, now trying to run into the parking lot. "What would happen if Mary went into the parking lot by herself?"

"She would get hit by a car and die," Cleo states.

"Uh, well, it could be dangerous, right? So we stick together."

Sometimes conformity can be a protective mechanism. If everyone is heading in the same direction, you figure someone must know what they're doing. They can't all be wrong. But this overwhelming psychological pressure to conform kept me in True Happiness for so long, doubting my own instincts. Cleo nods and quiets, satisfied for a minute. She turns her large brown eyes to me again. "But what if it's a really wise bird?"

She asks this because my mother reads her Indian fables, and the fables always feature wise animals and foolish animals. I explain to my daughter that there is no such thing as a "wise" animal. We splinter off into a discussion of instinct, but I am still watching the geese, eyeing the one at the end flying just slightly too far from the rest, thinking she will have to get wise fast if she wants to break apart from the flock. She'll have to trust herself to pick a direction and go.

Months after Charlie moves out, he comes back crying, saying he made a mistake. I consider letting him move back in because, in spite of everything, we built IKEA furniture together in our college apartment and painted our daughters' rooms together while expecting our son. The circumstances of our union may have been strange and unexpected, but I've borne this man's children, and family means something.

"So you'll let him move back in," my therapist says. "And then what?"

I shrug.

"Let me suggest a scenario. You'll have a need, and he won't meet it, and you'll let it slide. You'll have another need, he won't meet it, and you'll let that one slide, too. By the fiftieth time this happens, you explode and everyone is pointing a finger at you, calling you crazy because you had this big dramatic explosion, and they can't see the fifty quiet things he ignored before that. It's like shaking a soda bottle over and over."

I get chills when she says this. Because now that Charlie has moved out, I don't get angry anymore. I've spent our marriage thinking of myself as a controlling, bitter woman, but without a man restricting my choices, I find my life blissfully free of conflict.

My therapist is not the first one to suggest that, too often, we pathologize expressions of pain instead of addressing the cause of the pain. Except last time I heard this idea, the man who said it didn't tell the story with a soda bottle. He told it with a fork and a video camera, but the basic point is all the same. Sometimes it is not enough to correct the maladjustment inside you. Sometimes it is not enough to say to yourself, I am loved, I am happy, I am grateful. Sometimes you have to leave the town where people keep killing themselves, leave the man who keeps telling you that you are broken, leave the husband who would place you back in the kitchen for another decade. Sometimes it is not enough to contort yourself into the strict confines of good daughter, good mother, good wife, good Christian, good girl. Sometimes you have to step outside the circle. Because not every single problem exists exclusively in your mind.

Sometimes you have to take out the fucking fork.

31

December 31, 2019

I shift a case of IPAs from my right hand to my left as Venkat rings the doorbell of an inconspicuous Brooklyn brownstone. In the ten years since my visit to Stanford, we've upgraded from stolen frat party kegs. A buzzer rings, and we climb up a narrow stairway to his friend's apartment. Venkat tells me we're in Bushwick, that Liv's apartment is in a great location, only blocks away from some of the best clubs, and I nod as if I know things about Bushwick and clubs and IPAs.

The door opens to a woman in cheetah-print pants and a bold red lip. "Oh, my God, Venkat! You're back! I wasn't sure you were coming." Her voice is rich like warm soil.

She pulls my brother into a deep hug, and I experience a sinking sensation in my stomach as I stand there awkwardly in the hallway with our beer. I don't know who this woman is, and from the way she hugs my brother like a long-lost friend, I realize I don't know my brother, either.

"You must be Venkat's sister!" she exclaims as she hugs me, too, warmly and intentionally.

I wonder how my brother described me, how he thinks of me. I haven't thought of him for years. I catch his eye over Liv's shoulder and see the same realization on his face, that I've never met any of his friends. He's never seen me in a social setting as an adult. Venkat and I are awkward, fumbling with the space between us, wondering when and how it was built and how to best dismantle it.

Inside, Liv's apartment is everything I have thought of as "Brooklyn" before I ever got on a train to confirm: tastefully arranged houseplants and fairy lights, a bike against the wall, friends lounging on floor cushions while Frank Ocean pulses gently on the Bluetooth speakers in the background. I set the beers in her fridge as another girl squeals at Venkat and pounces on him.

"VENKAT! Oh, my God! You didn't tell anyone you were back! I hate you! Where have you been?"

She whips out her phone and takes selfies of the two of them and sends them to group chat before Venkat can protest. The churning in my intestines is now a mixture of fascination and nausea. I'm not a part of any group texts. I don't have any friends who would scream with excitement upon seeing me. I don't have friends, actually. What I had instead was Bob, Charlie, and the church. Even Penelope and I found we had nothing in common without Bob uniting us. One by one those pieces of my life have fallen away, leaving nothing in their place.

I pour myself a drink that has cranberries in it. Six months out of the church and I still can't tell the difference between wine and hard liquor. I have no idea what I'm drinking, but whatever it is, I'm certain it will ease the stress of relearning how to socialize. It's been years since I was in a room full of people my age—and I'm guessing here they don't make conversation by sharing their favorite Scripture story they read this past week. I don't know where to stand or what to do with my hands. Now that I've settled the lawsuit and officially filed for divorce, I have more experience talking to attorneys than twentysomethings in Bushwick.

"How do you know all these people?" I whisper to Venkat.

"Okay, so"—he winds up for the explanation—"I think Liv and Bilal met on Tinder and they didn't date but just became good friends and thought it would be great to get their friend groups together. I was friends with Bilal. Like I said, Harper used to live with me, Blake, and Aria. I'm not sure how I met Sigrid and Eric. Maybe through Liv? And Liv and I became close because we planned a hiking trip and we were the only ones who showed up because everyone else flaked. They all went to a surf camp in Costa Rica once, but I didn't go because I didn't know how to swim." He pauses and looks at me. "We should really learn how to swim this year."

There is a long list of things I should learn this year. With Bob I could only ever see one step ahead of me: taking out the trash tonight, putting the kids to bed, preparing for church. With my head finally above water and the entire world once more in focus, the view is dizzying. Suddenly facing all my choices at once leaves me greedy and overwhelmed, hungry and exhausted. I should learn to swim, but my initial goals are much more modest: deciding what kind of food I want to eat tonight, choosing the outfit I want to wear. All I can think of is what food Charlie is most likely to like, what outfit he'd want me to wear. Without his or Bob's voice in my head, I don't even know what I want in the silence.

I wander into the kitchen and offer to pour chips into a bowl to avoid the pains of reacclimating to small talk. Liv and her friend stir two pots on the stove, and ladle mulled wine into crystal glasses. Liv taps on hers with a spoon to get everyone's attention.

"Happy New Year, everyone! I had a very tough year with my apartment burning down as you all know, and this year, I want to live with more intention. So, I thought it would be fun for us to discuss what we've learned this year and what we hope to accomplish going into 2020."

Ruby talks about a promotion she received, a big step up in her career as a graphic designer, and how she hopes to cope with imposter syndrome in the year to come. Abigail, a girl with tattoos and a septum piercing, talks about a difficult apartment move and how to navigate conversations with her roommates going forward. I get the name of her tattoo artist before we leave. James describes getting out of an eight-year relationship and jokes about how his ex-girlfriend took custody of their rabbit. I try not to think about the custody battle that awaits me at home and instead bond with James over the fact that we're both escaping eight-year relationships at the same time. Venkat is in a different room of the apartment and I don't hear what he talks about, but everyone in my group looks at me expectantly.

"Well . . . I had kind of a tough year."

"Do you want to share more? No pressure, but we all just poured our hearts out." James laughs.

I hesitate. I blend in with the Bushwick crowd. I'm wearing a black top with cutouts underneath my chest and I'm not used to exposing the skin, but it's a cute top and I probably look like one of them. They expect my story to be like theirs. But if I want the kind of community that Venkat has, I suppose it starts with a gesture of trust. Maybe Bob was wrong. Maybe the world isn't full of unloving people in pain. Maybe I am not as difficult to understand as he made me believe.

"Um, okay, so it's been hard advocating for my son because of his special needs—"

"Wait, you have kids?" Ruby blurts out.

"Who's watching the kids?"

"Yeah, I have three. My mom's watching them. And I got out of a cult a couple months ago—"

"Hang on, you were in a cult??"

"Yeah, I'm writing a book about it. And I filed for divorce—"

"Wait, can we rewind to the cult thing?"

"Can we read the book?"

I laugh and field their questions with a blend of forthright obliqueness, disclosing bits of information that feel comfortable, and keeping them guessing at the rest. It feels natural and fun, unlike the excessive intimacy and lack of filter Bob and True Happiness required. The apartment fills with laughter and acceptance—none of the judgment Bob promised was waiting for me in the real world.

James sidles up to me. "I remember when Venkat lived here he mentioned having a sister who also lived in the city and Blake was like, 'Yo, is she hot?' and he said, 'Bro, she's married and has a kid.'"

I grin. "I'm not married anymore."

After everyone leaves, Venkat, Liv, Bilal, and I get Ethiopian food at a place around the corner. Manhattan glints across the river and I wonder how many people I didn't meet because of Bob's influence, how many people I will never know, how many opportunities I will never get back and am almost crumpled by the thought. Venkat and I ride the train two hours home to Connecticut and he laughs at his group text blowing up with friends berating him for coming into the city without even seeing them. I feel afraid again, worrying that people will never want me the way they want him, how they fight over the chance to see him. Amma laughs whenever I voice these concerns and says, "Veena, relax. You just got out of a cult. It will take time. Pretty soon you will have more texts than you can keep up with and you'll regret ever saying this."

It's hard to believe her, but regardless, I have my brother back. When we get home, I kiss my children, asleep in their beds. I thank Amma for allowing me to rediscover my life as a young person. Amma brushes me off, minimizing her sacrifices as always, telling me there is no greater joy for her than watching my children, that it's good for me to get out.

That night, Amma, Nanna, Venkat, and I pile on the couch and Nanna starts telling a story we've heard a thousand times, of when a tiger wandered into his village and all the men had to beat drums to scare the tiger away. Amma starts telling me everything she's bottled up for the past ten years, how she always hated Charlie but didn't want to say anything that might alienate me, all of the crazy things Bob told her. I don't know how most families deal with their trauma, but our night ends with the four of us laughing so hard we cry.

"Do you want to be right or do you want to be happy?" Amma yells, imitating Bob. "And I'm so scared, I can't say anything to disagree. Do this, your daughter will die. Do that, your daughter will die."

Venkat and I are on the floor, wheezing with laughter. The whole thing is ludicrous now that we're on the other side.

"I had no idea you guys were talking to him that much," Venkat says. "I feel like I shouldn't be laughing but . . ."

He and I make eye contact and again disintegrate into laughter. Between the cult and my marriage, we have enough stand-up material for a lifetime.

That weekend, I go on a hike with Nanna, on a trail at the top of my street. He collapses into tears in the middle of the woods without warning, rocking back and forth on a log and covering his face. It is only the third time in my life that I have seen him cry. I hang back in alarm, uncertain how to respond until I hear him sob, "We took you to that bastard. All you wanted was for us to listen to you, and we forced you to go see that fucker."

It's satisfying to hear these words, but even in retrospect, it had to be this way. I haven't forgotten what it was like to be nineteen and hopeless and have no options in the world. Maybe Bob was right, and if my parents hadn't brought me to him, I would have wound up dead or permanently institutionalized. And while it messed me up in other ways, while it went too far, it also worked. It jolted me off the track I was on.

In a couple weeks, before 2020 really hits, Liv will invite me out to a club down the block from her apartment to get me "out of the woods." The night is Lunar New Year themed and we will slather ourselves in body glitter and Liv will make a headdress adorned with a Styrofoam moon in all its phases. I'll take selfies of us and text them to Venkat, who by that time will be in Brazil. I'll discover many things that night: I still love to dance, drinks at the bar are overpriced, and it's easy to belong in a place where there are different kinds of people. And in a couple of more weeks, I'll finally tap into the dreams I've put on hold and reapply to college.

When I am accepted by Columbia University, I jump up and down with Amma and Nanna in the kitchen, just like I did the last time I was readmitted to college. Education is the only thing that can make us this giddy because I finally understand what they've been trying to tell me all these years: having a degree means having opportunities.

My excitement is quickly overshadowed by the sobering realization that Columbia does not offer need-based financial aid to nontraditional students. I drop into a chair and start running numbers in my head while Cleo and Mary race in and out of the kitchen, squealing. Before I can spiral, Nanna places a hand on my shoulder.

"Veena," he says, "this is a moment to celebrate. We'll loan you the tuition money."

"But I've just started becoming independent," I argue. "I can't go from being dependent on my husband to being dependent on you."

Nanna nods. "Ultimately, it's your choice," he says. "But we're your parents and we want to help you."

In his voice, I can hear that his respect for my decision is genuine. His response creates room for me to reconnect with my own desires. I want to attend this university and finish my degree. I want it more than anything—enough to accept his financial help.

Nanna then smiles and lightly touches my hair, though he is not a physically affectionate person. "You remind me of my mother," he says finally. "Your stories are so similar. She also finished her degree as a single mother of three. Bamma will be so happy when we tell her that you're going back to school." He laughs and says that we do not need to tell her about my divorce. "We are so proud of you, Veena. We always have been."

I am not present when he tells Bamma, but I can feel her pride and mine burning a hole through my chest.

32

2021

"A huge problem with modern psychology research is that ninety percent of it was conducted in WEIRD countries: Western, educated, industrialized, rich, democratic," my professor says, wheezing. She's wearing a mask and we're in that transitional period post COVID, where classrooms are still half empty and we're all readjusting to in-person socialization. I'm in transition, too, completing my undergraduate degree as a twenty-eight-year-old single mom. "And of that ninety percent, the vast majority of psychology research has been conducted in the United States. Researchers assumed that America was representative of the world at large; but the more global research is conducted, the more it's becoming clear that American culture is not representative. In fact, American culture is actually an extreme outlier. The majority of the world is much more collectivist."

I sit up with renewed interest, and my wooden chair squeals in the lecture hall at Columbia University. For the first time, I've been considering that I do not need permission from a system of authority to analyze my own life, that any authority inherently implies a particular value system, that I have allowed my mental health to be evaluated from the perspective of Bob's white male Christian standpoint. Bob led me to believe that every struggle I faced existed solely in my mind. In contrast, the entire premise of cultural psychology is that an individual's mind is inextricable from its environment, that culture shapes the framework of morality—the sense of self, the social scripts. Now that my mental health has stabilized, I've begun to focus less on modes of therapy and instead on creating room for discovering my own values.

My professor is a Black woman who has spent years studying diversity and intersectional identities. She delves into the budding research on bicultural individuals and acculturative adjustment strategies: assimilation, separation, integration, and marginalization. When you enter a different culture, the strategy with the optimal mental health outcomes is integration: maintaining your heritage culture while adapting to aspects of the new culture. At the opposite end of the spectrum is marginalization, individuals who identify with neither culture, and thus experience the most acculturative stress.

Take one teenage girl in the throes of acculturative stress. Add a high school with a rampant suicide problem. Add college bullies and a white savior. Cover and let rise. Or rather, let sink. It's impossible to isolate what elements catalyzed which reaction, but I know how the story played out.

The class ends, and I slide out of my seat. The first-time undergrads, the eighteen- to twenty-year-olds, congregate around me, like the Young Women of the church did, sharing their heartbreaks and struggles and hopes and dreams. Their attention and deference makes me jumpy and awkward around them, intimately aware of how indestructible they believe they are and how vulnerable their reality is—how easy to warp. Watching them reminds me of the first time I saw a baby bird, its translucent skin functioning as a paper-thin barrier between their lifeblood and the rest of the world. Their veins, like thick blue slugs, so *available*. The undergrads remind me of me. I want to tell them not to trust so easily and not to love so deeply, but at the same time, I want them to continue slopping up their youth as long as life allows them.

I have five missed calls from the nineteen-year-old who asked me what the difference is between an Uber and an UberX when she moved to the city, and a string of ten memes DMed to my Instagram account from another girl in my Thinking and Decision-Making class. A girl sitting next to me on the library steps compliments my outfit.

The way I make friends at college is as effortless and accidental as it was grueling the first time around: my classmates and I follow each other on Instagram. They read my essays online—the one about my sex life or the one about my divorce—and send me incredibly heartfelt DMs about how I've helped them finally understand what their single mother must have gone through or how I have inspired them in some way. I send an awkward but grateful reply and that is all it takes. Things have changed since I was last in college.

Lately my life feels like it could be summed up with the *Hannah Montana* theme song, "The Best of Both Worlds"—between my time in New York City attending college classes and my time in Connecticut at home with the kids. Mary is four and Cleo is seven. Cleo sits on a counter stool in the kitchen and kicks her legs back and forth. Mary scrambles onto the stool next to Cleo and folds her tiny knees under her. I pour a pile of tiny colorful tubes on the counter in front of them.

"Girls, do you think this"—I hold up what looks like a little pink pill—"can ever become anything else?"

I pass it to Cleo, who turns it over in her hands and says simply, "No."

Mary grabs it and declares, "No! It's too small."

When we attended church, I used to spend Mondays teaching the kids a Bible lesson with an activity and a snack. Now that we've left, I've been trying to teach the kids basic principles of psychology to give them the life skills that I never had.

"Are you sure? You don't think this little pink thing can ever grow? Okay, that is called 'fixed mindset.'"

The analogy isn't perfect, but then again, my daughter is seven. She won't remember the academic terms I bring home from my child psychology class in an overzealous attempt to reclaim the experience of motherhood. I'm still haunted by feelings of self-doubt and inadequacy when it comes to my children, but in moments like these, I start to believe that maybe I can raise these little people. I give them a watered-down explanation of fixed mindset that goes over their heads: it's believing your basic qualities, such as intelligence and talent, are unchangeable over time. According to my textbook, fixed mindset is associated with negative mental health outcomes—though I don't share that part.

I fill a bowl with water and bring it back to the counter. "Put the pink thing in the water and let's see what happens."

Cleo gently places it in, and for a moment nothing happens. Then the plastic casing unfurls, and the sponge expands into a little unicorn. Cleo's face lights up. Mary claps her hands. "More, Mom! Can we do more?"

"Hang on!" I pick up another compressed sponge. "Now what do you think? Can this little tube grow into something beautiful?"

The girls shout, "Yes!" and grab at the desiccated sponges. Cleo dumps five more into the bowl.

"You are like the sponge," I tell them. "All you need is a little water to grow into the best version of you."

Growth mindset is believing that characteristics such as talent and intelligence are skills that can be improved through effort. Developing a growth mindset is a skill itself—one that leads to improved resilience and therefore positive mental health outcomes. My kids don't understand these academic nuances, but they will remember this day with the unicorn sponges. With any luck, they'll grow up embracing change, understanding that failure is a necessary step toward progress. And when tragedy inevitably strikes, hopefully they will know that bad days can give way to mediocre ones and eventually to days of contentment once more.

I'm trying not to engage in what-if scenarios about my past anymore. But sometimes I still wonder if I could have avoided the True Happiness Company if I'd had access to the kind of support that would help develop my ability to process my own emotions and troubleshoot my thought patterns from a young age. I spent so long as a teenager searching for one big answer to my existential distress; but the more time passes, the more I derive my satisfaction from a kaleidoscope of little joys: teaching my children; pursuing my passions; developing lush, layered friendships that don't come at the expense of my values.

The next Sunday, I turn the house into one big game of *The Floor Is Lava,* in order to illustrate the value of leaving our comfort zones.

Hugo's third birthday falls on the same week as Holi. The beginning of March still feels like winter, but inside my home, the frost has melted. Hugo knocks over the teddy bear–shaped Costco-sized container of animal crackers on the dining table, stuffs three in his mouth, and runs away with two handfuls before I can stop him. He eats with urgent abandon now, as if to make up for the two years of his life when he could not eat independently. His feeding tube was finally removed last year. His pediatrician cried at our most recent well visit and told me she never thought he'd be able to walk. None of the genetic panels on Hugo returned any clear answers, but her best guess is still a genetic abnormality. I'm learning to live without clear answers in life.

I chase Hugo into the living room, telling him in American Sign Language to stop and slow down. He doesn't respond verbally or in sign but stops long enough for me to pry out the crackers. Cleo and Mary beg for a snack. I panic slightly, hearing Bob's voice in my head telling me that there is a right way and a wrong way to parent, and I wonder if saying no to snacks right now is overly restrictive and will lay the groundwork for eating disorders in their future or if saying yes is overly lenient and will teach them that there is no order in the world and make them incapable of following rules in the future. It's been two years, but it takes time to rewire my brain. To my kids and my parents, it just looks like I take too long to answer simple questions. I hand them each a cracker, and Nanna runs into the room to tickle Mary as I hang up the rest of the balloons.

I put a playlist of top Bollywood hits, curated by my cousin, on the kitchen speakers and rearrange the juice boxes and decorative straws, glancing at the clock, convinced—as I am convinced every time I invite people over—that no one will come. But people do come. Charlie shows up with the paper plates. The kids' pediatrician arrives. A mom I met at the gym comes with her husband and two daughters, bringing houseplants and beer. Our half-Indian, half-Irish neighbors stop by with a bottle of wine. Another family we met at Cleo's preschool, half Guianese and half white, bring their girls. The mom I met at the same preschool, the first friend I made after True Happiness, arrives. It took some time to convince myself that she's not judging me, but here she is, with her boys and husband and birthday presents for Hugo.

I usher everyone into the basement and offer a brief explanation of Holi. My speech is more for myself; everyone already knows the North Indian celebration, but it's one I've never experienced. I never went to the Holi party at college. I never went when Amma took Cleo to the Holi celebration at the temple. I turn the music back on and all my friends in this strange town start throwing colored powder at each other. It smears into faces and cheeks. Dust clogs the air, and we open the back doors and spill onto the patio. My friends laugh and drink, and the children squeal and dance. Nanna carries Hugo on his shoulders like a king.

I see Charlie in the corner on his phone and the sight brings me back to that Thanksgiving dinner when we first started dating.

"Hey," I say. "Question for you. In the time that we've been together . . . did we have any tender moments?"

A friend recently asked me this question about Charlie and me, and I haven't been able to get it out of my head. Because as much as I've racked my brain, none come to mind. I haven't shed a single tear in the divorce process.

Charlie grins. "Gee, thanks."

"No, really," I continue. "Can you think of any?"

He shrugs as he slips his phone in his back pocket. "Hmm . . . I think we went to the aquarium once in college?"

We were nineteen at the time. A weight lifts off me at the realization that our memories finally line up: neither one of us can easily recall a moment of softness. Cleo runs to me, crying, and I clear dust out of her eyes.

"You're a great mom," Charlie says.

I stop and look at him, exhausted by the process of talking through our attorneys and confused by the abrupt display of emotion, still unable to reconcile the awkward kid from the college debate league with the person who so recently told me I was a danger to my kids.

"Our kids are lucky to have you. You sparkle."

I don't quite know what to make of his compliment and I'll never really understand what to make of our marriage. In a year, one week after our divorce is finalized, he'll marry the coworker who was "just a coworker." When he does, I'll feel relieved that we are both moving on from a relationship that probably never should have happened.

Today, Cleo interrupts to say she wants a Polaroid with her entire family in it. Amma, Nanna, Mary, Hugo, and I all line up next to her, but she insists on Charlie being in the photo. Venkat is in Brazil. Someone takes the camera and the shutter clicks.

Now that I've filed for divorce, my life has taken shape as the house has fallen into disrepair. The gutters leak. Mice keep chewing through the oven wires. The garden is a jungle with weeds and poison ivy stalks taller than my children. I tried to weed it once and came away with a rash so bad it looked like I'd been burned across the chest. The scars faded but slowly.

It's impossible to say if the mark they left will ever fade completely. Learning self-reliance is a slow, grueling process. But still the flowers bloom every year. First the daffodils, then the daylilies, the peonies, then the roses. Spring always comes.

At bedtime every night, Cleo asks me questions:

Why are you and Daddy getting divorced?

What happens when we die?

Who is Bob Lyon?

How come we're not Mormon anymore? Is Jesus real?

I take a deep breath (I take many) and give the answer a child psychologist helped us prepare: that her father and I decided we can love her better separately than we can together but we both love her very much. (I also tell her that her dad and I were very young and that she is not allowed to marry before the age of thirty.) I tell her no one knows what happens when we die, or if God and Jesus are real, but that some people believe they are, and it inspires them to be kind and gives them hope. I offer to take her to church or explore other religions with her and we spend many a night down this rabbit hole, asking Amma about reincarnation or reading up on nirvana. I tell her Bob Lyon is someone I used to trust, who I don't anymore. He is someone who doesn't matter.

Then she asks: *What is the meaning of life?* And this one continues to stop me short.

I still think about Kate, about Sarah Rose, and the epidemic of suicides I witnessed all around me in high school. After casually trying to kill myself for so long you'd think I'd have some grand answer to it all. I tell my daughter that some questions are too big and too bright for us to face head-on, that we can decide on our values and preferences and build meaning into our actions. That a day can be broken down into a string of tiny joys and moments of gratitude. I tell her that when problems seem overwhelming, they, too, can be broken down into a series of smaller problems, and small problems have solutions. I tell her building a life you love is like building a home: it takes time, constant adjustment, and you have to replace the roof every ten years. Sometimes you change your situation and sometimes you change your mindset and being able to tell the difference between the two is crucial.

For the record, my daughter still hates my open-ended responses. She rolls her eyes and says, *Fine, I'll just ask someone who knows.*

I tell her to let me know when she finds the answers. I also tell her: *When you do uncover the answers, don't trust absolutes.* Truth is never as clean as we'd like.

ENDNOTE

My goal in writing this book was to take the reader on my journey as closely as possible to how I first experienced it unfolding in real time—which is to say, for it to be confusing, ambiguous, and almost impossible to see the patterns and power dynamics at play while in the thick of it. Throughout this story, I've inserted my analysis as sparsely as possible in an attempt to preserve the ambiguity and disorientation I felt. To communicate what it feels like—in real time—to fall under someone's manipulative influence. To give voice to the surreality of looking back and being able to pinpoint the moments you were leveraged into submission with the clarity that is not available at the time. The changes feel almost imperceptible as they happen and then suddenly appear extreme in retrospect.

Nine years later, after finally extricating myself from the tight-knit community that enmeshed my young adulthood, I've become fascinated by the trajectory of my own life, the way some people binge documentaries of Jonestown or NXIVM. I completed a psychology degree at Columbia University to better understand the dynamics that shaped my life and learned a great deal about how mental illnesses are categorized, how culture and race impact social norms, and how humans process decisions. What I've learned has reshaped my understanding of myself and my life. I'm by no means an expert—nor do I speak for any race, gender, or subset of demographics—but I'll offer my perspective here in the hopes of beginning a conversation.

In her book *Cultish,* Amanda Montell describes the psychological process behind obsessing over cultlike groups: our amygdala, the part of the brain that manages the fight-or-flight response, is trying to assess whether these events pose any direct danger to us. "We're scanning for threats, on some level wondering, Is everyone susceptible to cultish influence?" Montell writes. "Could it happen to you? Could it happen to me? And if so, how?"

In this endnote, I want to return to the question: How did I fall for that?

I began writing parts of this book when I was still under Bob's influence. The story was: I was depressed, and he saved me. His manipulation was so effective and enduring that even after I realized True Happiness was a cult, I still tried to take too much responsibility for what had happened. I must have been more gullible than I thought. But as I entered therapy and continued to write, the clearer Bob's tactics came into focus. There were the cultural and racial dynamics he leveraged, psychological principles of coercion. But key to it all was his ability to physically alter my circumstances: by threatening to have me kicked out of college or ultimately institutionalized if I didn't call him daily, by manipulating those close to me to enforce his rules. Once I was required to stay in constant contact with Bob, multiple overlapping factors left me susceptible to his manipulation: I was a nineteen-year-old without a fully developed prefrontal cortex—the part of the brain responsible for reasoning and risk assessment that does not fully develop until around age twenty-five. I was suicidal and desperate; and as an Indian American woman, I was taught, both by my parents and by cultural scripts I inherited, to defer to figures of authority.

By leveraging these vulnerabilities and his knowledge of coercive techniques—forced silence, prolonged eye contact, extreme language to present each choice as a false binary, mixed put-downs (criticism coupled with a compliment to condition me to rely on his approval)—he was able to cultivate undue influence over me as my "therapist" and confidant, isolate me from my support system, and use Charlie to institutionalize me at will. By the time I got pregnant, and Charlie involved Bob in the conversation, Bob had established enough sway over me to impose his religious morality upon me by presenting it as the objective, singular path to happiness. Insisting I stay with Charlie was yet another technique, known as narcissistic triangulation, in which a person introduces a third party into a relationship to divert any negative attention from themselves. This establishes a dynamic whereby the two triangulated parties (Charlie and me) only feel capable of communicating successfully with each other through the manipulator (Bob). Once Bob married us, he'd placed me in a position where my husband had decision-making authority over me by way of overseeing our finances. With my parents living across the country, I had no access to regular childcare. Without childcare, I was unable to pursue my education. Without an education, I couldn't pursue a career; and without a career, I remained financially dependent on my husband. This double bind left me virtually unable to leave the house without his permission. Which in turn left me isolated and stunted my social and emotional growth, leaving me susceptible to further manipulation.

As I begin to tell my story I find that some people—educated, intelligent, and thoughtful people—are deeply invested in the idea that, despite my circumstances, I remained in control of my choices. To me, these responses are yet another by-product of the victim-blaming culture created by the systems of power that leave women and marginalized groups susceptible to such influence to begin with. If a minor gets groomed by a high school teacher or college professor, we would not describe her as "technically in control of her choices." If a child is raised in an abusive household and unable to escape, they are not simply choosing to stay. And if a vulnerable teenager struggling with mental health issues is groomed and molested by a sixty-year-old man positioning himself as a figure of authority, trying to argue that she has control of that situation is, at best, a questionable endeavor. I can assure you I did not choose this particular life experience from a menu. I take this stance less because I am attached to a particular version of my history and more because of the implications for how we treat young women in similar situations. The common denominator of these situations is an extreme power imbalance.

With regard to Montell's questions ("Could it happen to you? Could it happen to me?"), well, maybe you won't wind up in a virtual self-help cult headquartered in the middle of nowhere Georgia, but whether at the hands of an abusive romantic partner, a questionable mentor, or an overly tight-knit company, we are all susceptible to some degree because we all share the same basic need for belonging. It's not the hyperbolized "brainwashing" as commonly portrayed in pop culture, where some charismatic leader can say a few magic words, wipe clean someone's personality, replace it with their own, and no one is immune. The reality is far more complex. It takes a specific set of vulnerabilities, an intimate knowledge of how to exploit them, an ability to alter someone's physical circumstances, and buy-in from trusted family members and friends. But when enough of these pieces stack up in the right way, it is indeed possible to alter a person's reality. Especially when you throw in a false diagnosis and wield it to perpetually undermine that person's trust in their own judgments.

I could talk for hours about the specific cultural factors, psychological processes, and linguistic tactics Bob employed. Instead, I want to address my misdiagnosis. By now, the ways in which Bob's misdiagnosis led me to doubt my own intuition should hopefully be clear—in addition to the way this misdiagnosis was weaponized against me; all Bob had to do was tell the head psychologist at a New York City hospital that I had borderline personality disorder to discredit and institutionalize me at will. In addition to being personally harrowing for me at the time, the doctor's complete disregard of my story following a single phone call also raises a serious alarm about how the mentally ill are treated within our system.

One of the questions I'm still asking myself is: Who gets to decide what is normal? With respect to the mental health system, every diagnosis of mental illness assumes a certain baseline of normalcy. With borderline personality disorder, one of the symptoms is excessive risk-taking, in areas such as spending habits and sexual behavior. Excessive to whom? Based on whose value system? Whose environment? A social risk for a young white man from the affluent suburb of Greenwich, Connecticut, might present very differently than a social risk for a Black woman raised in inner-city Baltimore. More important, our perceptions of acceptable risk from these two circumstances vary greatly based on our own upbringing and biases. Let's say both our imaginary individuals have unprotected sex that results in a pregnancy. One has the power to make it go away, one doesn't. Whose risk is more likely to be labeled as "excessive"?

Even when evaluating a symptom as apparently clear-cut as a suicide attempt, there are rich and varied cultural scripts, environmental factors, and individual situations we must take into account. I now notice a large precedent for female suicide threats in messaging I absorbed as a child. In the Hindu religious text the *Ramayana,* Kaikeyi, the second wife of King Dasharatha, threatens to kill herself when her son is not crowned king. (And it works; her son is crowned king in response.) In this instance, a suicide threat functions as an apparently rational political tactic rather than a symptom of mental illness. In Bollywood movies, even comedies such as *Andaz Apna Apna,* heroines faking or threatening suicide as a form of leverage is a common trope. (The vast majority of Bollywood movies are written by men, so this trope may not reflect real-life suicidal behavior among women but rather male perception that this behavior is common among women.) I cite these examples not to suggest that suicide threats are okay or desirable but to illustrate that from an early age, I was repeatedly exposed to messages that normalized suicide threats. Combine that with the degree to which suicide was normalized in my hometown, and I no longer think of my past self as a person who had an extreme reaction to a difficult situation but as a person who reacted more or less in line with the messages I'd absorbed.

Even the term "mental disorder" implies a dysfunction that exists solely in the mind and risks leveling the complex interplay between an individual's mind and circumstances. According to attribution theory, whenever we make a determination about why something has happened, we make a subconscious choice to attribute it to something internal and inherent to us, or to something external (though some combination of the two is usually most accurate). When we label individuals with disorders or mental illnesses, we risk overemphasizing internal factors and crowding external factors out of the conversation. Or in slightly different terms, we focus on nature to the exclusion of nurture.

As an impressionable teenager, I internalized the diagnosis of situational depression and overgeneralized the symptoms; since my reaction to my classmate's suicide was labeled disproportionate, I assumed that many of my emotional reactions were disproportionate. In other words, I (mis)interpreted my diagnosis as clinical proof that I have a tendency to overreact. Once you account for the way I'd already been conditioned to doubt my own judgments as a young woman of color, you get a very clear picture of why I was ready to accept Bob's misdiagnosis and dismissal of my instincts.

I believe it is very important—particularly where young people are concerned—to differentiate between an individual and the symptoms they present on a given day. When delivered without the appropriate nuance and consideration, diagnoses can blur that line and encourage a fixed-mindset approach to mental health—which can make a temporary state feel like a permanent characteristic, thus making attempts at change feel futile. In many instances, diagnoses may be beneficial on a personal level or medical level, such as in cases where medication or other diagnosis-dependent treatment is the most appropriate course of action. However, I believe that, in general, caution is warranted when branding women or any other marginalized group with diagnoses that effectively state that our perceptions or reactions are extreme or not based in reality. Again: Whose reality? The power of these diagnoses in silencing the voices of the already marginalized, neglected, and overlooked should not be underestimated. Whether they are issued by a reputable medical professional or a narcissistic cult leader, these labels are incredibly difficult to overcome, both internally and externally.

All this is just one take—my take—on my past. My point here is not to argue that there was no genetic or neurological component to my experiences but rather to illustrate the difficulty of extricating and isolating the myriad relevant situational and individual factors—and moreover, to suggest that our motivation for doing so in the first place warrants further scrutiny.

In 1851, American physician Samuel A. Cartwright posited the mental illness drapetomania. The symptoms? A desire to flee captivity. The affected population? Enslaved Africans. Even the basic human desire for freedom was at one point pathologized because doing so served the white men who benefited politically, economically, and socially from slavery. History is full of examples like this. "Crazy" has long been a gendered term used to subjugate women into demure, acceptable forms of behavior. Most of us now know that even the word "hysteria" is derived from the Greek *hystera,* which translates to "uterus." When my ex-husband explicitly and implicitly labeled me hysterical, and treated me as such—per Bob's urging and instructions—I do not believe he was behaving maliciously, with conscious intent to harm me. To me, that makes it more insidious. I believe my ex-husband did nothing more than act in pure self-interest, by simply following a cultural script available to him as a white man—one that he never bothered to question. It was convenient and easy for him to take total control of our finances and to prevent me from obtaining my education and working outside the home. Not paying for childcare allowed him to spend money on other priorities—such as a big house—and all the while, he was doing the "right" thing by supporting us financially anyway. I think, though, that some part of him knew this was problematic. Continually pointing out my "craziness" became a trump card he could pull at any moment to invalidate my needs and validate his.

I give you my take on my past to illustrate how people—and women of color in particular—can be influenced to doubt their own judgments. To anyone in a situation that bears any similarity to mine, remember this: in order to effectively triage the root cause of unhappiness, we must account for external factors as well. Maladjustment to the system may be a symptom of a broken system rather than a broken mind.

As a woman who was cast at an early age into the role of good daughter, expected to dress modestly, not talk too much, not fight too much, not question too much, and come home on time, is it any wonder that I was susceptible to a man who trained me to do just that, to stay home, to cover my body with religious garments, to give my husband sex whenever he asked for it, to obey? I simply fulfilled the social script I was given.

In some ways, it's a perfectly normal story—but I guess that depends on your definition of "normal."

ACKNOWLEDGMENTS

Thank you, first and foremost, to my parents and brother for your wholehearted love and unwavering support and for your generosity of spirit in being so totally chill about my decision to make a career out of airing our family's most difficult moments. I never could have gotten through those moments without you, let alone written this book. Thank you for teaching me what love actually looks like. To my children, whenever you're old enough to read this: I adore you and cannot imagine my life without all three of you. Thanks for rolling with your mom's weird job. Who knows, maybe one day you'll write your own memoirs about it.

Thank you to my acquiring editor, Chayenne Skeete, for cold emailing me, for your refusal to take no for an answer, and for finding me a home at Random House. Thank you to my agent, Mariah Stovall, for your thoughtful support and for guiding me throughout this journey. Thank you to Miriam Khanukaev, half editor, half wizard, for understanding and believing in my vision, for helping me hone this manuscript into a truer version of itself. Learning from you has been a privilege that has made my writing clearer, more deliberate, and better paced. I'll never look at pronouns the same way again. My sincere gratitude to Hilary Redmon, Julie Tate, Carolyn Foley, and the entire team at Random House.

This book was brought to life by a series of coincidences and kind strangers. I'd like to thank the student staff of the *Columbia Daily Spec-*

tator: Joy Fan, Claudia Gohn, Sarah Peters, Teresa Lawlor, Cole Cahill, Annie Cheng, and Sarah Braka (among many others!) for encouraging me to write the essay that started it all. Thank you to Alexandra Cohl, for that short but consequential call where you taught me how to use Instagram and suggested I post that essay. Smita Sen, for reading, loving, and sharing my essay with Chayenne when it came across your feed. Thank you to my mentor, Allison Dickens, for convincing me that I was not, in fact, being catfished, and that I should indeed pass along my latest draft.

Writing has a reputation for being a solitary act, but after spending nearly a decade in a cult, I have had quite enough solitude, thank you very much. So, I'd like to thank my remarkable community of writers because this book has truly been a communal effort, in more ways than one. Thank you, Isabela Carvalho, for your sharp instincts, for editing the entire book, for your podcast recommendations and your ten-minute voice notes that rival the podcasts. I can't wait to read your book next. Thank you, Natalie Ponte, for being my first post-cult friend and my first reader for basically everything. To Jessica Coleman, for your insight on a very different version of this book years ago, back when I thought Bob saved my life. To Julie Sarkissian for your life-changing metaphors and Michelle Ruiz-Andrews for the library dates. To Ruben Reyes Jr. and Emma Levy for keeping me sane.

Thank you, Neighbor Matt, for letting me trauma-dump on your couch as I read the entire manuscript out loud, for falling in love with me because of it, and bearing with me through the highs and lows of the editing process. I hope you still think dating an author is cool.

A heartfelt thank-you to my brilliant professor Katherine Fox-Glassman, for shaping my entire understanding of decision-making and mental illness and reading through the endnote multiple times. I frequently think about the principles you've taught me in the course of my everyday life and consider myself unbelievably lucky to have benefitted from your knowledge and generosity.

Ashleigh Owens, you are a source of constant joy and my biggest hype woman. I am eternally grateful for your enthusiasm, precision of thought, and willingness to come over at midnight and talk through the finer points of copy.

To all the therapists who have tried to keep me alive over the years—even when I was a poor sport about it—thank you. Mrs. Meyer and Mr. Steve, you were right. Things really do get better.

ABOUT THE AUTHOR

VEENA DINAVAHI is a first-generation Indian American writer raising three small humans in the woods of Connecticut. Her personal essays have appeared in *The Rumpus* and *PULP.* She holds a BA in psychology from Columbia University and works in the fashion industry. *The True Happiness Company* is her first book.

ABOUT THE TYPE

This book was set in Fairfield, the first typeface from the hand of the distinguished American artist and engraver Rudolph Ruzicka (1883–1978). Ruzicka was born in Bohemia (in the present-day Czech Republic) and came to America in 1894. He set up his own shop, devoted to wood engraving and printing, in New York in 1913 after a varied career working as a wood engraver, in photoengraving and banknote printing plants, and as an art director and freelance artist. He designed and illustrated many books, and was the creator of a considerable list of individual prints—wood engravings, line engravings on copper, and aquatints.